DATE DUE			

A FIELD GUIDE TO CONSERVATION ARCHAEOLOGY IN NORTH AMERICA

A FIELD GUIDE TO CONSERVATION ARCHAEOLOGY IN NORTH AMERICA

Georgess McHargue and
Michael Roberts

With an Introduction by Thomas F. King, Ph.D.

Drawings by Georgia Lee
Charts and maps by Barbara Page

J. B. LIPPINCOTT COMPANY/PHILADELPHIA AND NEW YORK

U.S. Library of Congress Cataloging in Publication Data

McHargue, Georgess.
A field guide to conservation archaeology in North America.

Includes bibliographical references and index.
1. United States—Antiquities—Collection and preservation. 2. Indians of
North America—Antiquities. I. Roberts, Michael, birth date, joint author.
II. Title.
E159.5.M32   930'.1   77–21558
ISBN–0–397–31724–7   ISBN–0–397–31725–5 (pbk.)

THIS BOOK IS DEDICATED
TO W. R. McHARGUE,
NEAL E. McHARGUE,
AND THE MEMORY
OF JOHN BATES ROBERTS,
WITH LOVE AND GRATITUDE.

Acknowledgments

The authors would like to acknowledge the truly heroic contributions of those professional archaeologists who read through the manuscript and undertook to correct factual errors and make philosophical comments. They are Dr. Laurel Casjens of the Peabody Museum, Harvard University; Dr. Tom King of the National Park Service (who also supplied the introduction); and Dr. Barbara Luedtke of the University of Massachusetts, Boston.

In addition, we received valuable help with particular sections of the book from Dr. Jeffrey Brain of Harvard University; Dr. Dena Dincauze of the University of Massachusetts, Amherst; Dr. Robert Hoover of the California State Polytechnic College; Dr. Charles Nelson of the University of Massachusetts, Boston; Dr. Maurice Robbins, Massachusetts State Archaeologist; and Martin E. Weil of the Department of Northern and Indian Affairs, Canada. Needless to say, none of these individuals bears the slightest responsibility for the errors of fact or interpretation that have doubtless crept into the finished book.

We also wish to thank the Bronson Museum of Attleboro, Massachusetts, for permitting us to photograph their collection, as well as Georgia Lee for her beautiful and lightning-fast drawings of artifacts, Barbara Page for making visual sense of our chaotic sketches for maps and charts, Whitney Powell for much good counsel on matters graphic, Frank McManamon of the Massachusetts Historical Commission for permission to extract from his summary of U.S. archaeological law, and Fred Turchon for "a generally cheerful attitude."

We would also like to thank Ellen Stuttle for editorial devotion in the face of power blackouts and other insanities.

Finally, the authors extend to each other their awestruck mutual appreciation for having stayed married during and after the whole undertaking.

Contents

Introduction

In the late 1960s Alex Apostolides, a Los Angeles writer-photographer, began spending his weekends on an archaeological survey of a mountain range in the Mojave Desert. He didn't dig; he surveyed, recording rock art, campsites, trails, and village sites in notes and photos. He came to understand the prehistory of his area like no other living person. He helped place the range on the National Register of Historic Places. This gave it special protection (ineptly administered, Alex assures me at every opportunity) by the federal government.

Marian Parks of Corona del Mar, California, became concerned about a federally financed sewer system proposed for a canyon area near her home. The sewer route had not been fully surveyed by archaeologists, and construction would almost undoubtedly damage archaeological sites. Moreover, what about the urban growth that would follow? Enlisting the aid of amateur and professional archaeologists in the area, Ms. Parks twisted the arms of local, state, and federal agencies until they took action. The whole route has now been surveyed, and steps are being taken to protect endangered sites. Ms. Parks is still fighting to get the government to consider what urbanization may do to the archaeology of the area, but she is making progress.

The San Luis Obispo County Archaeological Society, tired of the way professional archaeologists had neglected its area, launched an ambitious county-wide survey in 1968. Now San Luis Obispo is one of California's best surveyed counties; professional archaeologists are on the staffs of local colleges, a museum has been created, and archaeological sites are protected by local government. Among the members of the society who assured its organized, vigorous attack on the problems of local archaeology was a young engineer named Mike Roberts.

Now Roberts—who has lost his amateur standing to become a Harvard-based professional—has happily teamed up with Georgess McHargue, who is adding archaeological skills to her already impressive talents as a writer. They have prepared this book for people who would like to emulate the San Luis Obispo Society, or Marian Parks, or Alex Apostolides, or the hundreds of other avocational and professional "conservation archaeologists" across the country. This book is a welcome relief from the long, long list of works that portray archaeology as a discipline dedicated to digging. I would not claim for a moment to agree with everything that Roberts and McHargue say in this book, but our differences over particulars are of little importance. Conservation archaeology is not a creed with a single dogma; it is an exciting, challenging approach both to doing archaeology and to being a citizen, and it presents us with our best chance for saving a respectable portion of our past.

A conservation approach to archaeology is very different from the exploitation of archaeological sites that has traditionally been archaeology's stock in trade. Conservation by no means forbids archaeologists from investigating and learning from the remnants of the past, but it does require thinking before digging—about whether digging is necessary, whether there is not some other, less destructive or more productive way to learn.

One of the beauties of conservation archaeology as Roberts and McHargue present it is that everyone can take part. There are more and more professional archaeologists who do conservation-related work—in the preparation of environmental impact statements, and in federal and state environmental and historic preservation agencies, for example—but we need all the help we can get from the public. We need the peoplepower that only trained and dedicated volunteers can supply. We need the special skills in physics, chemistry, engineering, computer programming, scuba diving, aerial photography, and a host of other useful disciplines that we haven't learned ourselves. We need the eyes and ears of citizens in the communities of the nation, to look out for archaeological sites and the activities of modern society that destroy them. And we need people who are willing to raise their voices, as responsible citizens of our democracy, in defense of the past.

The fact that the past has much to teach us is commonly understood. Really living with this fact, however, requires some adjustments in our ways of thinking about our society in general and about archaeology in particular. We have been studying and learning from the archaeology of this country ever since our first archaeologist, Thomas Jefferson, dug into an Indian mound in Virginia in 1784. But at the same time we have been tearing up the documents from which we are trying to learn—bulldozing them for roads, houses, and reservoirs; knocking them down for urban renewal; and digging them up without really thinking about how necessary their excavation might be. Conservation archaeology is a more productive, more responsible way to learn—a method of coming to grips with the real value of the past.

From the desert—in west Texas, this time—Alex Apostolides wrote me recently:

Restless, Sunday, went out and found another ceramic site not twenty minutes from the house, sherds sprawled over some one hundred meters in a quiet sandblown cove tucked in among the mesquites of what must have been a huge grove, once upon a time. "They" haven't touched it yet, but you can hear the sound of weekend engines on the roadway not too distant. People in this country have too much leisure time. Or, it's not so much that they have an overabundance of leisure time; it's that they don't know what to do with the time they have, damn them. Make a lot of noise, tear up the countryside, scatter beer cans in your wake. That's no kind of civilization.

Conservation archaeology represents a different vision of civilization. Like preserving the natural environment, like maintaining the character of urban neighborhoods or restoring elegant old buildings, the conservation of archaeological sites and their information maintains and enhances the quality of our collective life. I don't know if Alex gets as much of a thrill out of finding his ceramic site, recording it, and leaving it alone as "they" do racing their trail bikes or digging for artifacts, but I think he makes a much more substantial contribution to our future. I hope this book will help many people discover how they can make such contributions.

Thomas F. King
Washington, D.C.
March 4, 1977

I
Preliminaries, and Potshots at Pothunters

Archaeology has a wonderful reputation—for all the wrong things.

In old movies, archaeologists are lean and handsome adventurers or lean and unworldly graybeards who discover idols with emerald eyes, struggle in the toils of the mummy's curse, or rescue maidens from enslavement by survivors of lost civilizations in hidden valleys. In cartoon drawings, archaeologists have humorous confrontations with *Homo neanderthalensis,* find the paint still wet in the caverns of Lascaux, or are bemused by unearthed artifacts of a size suitable for giants.

Of course, these caricatures are just lazy-minded oversimplifications, like the Absent-minded Professor or the Tight-fisted Scotsman. Yet, though we may smile, we have been more deeply influenced by the caricatures than we think. Ask some of the people you meet on the street to describe a group of archaeologists at work. Your informants may talk about palm trees or pyramids, rain forests or ruins, but what they almost certainly will not mention will be farmers, bankers, housewives, and high school students doing archaeology within a few miles of their homes. Like astronauts, archaeologists are popularly supposed to be a class apart, and in our mind's eye they are *elsewhere.*

Understanding why and how these ideas about archaeology are distorted will help us to answer the question, "What is archaeology really, and how is it done?"

In Egypt's Valley of the Kings on November 26, 1922, archaeologist Howard Carter took his first look through a small hole in the door of a newly uncovered tomb. The burial, over three thousand years old, was that of the boy king Tut-ankh-Amen, and all Carter could manage to say when asked what he had seen was, "Wonderful things." What he had glimpsed turned out to be a treasure in gold, silver, gems, and artwork whose value is now placed in the millions by those who attempt to calculate it at all.

It was a great day for Howard Carter and his fellow investigator, Lord Carnarvon. It was a great day for art historians and students of life in ancient Egypt. It was, of course, a great day for the journalists of the world, who soon made "King Tut" a household word. And many observers said it was a great day for archaeology. But was it?

One major result of Carter and Carnarvon's discovery was that thousands, possibly millions, of individuals who had barely heard of archaeology before were suddenly impressed with one very much mistaken notion: Archaeologists dig up gold. This is about as accurate as to say that fishermen only spot giant squids or that doctors do nothing but heart transplants, but the idea was exciting and romantic, and it stuck.

Of course, the association of archaeology with treasure is also traceable to other spectacular finds, both before and after Carter and Carnarvon. There were the gold masks of Mycenae, excavated by Heinrich Schliemann; the Mesopotamian tomb of Queen Shub-ad; the ship burial at Sutton Hoo, England; and the jades from Chichén Itzá, Yucatán. The funeral equipment of Tut-ankh-Amen is not the only basis for the myth, merely the best known.

The treasure myth gives rise in turn to three smaller

myths, each romantic and in its way destructive. The first is the idea that becoming an archaeologist is a good way to get rich. On the contrary, if you are anxious to acquire sudden wealth, you would be better advised to sit by the ocean and wait for a talking fish to offer you three wishes. You will have at least as good a chance of getting rich as an archaeologist has, and you won't have to work nearly as hard.

Next there is the assumption that the only worthwhile archaeology is done in the expectation of making large, impressive finds—if not gold and jewels, at least magnificent statuary, unblemished pottery, or a lost city or two. This is perhaps the saddest part of the myth, because it leads the general public, including thousands of people who might make contributions to archaeology, to suppose that there is very little archaeology waiting to be done. In fact, the exact opposite is true: both in North America and elsewhere, there are vastly larger numbers of archaeological sites than present resources of money and personnel can serve to locate, let alone survey or, where necessary, excavate.

This brings us to the third myth, which states that archaeology is inseparable from digging. The spade is probably the only visual symbol that is widely associated with archaeology, and yet in recent years archaeologists have found themselves acting like retired movie gunslingers with their .45s: the shovels may not have gone to the rubbish heap, but in many cases they have quietly been hung back on the wall. There have even been instances in which archaeological sites have been deliberately left undisturbed or paved over with the express approval of archaeologists.

The change has come about because, to put it very simply, archaeologists have begun to recognize their own limitations and the terribly fragile nature of their material. The history of archaeology is studded with technological "if onlies." *If only* modern conservation methods could have been applied to the organic materials found in the first Egyptian pyramids opened by archaeologists. *If only* the infrared camera probe could have been used in the Etruscan tombs. *If only* pollen analysis had been available at the time of some of the great Scythian finds. The list of archaeology's new tools—dating from thermoluminescence for pottery, carbon-14 dating, tree ring analysis—is a long and, even more important, a lengthening one. Who knows what further advances may have been made in ten, fifty, or two hundred years? But will there be any sites left by then, unless we conserve them today? For the archaeologists of the future it will make little difference whether a site was professionally excavated or bulldozed into the sea. Once a site is disturbed, it is useless; it can never be restored to its original condition.

That is why this book is not going to tell you how to conduct your own excavation. Instead, we are going to focus on what has recently come to be called *conservation archaeology*. The basic premise of conservation archaeology is that archaeological sites must be regarded as a resource that, like oil, uranium, or redwood trees, must be used prudently lest the supply run out forever. Conservation archaeologists, therefore, need to have a much broader range of interests, tools, and tactics than was required by the conventional archaeologists of the past, whose first goal, if not to find and study *things,* was to find sites and dig them up forthwith.*

There is so much to do in conservation archaeology—in the field, the museum, and the laboratory—that digging has simply become less relevant. Furthermore, and with

---

*Those who endorse the conservation ethic in archaeology should certainly join the American Society for Conservation Archaeology—ASCA —whose address is listed in Appendix IV.

"Get them while they're young," or, One Reason Why Cultural Resources Are Important. The diorama was made by avocational archaeologist Virginia Barnhard.

certain limited exceptions (see chapter 11 on test pits), the process of planning and carrying out an excavation has grown much too complex for anyone, professional or avocational, without years of experience and training. The problem is that a badly run dig—where the workers do not know what they are looking for, where records are carelessly kept and finds improperly cataloged, where valuable evidence is therefore inevitably overlooked or destroyed— is much worse than no dig at all. Archaeology, it cannot be said too often, offers no second chances.

As it happens, the rise of conservation archaeology has been accompanied by increasing interest in the formerly neglected archaeology of North America. This neglect was partly a historical accident, because the first great discoveries about prehistory were made in the Nile Valley and Mesopotamia, and partly a result of the treasure myth to which we referred earlier. Because the objects commonly found in North American sites are made of stone or pottery or bone, but virtually never of gold, silver, or jewels, the tendency of the past was to concentrate on places where more spectacular (but not necessarily more interesting) things might be found.

It is none too soon for an increase in scholarly interest in the archaeology of North America. For example, it has recently been estimated that in California, an area especially rich in remains, *two archaeological sites are being destroyed every day* by construction projects, natural erosion, incompetent excavation, or just plain vandalism. Even if one revised that figure to two sites per state per week as a national average, the United States would be losing forever (since sites, unlike trees, will never grow back), 5,200 sites a year, and the figures are probably similar for Canada. Professional archaeologists are quite aware of this situation, but they are often helpless to do anything about it. There simply are not enough competent archaeologists to find, protect, and where necessary excavate all the sites before they are destroyed. The reason for this, ultimately, is that there is not enough money available to pay for the excavations, and that in turn is related to the fact that the public is not well informed about the nature and importance of North American archaeology. Sources in the United States and Canada recently contributed millions of dollars to preserve the monumental statues of Egypt's Abu Simbel from the floodwaters of the Aswan Dam project. Yet it is probable that few of those who responded so generously to Egypt's need would have recognized a complete assemblage of Early Archaic stone tools if they had uncovered them in their own backyard barbecue pits. One of the major goals of conservation archaeology, therefore, is to inform the public about the rich and varied cultural resource that is literally under their feet.

Enter at this point the amateur (or, as many prefer to be called, avocational) archaeologists. They are of every profession, age group, and background. Well-informed, responsible avocationals are conservation archaeology's first line of defense. They study their subject, survey sites and defend them against vandalism and commercial destruction, operate local museums, catalog collections, and engage in a wide variety of educational and research projects. They are sometimes more knowledgeable about local archaeology than the professionals. In addition, they may bring to bear on archaeological problems skills derived from law, journalism, engineering, art history, computer science, botany, geology, drafting, photography, and dozens of other useful fields. Because avocationals are on the spot and willing to donate their time and effort, they can and do play an indispensable role in conservation archaeology.

In practice, conservation archaeologists, both avocational and professional, operate on two levels and cultivate two rather different sets of abilities. First, of course, they need to know the techniques of field archaeology, with emphasis on site location and laboratory analysis rather than excavation. In later chapters we will speak in detail about such topics as how to find a site and what you should know before you go looking; how to record, map, and report sites; how to make a proper scientific collection of the artifacts you find; how to get professional advice about matters such as dating material or protecting endangered sites; and how to set up your own traveling display or small archaeological museum.

One of the most important contributions the avocational archaeologist can make to the field is her or his intimate knowledge of the local landscape, history, or weather conditions. Site location, for example, is not yet so much a science that archaeologists can do without a large dose of old-fashioned intuition, backed up by the kind of information that comes only from knowing the land. Perhaps this canyon is subject to flash flooding. It is therefore a poor place to look for an Indian campsite. On the slopes of this mountain there may be groves of beech trees and a year-round stream. Early inhabitants might well have gone there to gather nuts in the fall. An unusual salt spring in this valley would have been valuable to colonists when salt was scarce. And so on.

Another fascinating and important field of activity is called replication, meaning the attempt to learn more about other cultures by studying the *processes* by which their artifacts were made, rather than by merely cataloging the artifacts themselves. Once you have spent four frustrating hours attempting to chip a single edge, let alone a finished tool, from native quartz you will assuredly have a new respect for the original makers of the stone tools you see in museum displays or in your own collection.

Some conservation archaeologists content themselves with a private quest for knowledge. Increasing numbers of others, however, find themselves drawn into the public arena as well, because of the threat to archaeological resources posed by modern society's increasingly avid exploitation of undeveloped land. Both the United States and Canada have laws for the protection of historic and prehistoric archaeological sites, but they are often ambiguous in their meaning and restricted in their application. (See Appendix I for a summary of the more important United States and Canadian laws.) On the state and provincial levels there are also laws, and these vary widely, from almost complete protection of sites (at least on public lands) to virtually no protection. More often than not, the archaeologist finds that protection (in whatever form) extends only to those sites that are on publicly owned land or are to be used for publicly funded or licensed construction projects, while sites on private land are entirely under the control of the landowner. (There are exceptions, however.)

In cases where protective laws do apply, legally required archaeological work is usually done in stages. First the land-moving agency or firm must commission and pay for a thorough, competent survey for historic or prehistoric sites on the property, unless an adequate survey report has already been filed. It is not legally sufficient to say, as construction agencies have all too often been known to do, "The State Archaeologist has no sites listed here," or, "Professor Knowall of Wisdom U. says she went there one day in 1949 and doesn't remember finding anything." One of the most constructive things you, as a conservation archaeologist, can do when government agencies or firms contracting with government agencies refuse to carry out their responsibilities under archaeological law is to contact them or their administrative superiors. Your object is to convince them that a proper survey, done competently and early, is not only environmentally sound but is almost always less expensive for them in the long run.

The reason is twofold. First, there are some cases where excavation can be avoided altogether if archaeological information is available in the planning stages of a project. Consider a highway extension that can equally well be built on either side of a valley. If the south side contains sites while the north side does not, it may be possible for the Highway Department to satisfy archaeological requirements merely by commissioning a brief survey and locating its roadbed on the north side of the valley. Second, even if sites are found and there is no way to avoid destroying them, so that excavation is required, the rule that haste makes waste indicates why a well-planned, careful excavation is much more "cost-effective," in engineering parlance, than one conducted one step ahead of the bulldozer.

Another effective way for conservation archaeologists to make their point is to speak up at public hearings or town meetings when a project is in the planning stage. Some officials are genuinely unaware of their obligations under environmental law and are perfectly willing to cooperate once the situation is explained to them.

The next step of the usual archaeological review process is the filing of one of several types of impact statement (an assessment of the foreseeable effects of the proposed project). Here again, avocational conservation archaeologists have a role to play. Since impact statements are mandated and funded by public laws, the public has an inherent right to read and comment on them. You or any other citizen may monitor the accuracy of such statements and point out probable sites or types of negative impact to known sites that you believe have been overlooked. For example, a proposal to build a school athletic field on top of an archaeological site might be given an assessment of "no impact," without taking account of the fact that archaeological damage would result from using a cultivator on the site in the course of putting in a lawn. The courts have established that the right of review extends to the right to sue the agency or individual who puts out a demonstrably inaccurate impact statement. (This fact helps to explain why contract surveys and excavations are no place for beginners: those who write impact statements must be prepared to defend their conclusions in a court of law.)

We should pause here, however, to point out that conservation archaeology is not and should not be in the business of stopping construction just for the sake of stopping construction. Environmentalists, urban planners, and various community or special interest groups sometimes find themselves opposed to particular projects, and they may make useful allies for conservation archaeologists seeking to promote the wise use of a vanishing resource. However, the authors do not think it is in the best interests of archaeology for its advocates to get the reputation of being "spoilers" who have no regard for the jobs that are lost or the money that is spent when construction is delayed for archaeological reasons. Except in rare cases, it is not necessary to take an all-or-nothing attitude toward conservation. Rather, the aim should be to identify endangered sites and then, if destruction or damage is inevitable, extract the data in the best possible form through careful, responsible excavation by trained professionals.

Unfortunately, this kind of measured, well-reasoned approach is not always possible. No matter how alert you are to newspaper stories and public hearings on proposed construction, the time will come when you discover a site that is being destroyed before your very eyes through either natural causes (the collapse of a cliff face, erosion of a river bank) or human agency (bulldozers moving earth on private property). Now the conservation archaeologist has to find the best answer to the question, "How can at least some useful information be salvaged from this shambles?" Like medicine, archaeology is often forced to make the best of circumstances. If there is no operating room available, you make do with the kitchen table and a hunting knife. Thus, while it is all very well to be picky about field technique when conditions permit, there are also times in archaeological salvage when anything goes. If stone tools and pottery sherds are literally dropping out of a cliff face into the ocean or the bulldozer is warming up for its day's work, you may be reduced to snatching what you can and crying later. One of the authors has literally gone knocking on doors to turn out local residents for an unexpected salvage job. This sort of situation may be heartbreaking, but the volunteers certainly receive a quick education in conservation archaeology.

Between the planned scientific excavation and the salvage emergency lies a large middle range of possibilities. Perhaps a site slated for destruction is on private property and therefore probably not protected under the law. Perhaps the local university department of anthropology or museum staff may persuade the owner to allow a staff member to excavate without pay. Or the regional archaeological society may wish to excavate on weekends. On the other hand, the undisturbed and unendangered ancient campsite twenty miles from the nearest road should probably be left alone, a resource for the future. The site near but not on a proposed roadway may easily become desirable for residential or commercial use in the next decade. It should be brought to the attention of professionals who may wish to excavate it if it fits into their long-term research designs or promises to be relevant to pressing current research questions. However, the site on public land that is going to be flooded by the new hydroelectric dam next year is urgently in need of professional excavation at the earliest possible date. And so on. The important point is that each site must be assessed individually on the basis of the level of crisis involved. Waste is the cardinal sin of conservation archaeology.

We have gone some way toward answering the questions, "What is archaeology in general?" and "What is conservation archaeology in particular?" Before we are satisfied, however, we ought to take a brief look at one other thing that archaeology is not.

You probably cannot be involved in archaeology very long without coming across individuals who may call themselves archaeologists but who most decidedly are not. The correct name for them is pothunters, and though some of them are merely misguided, there are no more devastating destroyers of the continent's archaeological heritage.

Pothunters collect, for themselves or for sale, American Indian or historic period artifacts, especially pottery, projectile points, beads, carvings, bottles, and other items considered attractive or exotic. Some pothunters genuinely admire their finds as objects, but they care little or nothing for the cultures from which they came. Whenever they find a site (or, worse, hear about a site others have found), they grab their shovels and rush off to plunder the place before anyone can beat them to it. They dig without the least thought for the unique information they destroy, leaving behind only a hopelessly muddled mixture of early and late deposits (once neatly layered, or stratified, with the oldest on the bottom), so that the site is forever afterward useless to scientific archaeology. Pothunters have even been known to desecrate burials in their quest for funeral goods and to sneak into legitimate excavation sites at night to steal "the good stuff." Such people are no more doing archaeology than a man-eating tiger is performing lifesaving surgery on his victim.

Dr. Charles McGimsey III, Director of the Arkansas Archaeological Survey, has defined the pothunter as one who cannot pass the test of being "at least as interested in preserving archaeological data as in recovering archaeological objects." Anyone who wishes to be known as an archaeologist, therefore, must be careful neither to be a pothunter nor to come unwittingly under the influence of pothunters. Admittedly, this may be tricky because some pothunters are members of archaeological societies and other apparently respectable groups.

Yet it is not entirely fair to condemn pothunters out of hand. In one sense, they are not so much deplorable as merely outdated. More archaeologists than might care to admit to it are reformed pothunters, and many famous "antiquarians" and "collectors of antiquities" of decades past would today run the risk of being labeled pothunters. There is a long tradition behind the activities of men like Britain's Lord Elgin, who stripped the Parthenon of its sculptures and shipped them off to the British Museum with the well-intentioned purpose of saving them from the Turks. It is no fault of the Elgins and their colleagues that archaeology has changed from the pastime of collection into the science of interpretation and conservation.

The history of archaeology as a field of study has been a dynamic one. Springing from roots among European collectors (read "glorified pothunters") of the seventeenth century and earlier, archaeology in the nineteenth and early twentieth centuries was passing through a literal Golden Age when it was not easily distinguishable from treasure hunting. During this period universities and intellectual historians most often classified archaeology as part of art history or classics. Only gradually did its emphasis shift from the finding of things to the making of theories about man. The result is that today there might be more scholarly excitement generated by the discovery of a single twelve-thousand-year-old spear point in Massachusetts (in a context such that it could be accurately dated) than there would be over the discovery of a whole tombful of gold bric-a-brac in Lower Egypt.

Archaeology, then, has emerged as a branch of anthropology, and we may define it (with as much confidence as we may ever use in trapping a purely human concept in a definition) as the study of the material remains of human cultures. That means not only ancient or "primitive" cultures, nonindustrial cultures, or cultures geographically removed from our own, but literally *all* cultures, always, from the first hypothetical day of human prehistory to yesterday, and from the farthest reaches of the globe to the suburbs of Chicago.

Modern archaeologists and anthropologists have abandoned the once-popular notion that Human Progress is a ladder with Civilization (usually meaning Western European Christian civilization) at its top and Savagery at the bottom. They have found it more enlightening to study cultures, in the plural, than to search for evidences of something arbitrarily labeled Civilization, and to ask not, "Which culture produced the most elaborate artifacts for its ruling class?" but, "What are the many ways in which groups of human beings may live harmoniously with their environment, and what are the human or natural factors that may throw the system out of balance?" This last is the real question that animates the search for archaeological knowledge, and though such concerns may at times seem far removed from the niceties of artifact classification or the legal intricacies of Executive Order 11593, they are, in the last analysis, what archaeology is all about.

2
What Are You Looking For?

Before you set out to look for something, it is usually a good idea to know what the something is and where it is likely to be found. You will not discover many beechnuts at the beach or mango trees on Madison Avenue.

One of the major things that archaeologists look for is artifacts, not as an end in themselves, but as indicators of where to look for sites. But what exactly is an artifact? Strictly speaking, an artifact is any sign of human activity, yet many artifacts are too fragile to endure. You will not find the ripples from the wake of a bark canoe or the footprints of the Ghost Dancers. In more practical terms, you will also be very unlikely to find the remains of the canoe itself, long rotted back into lake mud, or the leather moccasin, now part of the dust of the prairie. With a very few exceptions, such as frozen tundra, arid desert, and dry or nitrous caves (which will be discussed in the description of the various archaeological regions in chapter 4), North America does not have the kind of climate and soil conditions that preserve organic materials (those of plant and animal origin). A combination of rainfall, bacteria, and soil acidity quickly destroys hides, wood, leather, bark, cloth, and grain. Bone, shell, horn, metal, and glass (the last two, of course, dating mostly from historic times* but also including native copper of the pre-Columbian period) often take only a little longer to disappear.

What remains on the ground surface often looks to the untrained eye like nothing at all. To the archaeologist, however, the same patch of ground tells as vivid, if not quite as legible, a story as a movie marquee.

Although the situation obviously varies from area to area and from site to site, the single most common material for remanent artifacts (those that are preserved in or on the soil when a site is abandoned) is probably stone, followed by pottery. During the tens of thousands of years from their arrival on the continent until contact with Europeans, the inhabitants of North America made many of their implements of chipped, flaked, or ground stone. The tools ranged from tiny, delicate points to capacious stone bowls weighing up to forty pounds, and the styles or patterns in which they were made tended to change over long periods of time or from culture to culture.

This fact is very important to the archaeologist, who can distinguish among the various styles the way you might be able to tell a 1958 Plymouth from a 1974 Ford. However, this evolution of artifact styles also gives rise to certain difficulties. For one thing, no one has yet been able to say with certainty whether the most important reason for changes in artifact design is time (vertical change) or differences between cultures (horizontal change). In other terms, if you have two Ford cars, is one merely a later

*"Historic times," as contrasted with prehistoric times, refers to the period for which written records are available. "Historic times" does not refer to a uniform time period, since writing appeared several thousand years ago in China and Mesopotamia, for example, while in North America the historic period does not begin until the first European contacts, that is, until the sixteenth or seventeenth century.

version of the other, like the Mustang and the Tin Lizzie, or are their differences due to the fact that they were manufactured in different places at the same time, like the American Pinto and the British Anglia? Both sides (vertical versus horizontal change as cause) have their ardent supporters, but the dispute is far from being resolved.

Another problem is the question of purpose or function. A Rolls-Royce doesn't look much like a Jeep, but both were made to serve as transportation. In the case of stone tools, we not only have dissimilar objects that may well have had the same function, we are not even able to say with certainty what any one tool may have been used for. The popular term "arrowheads" is definitely incorrect when applied to all but a minority of stone tools. (Most of the artifacts called arrowheads are more accurately termed knives, spear points, or dart points.) The early Americans needed a very large tool kit that included awls, scrapers, knives, spear points, throwing darts, axe heads, burins, adzes, drills, hammers, punches, reamers, needles, and choppers as well as arrow points, and we can hardly be positive about what a particular tool was used for, not having seen its maker at work with it. It is even likely that one tool had many functions, just as you might use a jackknife for whittling, cutting your meat, spreading butter, and playing mumblety-peg. We therefore issue this warning: Although various authorities provide elaborate typologies of stone tools, making minute distinctions on the basis of dimensions, number of cutting edges, and so on, these are really only conveniences for the purpose of cataloging. Don't be misled into thinking a particular tool *is* a scraper or whatever. The fact is that all such names are just guesses, however reasonable. (But see pages 166–67 for laboratory tests that may serve someday to settle the question.) You should also beware of the label "ceremonial object." Archaeologists have an unfortunate habit of applying this term to any artifact whose purpose they do not understand.

To return from the theoretical to the literal nitty-gritty of the stuff lying around on the ground—just how do you identify a stone tool in the field? Of course, many fully worked tools are unmistakably of human manufacture, but others may look at first glance like nothing but chips of stone. It is certainly not safe to assume, though, that any sharp-edged piece of rock is a tool. Natural events such as landslides and frost fracture often produce flakes that look like genuine tools. But there are differences. First of all, the makers of chipped stone tools knew that not all types of stone are suitable for the purpose. Soft stone like volcanic tuff, grainy stone like granite, and strongly layered stone like slate are all equally undesirable because they wear too quickly, or give a poor edge, or break unevenly. (Some tools were made of inferior stone, however, when that was the only material available.) Good stone for tools is both hard and uniform. The most commonly used of the many North American stone types are chert, quartz, obsidian, "flint" (in reality a kind of chert), and chalcedony. There are literally hundreds of possible materials, too many to list here, much less describe. However, they share one useful characteristic: when struck (percussion flaked) or subjected to pressure with a narrow instrument such as a piece of antler (pressure flaked), they produce a kind of fracture mark known as conchoidal. The term means shell-like—the mark shows rings like those on the outside of a clamshell. The best everyday example is the sort of chip often found on the edge of a thick drinking glass. The mark is characteristic of one caused by a sharp blow or heavy, steady pressure, and it looks quite different from the kind of breakage produced by frost, erosion, or faults in the stone. Figure 1 shows a stone tool with arrows indicating the marks of conchoidal fracture. (More will be said about methods of making stone tools in chapter 8.)

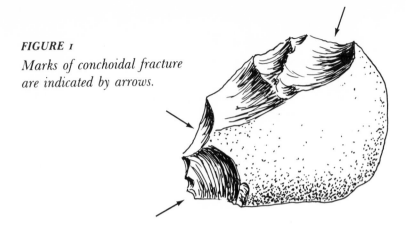

FIGURE 1

Marks of conchoidal fracture
are indicated by arrows.

Regular or patterned marks of conchoidal fracture, then, are the best field indicator of stone tools and may be used in doubtful cases to decide whether a piece of stone is an artifact or merely a natural accident. Some people become incredibly expert at spotting worked stone. Here is archaeologist Geoffrey Bibby's description of the abilities of his friend and colleague P. V. Glob as evidenced during the expedition that was to locate the biblical Land of Dilmun off the coast of Arabia:

> We were on our way to a ruined building, far from any habitation, which the air photographs had shown out here in the southwestern desert area.
>
> P. V., a little in advance, stooped down, and then turned and held out his clenched fist to me. "The expedition is off the ground," he said, and dropped a flake of flint into my outstretched hand.
>
> Now, I should explain that there are two main classifications of archaeologists. There are those who are crazy about potsherds, and there are those who are crazy about flint. I belong to the

first category, and P. V., though as good an all-rounder as I have met, belongs to the second. Your real flint enthusiast has a sort of second sight. He can see worked flint, not only at a distance where it is manifestly impossible to distinguish flint from stone, but, I am convinced, at anything up to an inch and a half below ground surface.*

P. V. Glob's piece of flint turned out to be an example of what is called chipping waste. Chipping waste bears the same relationship to stone tool manufacture as sawdust bears to carpentry. You can't have one without the other. One might say that chipping waste is an unsung hero of the archaeological saga, for whereas the toolmaker most often carries the tool away for use elsewhere, the chips produced in the toolmaking process are left where they fall, to the delight of future archaeologists. Chipping waste displays the telltale conchoidal fractures but is not a tool in itself unless it shows signs of wear. In that case it is called a utilized flake, meaning a flake or chip that was deliberately struck from the parent stone and used without refinement or retouching. Chipping waste is thus an artifact in the sense that it is a man-made sign of human presence. It is one of your best friends. Watch for it.

To be sure, tools and chipping waste are not the only kinds of stone artifacts. Other items include polished or ground stone bowls, carvings (usually small) in human, animal, or abstract form, jewelry, polished "axeheads," and atlatl weights (see Figure 2, page 38). There is almost no end to the uses to which stone was put in pre-contact North America.

*Geoffrey Bibby, *Looking for Dilmun.* (New York: Alfred A. Knopf, 1969), p. 48.

The second major type of remanent artifact is pottery. When well fired, pottery lasts almost as well as stone but tends to be found (alas) in fragments or sherds. North American Indian pottery styles are enormously varied. They show everything from the highest artistry to the most basic functionalism. Pottery may be plain or painted—black, red, white, brown, gray, tan, or any combination of these colors. Fortunately, pottery is easy to recognize and can hardly be confused with anything else except imported European earthenware of the colonial period or broken roofing tiles in areas of Spanish influence.

There are a few characteristics that are useful for distinguishing historic from prehistoric pottery. For example, a shiny glazed surface, the presence of colors other than those mentioned above (for example, blue and green), and the perfect symmetry achieved by the use of the potter's wheel are all signs of techniques introduced by European colonists.

But though pottery is not hard to identify as such, its classification is extremely complex. Vast tomes have been written on the subject of cataloging each style and its multi-

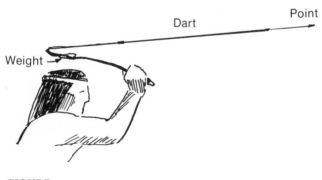

FIGURE 2
An atlatl in use

ple variants. No general description is really possible, but some typical pottery types will be described and illustrated in Appendix III, which discusses the artifacts of North America's various regions in some detail.

The third common material of ancient remains is shell. The shells of salt- and freshwater molluscs are not as permanent as stone, but where the soil is not too acid, they last a remarkably long time. Shellfish were useful to Native American peoples in a number of ways. On the most obvious level, shellfish are food. They neither bite nor run away, and must have been one of the tastiest and most easily available protein sources for those who were lucky enough to have access to suitable shores. Mounds of clam, oyster, mussel, abalone, or other shells are often very conspicuous on river banks, seacoasts, and lake shores. In addition, shellfish were often carried considerable distances before being eaten. Their white, chalky, razor-edged fragments make a startling contrast to the dark soil of forest floor or pastureland.

Shell had important uses for American Indian peoples. Whole shells and shell fragments were worn variously as pendants, necklaces, beads, gorgets (decorative placques worn on the chest), earpieces, armlets, and other items of jewelry and were sewn on clothing, inlaid into wood, stone, or bone, or incised with intricate patterns.

Even more significant for the archaeologist are the strings of shell beads that served as currency in parts of North America. Along the northern Atlantic coast, the hard-shell clam with its purple spot inside the lip *(Venus mercenaria)* yielded the well-known wampum. In the west the most prized source of shell discs was the Pismo clam *(Tivella stultorum)*. Also popular were the many varieties of olivella. Strings of shell beads traveled hundreds of miles into the interior along trade routes that are now being studied with great interest. Recent researchers have even shown that this currency, like our own, was subject to inflation and devaluation according to local economic conditions which are not yet fully understood. For this reason, it is doubly infuriating to archaeologists that these bead "necklaces" are among the favorite prey of the pothunter and the dealer in illegal antiquities.

Bone is another artifact material that may appear on the surface. Softer than stone, but harder than wood, bone was used by Native Americans for a variety of tools and ornaments. Bones (and of course teeth, claws, antlers, and horns) were made into pendants, beads, gorgets, and almost every other kind of adornment. Among bone tools, there were fishhooks, harpoons, shovels, awls, wedges, and more. In addition, one may come across engraved bone objects, the best known being those of the Eskimo.

The archaeologist must also be well acquainted with bone in the form of remains. Animal bones give important information about the food resources of the early North Americans, and human bones, of course, denote funerary sites. Because of the ethical questions relating to the finding of human skeletal remains (whether Indian or non-Indian), it is essential, at the very least, to be able to tell animal from human bones. More will be said about human bones and what to do about them in chapter 3, under Burial Sites.

A final class of remanent artifacts is made up of certain items used by the Native American peoples but not made by them. These are trade goods brought in by early white explorers, trappers, settlers, miners, and missionaries. Most common are the opaque colored-glass beads so familiar from designs on beaded belts and moccasins. Glass trade beads are of interest to the archaeologist not only as signs of occupation but because the various sizes and colors can tell us much about their origin and date—whether they were acquired from French, Spanish, Russian, English, or

Dutch traders, for example. Remember, however, that ready-made trade beads were a very valuable commodity, a fact you will appreciate if you ever try to make beads by punching, piercing, and polishing native materials such as stone, bone, or shell. As a consequence, beads were not left lying around like chipping waste, and it is unusual to find more than isolated single beads in the debris of an occupation site. (This is not true of burial sites, as pothunters have unfortunately discovered.)

Other trade goods that may survive on the surface are pearl buttons machine-made out of shell (very popular with some groups for decorating clothing), rifle flints, looking glasses, and occasional objects of worked metal, ranging from horse trappings to weapons to ornamental brass buttons. In damp areas, however, metals tend to corrode and disappear almost as rapidly as most organic materials.

European-made objects are of particular interest to those who study historic or industrial archaeology, those branches of the field that deal, in North America, with periods after European contact. Only recognized as subjects for serious study in the last decade or so, these new topics have already shed much light on the life of seventeenth-, eighteenth-, and nineteenth-century North America and have changed our ideas on such matters as the ethnic origins of early colonists, land settlement patterns, and the economic forces behind industrialization. They have helped open our eyes to the fact that almost any historic remnant is of potential interest—to the archaeologists of the future, if not to us. Certainly no remains of historic periods should be wantonly destroyed or exploited. From this perspective, the bottle hunters of today are not much better than pothunters. Even if your interest in archaeology is exclusively prehistoric, you should at least note significant finds of old glass or ceramics (to name only two of the most durable types of historic artifacts) and report them to the local historical society or historic archaeologist, if you know of one.

As a footnote to this discussion of remanent artifacts, one idea should be highlighted. It is that all artifacts are not of equal importance in the ultimate work of the archaeologist, which is not merely to find and catalog but to interpret the remains of the past. Some artifacts are so widely found and remain so nearly unchanged over such long time spans that their discovery tells us very little about the specific period during which they were made. On the other hand, some artifacts are firmly associated, through previous finds, with a particular period. An example is the fluted type of point called Clovis or Folsom, together with the unfluted but distinctive Sandia point (see Figure 4, page 64). These point types are typical artifacts of the period called Paleo-Indian and are the earliest positively identified remains of human occupation in North America. They have been found in the deepest and earliest layers of certain sites, and even, in a few famous cases, in association with the remains of extinct animals such as mammoths. The points called Clovis, Folsom, and Sandia thus have a special importance for archaeologists. Find one or more of these points, either on the surface or under many soil layers, and you can safely say your site is Paleo-Indian. On the other hand, in the absence of evidence to the contrary, a site *may* be Paleo-Indian, but this will be very hard to prove unless those points or other typical artifacts are found there. As you can see, it is of great importance to learn the typical artifacts for your area. They are the index tabs to your study of the past.

3
... And How Will You Know When You Find It?

Now that you have a basic idea of the types of artifacts you will be looking for, the next thing to consider is where to look for a site and how to decide what kind of site it is when you find it.

Of course the ideal answer to the question of where to look would be, "Everywhere." No one can state positively beforehand that a particular piece of ground does *not* harbor any remains. Nevertheless, it is clearly impossible to cover every square foot of even the most promising territory. The Valley of the Kings, for example, one of the richest and most publicized of all ancient sites, never has been and probably never will be excavated down to the last inch. The entrance to Tut-ankh-Amen's tomb was found in an area that had been familiar to archaeologists for decades —beneath an unprepossessing pile of rubble only slightly more recent than the tomb itself, where it had lain concealed for thousands of years.

Since, therefore, you cannot look everywhere, it is advisable to find ways to tell the likely spots from the unlikely ones. This means simply that the archaeologist must ask, "What parts of this territory would have been most attractive to its ancient inhabitants?"

It is one of the beauties of archaeology that the asking of this question opens up ways of looking at the natural world that we citizens of the industrial/atomic age have commonly forgotten. The land springs out of the prison of its map grids, alive with possibilities. From what direction are the prevailing winds in winter? In summer? A campsite will want shelter from the one and exposure to the other. Where is the nearest source of fresh water? Where *was* it before the white man polluted or diverted the rivers,

Archaeological sites may not look like much at first glance . . . but the trained eye can easily spot this Maine shell mound.

Courtesy of the Maine State Museum and Dr. Bruce Bourque

drained the wetlands, dammed the lakes? Which side of the
mountains gets the rainfall? Early farmers knew the most
favorable places for their plots of beans, maize, or squash.
How far up the river did (or, if we are lucky, do) the salmon,
shad, or alewives run? Along those banks may have been
temporary campsites for the spring fishing. If you broke
your favorite skinning knife just here, where would you find
the nearest source of good (conchoidally fracturing) stone
for making another?

Most essential of all, how could a family survive if they
were dropped off on this land without hot dogs, wheels,
polystyrene, stainless steel, or cigarette lighters? Could
they eat pinyon nuts, wild cherries, birds' eggs, fern roots,
freshwater mussels, seal meat? What forage would attract
the deer, the partridge, or the mountain goat for them to
hunt? Where could they shelter from rain, snow, or the
howling of wolves? Suppose they had human enemies.
Could they retreat to seaward spits of land, narrow canyons, natural caves? In every season of the year, in lean
years and fat, in peace, war, or religious festival, *how did they
live?* In searching for the answers to these questions, you
will begin, slowly, to see the land in a new light—as they
saw it.

You will need common sense, a keen faculty of observation, and a dash of intuition in your study of the environment. You will also need help from some more conventional devices. A local library probably has guides to the
geology of your region, with emphasis on the period following the last Ice Age. Geology is related in beautiful and
subtle ways to all the other facets of the natural world. In
its more obvious aspects, it can guide the archaeologist to
probable sites of ancient quarries (sources not only of
flaking material but of ochre for paint, pipestone, soapstone, or pottery clay) or help to rule out places, such as

recent lava flows, where sites would logically *not* be found.

Beyond geology, there are botany, zoology, climatology, and of course the science that links them all—ecology. In order to fill out a correct site report (see chapter 5), the type of plant and animal community surrounding the site must be identified. This in turn is helpful in site location for future surveys. It takes time, and a combination of study and field experience, to become fully familiar with an area's types of ecological communities. It takes even more time, study, and experience to be able to visualize what a place was like before it collided with industry or modern agriculture. Yet whether you are studying the American Indian peoples of prehistory or the early European settlers, it is well to remember that they all depended, much more directly than we do, upon the land for welfare and survival. To know material culture without knowing its environment is as impossible as to know fish while ignoring the ocean.

Another essential kind of written reference for the archaeologist who is preparing to go on a survey is the ethnographic source, as it is called—the historic account of Native American or early settlement life. It may have been set down by an explorer, a missionary, a newspaper reporter, a scientific surveyor, or even a painter like George Catlin, whose journals and pictures provide us with much unique information. There is a lot to be learned from these ethnographic sources concerning habits, customs, cultures, and events from roughly 1500 on. However, when the sources about Native Americans were written by those who were not themselves Native Americans, they must be read with considerable caution. Early writers were often hostile to, and almost always ignorant about, what they saw. The best ethnographic sources are those that simply describe, without trying to evaluate or explain, what the authors personally observed. The worst are those that tell sensational stories, repeat information given by third parties, or attempt to pass moral judgments on matters their authors manifestly do not comprehend.

Nevertheless, even the worst written records frequently contain fascinating and useful snippets. When British novelist Josephine Tey remarked that "Truth is not in accounts, it is in account books," she had in mind the fact that accounts of events reflect the biases of the writers, whereas the simple economic facts often tell a different story. Suppose you are reading an account of a westward journey taken by an educated trader in the first half of the nineteenth century. He has been received kindly by a small band of Sioux who have just carried out a highly successful buffalo drive. He comments with disgust on the "greed" these "savages" display in their eating habits. That he should react this way is understandable, since he has been brought up in a society with a stable agricultural economy, where Gluttony is reckoned one of the Seven Deadly Sins. Of much more interest to you is his casual remark that there are fewer dogs in the camp than seems usual and that a group of twenty-seven individuals, including children, consumed all or nearly all the meat and entrails of five full-grown buffalo. If you have read your other sources, you know that dog meat was the "food of last resort" for many Plains groups in times of scarcity, and you also know that the habit of gorging on fresh meat after a long hunger is very common among peoples whose main food source is large animals. You can now appreciate this anecdote for what it actually says about the amount of meat consumed per capita under these conditions, and for anything else it may tell you about the time of year, circumstances of the hunt, or method of meat distribution, without being sidetracked by words like "disgusting" and "gluttony." Be careful, however, that you don't fall into your own trap and decide that anybody who could kill and eat a dog must be despicable. How long has it been since you went a week without food? The point we wish to make here is that ethnographic sources must be read critically but also with due recognition of the fact that they are the closest we shall ever come to a firsthand glimpse of precolonial culture as a living body rather than as an excavated skeleton.

Historic archaeologists will of course spend even more time on original documents, if only because there are more of them. A modern reader has some of the same difficulties with historic sources concerning the earlier periods of our own culture as those encountered by the prehistorian seeking information about ways of life that have now have vanished. The problems may not be so acute, because at least the historic archaeologist "speaks the language" and because things have not changed utterly in three hundred years. However, this appearance of familiarity may itself lead to pitfalls. James Deetz, chief archaeologist for the excavation and restoration of Plimouth Plantation in Massachusetts, likes to tell this story: Wanting to know what furnishings to provide for their restored eighteenth-century houses, historic archaeologists turned to the old probate records, which listed the contents of houses whose owners had died and willed them to others. They found the usual quantity of beds, chairs, and chests, along with a surprising number of looking glasses. Each household seemed to have had several mirrors, which ought to have been luxury items in those days when almost every manufactured object was imported from Europe. The archaeologists dutifully researched mirror making of the relevant period and commissioned a number of authentic reproduction mirrors to hang in the restored Plimouth. Only by accident was it discovered later that in the language of the time "looking glass" was a euphemism for "chamber pot." The polite colonial clerks had caused the archaeologists to make several hundred dollars' worth of mistake.

A quite different kind of archaeological reading is to be found in books, papers, and journal articles published by modern researchers. These publications are referred to collectively as "the literature," but they are by no means to be confused with "real," or literary, literature. Archaeologists are no more immune than other professionals to the tendency to write in "technolese" rather than English. Thus an utterly haphazard sample derived from the contents page of the April, 1974, issue of *American Antiquity* (the journal of the Society for American Archaeology) reveals the following bewilderness of terminology: R-mode analysis, ceramic longevity, functional estimator, population aggregates, nearest neighbor analysis, and early millingstone horizon. Having said this, we can already hear the outraged squawks of the authors involved, declaring that these terms are either briefer or more precise than their alternatives and that they are perfectly understood by other archaeologists. Any or all of these claims may be valid on occasion, but the point we wish to make here is that the beginning archaeologist cannot expect to plunge headfirst into "the literature" without some preparation. And yet, a knowledge of the findings of others who have worked in your area is more or less a necessity, as it prevents duplication and makes you aware of the issues and problems that are especially relevant to you. The only answer to this dilemma is to proceed with caution. Begin with books for the general reader and then go on, perhaps to the newsletter of the local archaeological society. The more you read, the more your comprehension will increase, and it will not be long until—for good or ill—you too will be tossing off "biotic communities," "radiocarbon date coevalnesses," and "resource exploitations" with the best of them. Appendix II contains suggestions for further reading on a variety of topics ranging from the popular through the technical.

Another useful and frequently overlooked source of information on local archaeology is the unpublished impact statements filed by archaeologists in fulfillment of survey or excavation contracts. Public Law 91–190 (the National Environmental Protection Act) establishes a public right of review for all environmental impact statements. Copies of impact statements should be on file in the office of the State or Provincial Archaeologist and (in the United States) the State Historic Preservation Officer. See Appendix IV for addresses and pages 128–29 for further information about these officials.

The last kind of preparation you need before actually setting out to survey is a general awareness of how to evaluate what you find. Merely to say you have located a site is about as helpful as identifying an unknown animal as a vertebrate. Like vertebrates, archaeological sites vary in their distribution. Some types are found nearly everywhere, while some are found only in specialized environments. For example, you will almost certainly not discover any pueblos outside the Southwest. (If you do come across one in Alaska or Labrador or wherever, be sure to let us know. It won't be the first time sweeping statements have made archaeologists look foolish.)

The following kinds of prehistoric sites are nearly universal. (Historic sites vary widely and will be discussed separately.)

Occupation Sites

1. Permanent: These are the places where true villages were located. Though the types of housing and the layouts of such sites appear in bewildering variety, they have the common characteristic of having been settled communities that, if not occupied twelve months of the year, were lived in over long periods and returned to regularly. Permanent

villages are hard to identify positively from surface findings. However, a site that shows signs that many different activities were carried out there, especially if those activities would logically belong to several seasons, is very possibly a permanent one. The diagnosis is best made by collecting a wide spectrum of artifacts such as tools for woodworking *and* fishing *and* hide processing. Naturally, a source of fresh water is essential to a permanent village.

2. Temporary: The nature of a permanent occupation site becomes clearer when contrasted with findings at a temporary or seasonal camp. This type of site was used only for one major purpose, such as the taking of salmon in the spring, although it may have served as headquarters to several families for periods up to a month or two year after year. The remanent artifacts are usually those associated with one single activity, plus basics such as cooking utensils. Fresh water is usual, but is not absolutely essential to a temporary camp.

A word of warning: Size is not a reliable way to tell a permanent village from a temporary camp, at least not until you are thoroughly familiar with the habits of the local prehistoric population. In some cases, several small groups or tribelets regularly left their permanent villages to rendezvous with others for the purpose of exchanging news, trading, celebrating religious festivals, and the like. These gatherings, held perhaps once a year or once every several years, would leave occupation sites far larger in surface area than any of the nearby permanent villages. Because of their temporary nature, such sites are generally of less interest to archaeologists than even the smallest permanent villages, but some specialists find in temporary camps important clues to seasonal migrations and other population movements.

Trails

Man-made trails are very hard to tell from those made by wildlife or domestic animals. However, a trail that links two archaeological sites may be tentatively identified as man-made.

Quarries

These are the mines of the prehistoric population. The best indicator of whether a deposit has been used by man is the presence of broken stone tools.

Manufacturing Sites

Stone was not always worked where it was quarried. Other materials, too, were taken away from the site where they were gathered. Stone, however, leaves the most obvious signs at a manufacturing site—chipping waste again. In many areas, stone tools appear to have been manufactured in specialized locations that were neither villages nor quarries. One possible reason is that no one would want a house or front yard littered with razor-sharp stone flakes.

Rock Art

Under this term is included both rock paintings, called pictographs, and designs pecked or carved on rock faces, called petroglyphs. Rock art is not really universal in North America, but there are few areas that are completely lacking in sites of this type.

Rock art may be found in a wide variety of locations— inside rock shelters or caves (don't forget to look at the ceiling), on exposed cliff faces, on large boulders, on bedrock, or beside trails. Sometimes it occurs near village sites, but it may also appear miles from any other sign of occupation.

The meaning of rock art is a matter for much discussion among archaeologists, anthropologists, art historians, and modern American Indian groups. Of course, rock art was made by many different peoples at many different periods, and it ranges all the way from simple stick figures and handprints to the incredibly complex abstractions of central California and even to the huge dragonlike figures of the so-called Piasa rock (now unfortunately much damaged) that once brooded over the Illinois River. There is therefore no reason to suppose that rock art "means" any one thing. Some examples may be purely decorative, some religious, some magical; others may show the visions of shamans, record astronomical or prehistoric events, or mark the boundaries of clan or tribal territory. Be wary of any suggestion that rock art is Indian writing, or mysterious messages from Atlantis or outer space; it has plenty of simpler and more logical interpretations, some of which we have just listed.

Whatever rock art may have "meant" to the peoples who made it, it is clearly of great interest and should be carefully preserved from damage. If you come across a previously unknown or "lost" piece of rock art, the first step is to record it on film. Take several photographs from various angles and try to include something to indicate the scale of each picture, such as a person, a hand, or a meter tape. Make a note of the f-stop and shutter speed setting for each shot and keep this record with the developed prints for your final site report (see chapter 5). If the find is painted with colors, take color pictures as well as black and white. However, black and white pictures should never be omitted, as they are usually the only ones that can be printed in books and articles.

Next, it is a good idea to reproduce the piece directly

from the rock surface. If it is a petroglyph, a useful technique is to tape over it a piece of rice paper or similar high-fiber paper and then rub the surface with the side of a hard wax crayon (*not* a conventional "coloring book" crayon). The background will then appear in color while the carved-out areas remain blank. Hobby shops often carry excellent paper and wax crayons for this purpose. (Ask for supplies used in gravestone rubbing. Books on rubbing gravestones will give useful pointers on rock art technique.) It takes practice to give an accurate rendering of a petroglyph when the surface is the typically uneven one of a cliff or boulder.

If your find is a pictograph, it may be possible to reproduce it by taping over it a sheet of Pliofilm and tracing the design in color with waterproof felt-tipped pens. This technique is being pioneered by Georgia Lee of California and is much more accurate than other methods. Like stone rubbing, it has the advantage of causing minimal damage to the artwork.

There is one technique that, although sometimes recommended even by professional art historians and archaeologists, is very destructive and should never be used, no matter who advocates it. This is the outlining of a piece of rock art with chalk so that it will show up better in a photograph. The use of chalk has two serious shortcomings. First, outlining is very inaccurate and allows (or forces) the recorder to draw in or leave out doubtful lines. Even worse is the fact that chalk is almost impossible to remove, so that the mistakes of one well-meaning researcher are left to confuse archaeologists of the future. A much better way of enhancing contrast for photography is to wet the pictograph with water (carried in a squeeze bottle for the purpose). This sounds risky, but remember that these paintings would not be there at all if their materials were not relatively waterproof.

Burial Sites

As a distinct type of site, not associated with other kinds of occupation, prehistoric North American burials range from single sites to fairly large cemeteries. There are even a few "burials" that are above ground, such as those reported from the Aleutian Islands, where permanent frost makes it impossible to dig. In some cases "burials" have been found in caves or other natural cavities.

Obviously, the only way to identify a burial site is by finding human bones. As we said earlier, the ability to differentiate human from animal bones is basic equipment for the competent archaeologist. However, burials, by definition, are not often found on a surface survey. Only if you are dealing with erosion or with construction projects are you likely to come across burials.

Once human remains *have* been found, certain questions immediately arise. Many (not all) American Indian groups strongly oppose the excavation or disturbing of remains which they regard as those of their ancestors. They point out that when a Christian or Jewish burial (to name only the continent's largest religious groups) is accidentally uncovered, the appropriate priest, rabbi, or minister is usually summoned and the bones reinterred with all due reverence. Simple justice would seem to require that equal respect be paid to the bones of the first Americans. Many Indian groups are particularly outraged at the practice of displaying bones in museums. "Would you do that to *your* grandfathers?" they ask, and go so far as to call those who condone such proceedings members of the "Vulture Culture."

Archaeologists and physical anthropologists, on the other hand, argue that in most cases bones that are sufficiently interesting for display are hundreds or even thousands of years old; that they often belonged to peoples who were not the direct biological ancestors of any modern Native American group; that the study of bones can give valuable scientific information about prehistoric health, diet, and population distribution; and that, in any case, reburial in the same spot is often impossible because the original sites are doomed by construction.

Without entering into an extended discussion of the subject, the authors would like to say that they find some merit in the arguments of both sides. Certainly archaeologists have sometimes been high-handed and insensitive in their relations with Native American groups. Wholesale removal of relatively recent skeletal remains (less than, say, 250 years old) to boxes in museum basements is of doubtful scientific validity, even aside from the human questions involved. On the other hand, some American Indians have become so upset by the situation that they have announced opposition to *all* archaeology of prehistoric North America, whether of artifacts, sites, burials, or anything else. In the face of this know-nothing position it is hard to see how anyone—American Indian, white, black, or Oriental—can come to understand the true cultural contribution of Native Americans. This contribution has too often been ignored, belittled, or deliberately concealed. The philosopher Santayana's dictum that "Those who do not study history are condemned to repeat it" applies all too aptly here. American Indians have been uprooted, regimented, exploited, murdered, and systematically deprived of cultural identity once already. One can hardly think of a greater irony than for this tragedy to happen over again through a misunderstanding of the goals of archaeology.

On a practical level, and until agreements are reached among the many interested parties concerning disposal of remains, any burials discovered should be reported promptly both to the local archaeological society or university department of anthropology and to any Native American group active in the area. *Above all, human remains have no place in the individual's private collection.*

4
The Uncyclopedia of North American Prehistory

We are going to have to begin by saying what this chapter is not. It is not "Everything You Will Ever Need to Know about Prehistoric Archaeology in North America." It is not a substitute for extensive further reading about the archaeology of your particular area. Far from being the encyclopedia you would need to cover even a fraction of what is known on the subject, it is in fact a kind of uncyclopedia, whose main purpose is to help you find the information you need by making you familiar with the kinds of subject headings you might look for in a library card catalog.

To make things easier to follow in this lightning tour of the continent's archaeology, we have designated eight major cultural areas, each of which will be treated separately. Additional information on and illustrations of the typical artifacts of each area appear in Appendix III.

More often than not, informational books, and even uncyclopedias, overwhelm readers with a flood of facts, leaving them with the impression that everything worth knowing is already on file. Yet the fascination and the fun of any field of study lie in approaching the *un*known, and beginners as well as professionals can profit from focusing on a particular problem. For this reason, we have chosen to put our emphasis on long-term research problems, rather than on artifact typologies and cultural sequences, many of which are under dispute anyway.

Archaeologists are not agreed on what to call the periods or phases of prehistory in North America. In biology, one may be sure that phyla are divided into classes, which are divided neatly and sequentially into orders, families, genera, and species; but although some archaeologists write in terms of phases, periods, cultures, horizons, and so on, very few use these terms in the same way. The best archaeology can offer, as of now, is the concept of the *tradition*.

A tradition may be defined as a way of life or, rather, as the form of the artifacts that represent that way of life through time, as distinct from the people or tribe that uses the artifacts. The reason we use this term is that we are seldom sure whether a new way of making tools or pots means that new people have moved into an area or that the descendants of the original peoples have simply changed their way of life and ideas of design. All that can be reliably said is that when artifacts change substantially we must speak of a new tradition. Nevertheless, no one can blame you if you are confused by the statement that the Adena Tradition is part of the Northern Subtradition, which arose within the Woodlands Tradition of the Eastern Woodlands. It may, however, be some comfort to know that in the broadest possible terms North American prehistory does follow a general progression from the Paleo-Indian Tradition (characterized by spear and lance points) to the Archaic Tradition (not always so termed, but characterized by the appearance of atlatl points) and so to the post-Archaic Tradition (characterized by the appearance of arrow points and a general diversification of life-styles).

THE EARLIEST AMERICANS

The story of early North America begins with a question mark. We do not really know when *Homo sapiens* first set foot on the continent. Not so long ago, Ales Hrdlicka, Curator of Anthropology of the U.S. National Museum (the Smithsonian Institution), took a public and irrevocable vow that there were no possible circumstances that would ever persuade him and his numerous followers to accept any date earlier than ten thousand years ago for the first cross- ing of the Bering Strait. And that was considered to be that. More recently, however, the generally accepted date has been pushed back to between twenty and forty thousand years ago, and a few controversial readings have suggested dates of more than sixty thousand years ago.

Originally, it was thought that early migrants arrived on foot from northern Asia at a time when the last Ice Age had lowered the sea level and exposed a land bridge across the Bering Sea. According to this view, the new arrivals would have been cut off from the rest of the continent by the glaciers of the so-called Wisconsin period *except* during a warm phase called the Two Creeks interstadial, when they could have traveled south and east down a corridor be- tween the Wisconsin and Laurentian ice masses, toward the region of the Great Plains. The date of that temporary corridor was originally accepted as ten thousand years ago. Later geological findings, however, indicated that there were several of these glacial retreats, some much earlier than ten thousand years ago. Furthermore, some research- ers, led by Louis Brennan, have suggested that immigrants could have gotten around the ice by simply traveling down an ice-free corridor that ran along the continent's west coast at a level that is now under water.

A widely held hypothesis (which is as of now only a hy- pothesis) about the culture of the earliest Americans holds that they were the makers of certain types of very simple, basic artifacts called pebble tools. Generally chipped from rounded, water-washed pebbles by striking alone (percus-

Pebble chopper

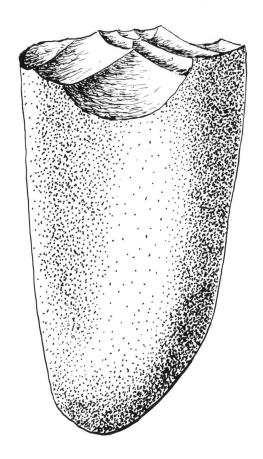

FIGURE 3

sion) rather than by a combination of percussion and pressure flaking, pebble tools have been found at scattered sites all over North and South America, sometimes in association with what may be crude hearths. Carbon-14 dates from some of the latter tend to support the idea that the pebble tool makers were at work twenty to sixty thousand years ago, but some archaeologists feel that the charcoal tested came from natural burning and that the "tools," likewise, were products of natural fracture. In that case, the date of first occupation would of course be pushed forward again.

Supporters of the earlier dates point out that these pebble tools are unusual in being chipped on one side only (unifacial) and that very similar types of tools from much the same period have been found in eastern Asia. Was it indeed the makers of these tools who came first to North America? We need more data from more and better-documented sites.

Some researchers think that between this hypothetical settlement of pebble tool users and the first firmly dated sites of projectile point makers there may have been several additional influxes of migrants, carrying with them variations on the pebble tool technology.

THE PALEO-INDIAN TRADITION

The first really solid dates for archaeological sites in North America cluster around 10,000 and 9000 B.C. Those dates are associated with the appearance of points of the Paleo-Indian Tradition. These points are flaked on both faces (bifacial), long and graceful in shape, excellent examples of the flint knapper's art. Many of them are also fluted, which means they have a long thin flake removed lengthwise from base to point.

It has taken more than a decade of persistent effort for a few modern flint knappers to be able to duplicate the appearance of this fluting, yet fluted points appear to be the earliest items in the North American archaeological sequence (if one ignores the alleged pebble tools). How do we account for the sudden appearance of these highly sophisticated points? No similar artifacts from a comparable time have been found in Asia. Were the fluted points nevertheless brought in by new migrants? Did they develop independently, almost overnight? If so, why haven't we found their "ancestors," the experimental models and evolutionary forerunners that should logically have preceded them?

We do not really know. All we can say is that already at this early date there were two sophisticated traditions, the Old Cordilleran and the Big Game Hunting traditions. Together they are termed Paleo-Indian.

BIG GAME HUNTING

The Big Game Hunting Tradition in general appears to have flourished over an enormous area of North America, comprising roughly the Great Plains from Wyoming southward, the Eastern Woodlands, and the Southwest. (Most of Canada was at that time covered with glaciers.) The Big Game Hunters seem to have lived by following mammoths, mastodons, and other large game. These species, some of which are now extinct, fed on the well-watered vegetation of the period.

Three major point types are found, each associated with a slightly different form of the tradition.

The Clovis point tradition is known mainly from kill sites of mammoths, cattle, horses, or bison, singly or in small groups. Clovis points are rather frequently found on the surface in the east, less frequently so in the west (where the tradition may have originated). Eastern sites are therefore harder to date. The Clovis point itself is a large point for a thrusting spear, with a shallow trough or flute running lengthwise on both faces. The flutes generally run no more than halfway from base to point. (See Figure 4.)

Of the Sandia point tradition, only two sites are known —a cave (presumably a habitation site) in Sandia, New Mexico, and a possible mammoth kill site found on the surface not far away. The Sandia point (see Figure 4) is slightly smaller than the Clovis point, on the average, and not fluted. It has a characteristic shoulder or bulge on one side at the stem end and may or may not be contemporary with the Clovis point.

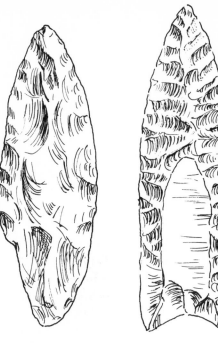

Sandia point   Clovis point   Folsom point

FIGURE 4

The Folsom point tradition has been identified at kill sites of numerous bison of an extinct species. There are also campsites, frequently near a kill site. The Folsom point is of slightly later date than the Clovis point. It is also a little smaller, with long flutings often extending the full length of the point. The base is curved inward as if a small bite had been taken out. (See Figure 4.)

Research Problems

A list of research problems for the Big Game Hunting Tradition as a whole, including the Clovis, Sandia, and

Folsom point traditions, might go like this: When and where did the Big Game Hunting Tradition originate? Was the Sandia point earlier than, later than, or contemporary with the Clovis point? Where are the other Sandia sites, if indeed there are any? What are the relative dates for Clovis points in the east and west? Are there really two subtraditions of Big Game Hunters, one concerned with grasslands, the other with a forest environment? Is it possible that the Clovis point originated around the glacial lakes of the Great Basin and moved eastward in the pursuit of game as it followed the retreating forests? Or did it originate in the east and spread westward? Did a change in the type of game hunted motivate the change from the Clovis to the Folsom point? What was the relative importance of plants as a food source?

OLD CORDILLERAN

The other division of the Paleo-Indian, namely the Old Cordilleran Tradition, apparently arose independently and had its center in the comparatively restricted area of the Cascade Mountains in the Pacific Northwest and the Interior Plateau, particularly in the valleys of the Columbia River and its tributaries. Old Cordilleran sites are mainly temporary camps beside river rapids, possibly for fishing. No particular big game species are associated with them. Typical points are of narrow leaf shape and unfluted. (See Figure 5.)

Research Problems

Research problems of the Old Cordilleran tradition include the question of its dates relative to the Big Game Hunting Tradition. Also, is there a genuine relationship to similar-seeming points from southern California and the

Old Cordilleran point

FIGURE 5

Mojave Valley? Is the Old Cordilleran point even, perhaps, ancestral to the fluted point? How does the Old Cordilleran differ from the Big Game Hunting in its choice of sites and its hunting patterns? And how did those differences affect the group's organization?

And here is one overriding problem for the entire Paleo-Indian Tradition: Was it change in climate that killed off the native American horses, mammoths, camels, and other animals at this period, or was it overhunting by human populations, epidemic disease, a combination of factors, or none of these?

We must note that the Paleo-Indian Tradition does not disappear at this point in our story. It merely divides and diversifies into local variants, which will be described in the following sections devoted to specific areas. A decisive change was about to take place, not only in North America, but over the whole planet. For the last time the glaciers began to withdraw. A warmer climatic phase released the enormous quantities of water once locked in ice masses, and the seas rose. The land bridge from Asia to Alaska disappeared forever, initiating a ten-thousand-year period of comparative isolation for the descendants of the daring migrants who had found a new world. (New arrivals continued to cross the straits by boat, however, the most recent probably being the ancestors of the Eskimo.) Certain game species died off at this period, but as if to compensate the wandering hunters, climatic conditions gradually stabilized and vast new territories emerged from beneath the ice. Rich and glorious variations of wet and arid, flat and mountainous, coastal and landlocked, arctic, temperate, and semitropical landscapes unfolded themselves across the continent, each offering man its own opportunities and challenges.

THE SOUTHWEST

The modern, postglacial climate of this region is semiarid, but the land is carved and watered by a number of fairly large rivers, whose action has created the spectacular and colorful buttes, plateaus, and canyons for which the area is famous. Archaeologically, the Southwest is centered in Arizona and New Mexico and includes adjacent parts of west Texas, southern Colorado, Utah, and Nevada, and southeast California. (Artifacts of Southwestern traditions can, of course, also be found across the border in northern Mexico, but that is outside the scope of this book.) In many cases the dryness of the climate has preserved organic materials such as wood, cloth, and matting.

In the Southwest, the later forms of the Big Game Hunting Tradition evolved unfluted points that are found associated with nonextinct game. Then developed a seminomadic way of life known as the Western Archaic or Desert Tradition, in which hunting for small game and the gathering of seeds played a major part. During this period, basketry appeared, and point types were slightly modified and became somewhat smaller. The mano and millingstone, a flat grindstone and base combination, came into use also. (See Figure 20, page 251.) The tradition persisted with little significant change until about the time of Christ.

The Western Archaic then faded out, and the population appears to have taken up a more sedentary way of life, which may be divided into three major traditions—the Mogollon, the Hohokam, and the Anasazi. The change seems, in general, to have been precipitated by the introduction of agriculture from Mexico, where evidence indicates corn was domesticated as early as four thousand years ago.

The first signs of a settled way of life in the Southwest occur in the Mogollon Tradition, which was largely centered in the southern mountain valleys between Arizona and New Mexico. The Mogollon evolved through several cultural phases until it was apparently absorbed by the Anasazi. Pottery, pit houses, and the bow and arrow are found in the region dating from this time, and crops were watered by the runoff of seasonal rainfall. The dead were buried in the earth, sometimes inside the houses.

In the lower Gila River area of southwestern Arizona the Hohokam Tradition developed, apparently slightly later than the Mogollon. Crops were watered by the natural floodwaters of the Gila. House pits, pottery, and the bow and arrow were in use, and the craft of stone carving was highly developed. A technique was invented for etching patterns on shell with acid derived from cactus, fully three hundred years before etching came into use in Europe.

Like the Mogollon, the Hohokam Tradition also passed through several stages of development. The fact that the custom of burial by cremation persisted in the area may indicate that the tradition survived the threat of assimilation posed by the expansion of the Anasazi. The modern Pima and Papago cultures may be direct descendants of the Hohokam.

The homeland of the Anasazi Tradition was the northern part of the region, around the "four corners" of Arizona, New Mexico, Colorado, and Utah. The date of the Anasazi's origin is later than that of the Mogollon, and possibly later than that of the Hohokam as well. The tradition evolved through numerous phases and survives today in modified form among the Hopi.

The earliest phase of the Anasazi marks a transition from the Western Archaic into a proto-agricultural way of life, featuring basketry and saucer-shaped house pits, but no pottery. The crops were not the same as those of the Mogollon and Hohokam, and may have been introduced from the Mississippi Valley rather than from Mexico. As time went on, house types became more elaborate, being built over pits lined with stone slabs. Pottery and the bow and arrow appeared. These two early phases of the Anasazi Tradition are often called the Basketmaker Subtradition. The next four phases belong to a new subtradition called the Pueblo.

The first sign of change was a sudden proliferation of housing styles. For a while anything went. Houses were round or rectangular; above ground, below ground, or half

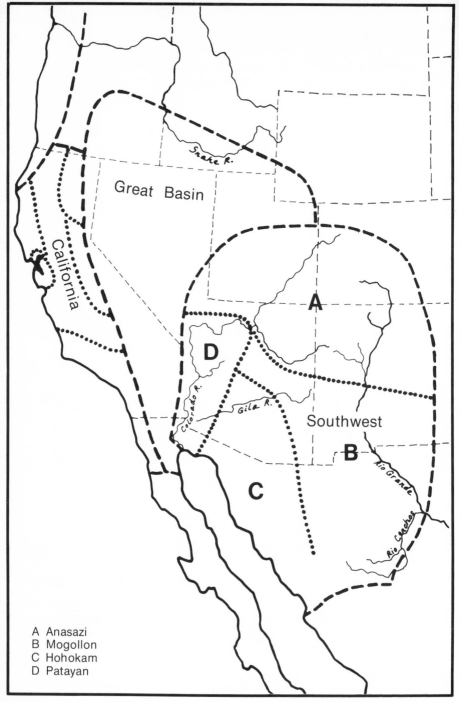

A Anasazi
B Mogollon
C Hohokam
D Patayan

FIGURE 6

and half; made of clay-daubed wattles, stone slabs, adobe brick. However, a tendency is discernible toward single-storied, many-roomed dwellings built of masonry. Pottery styles also became more diverse, with corrugated ware coming into use for cooking. The first kivas (underground structures, possibly for religious purposes) also appeared.

Next came a phase in which the favored style of building had definitely settled on the pueblo, a many-roomed, many-storied masonry structure placed either against a cliff face or on a valley floor. During this phase, the Anasazi Tradition greatly expanded its influence, and artifacts of pure Anasazi type are found even outside the Southwest, in the Great Basin. Pottery became ever more elaborate in design and color.

Though the next phase saw a retreat of the tradition into a somewhat smaller territory, the construction of pueblos reached a peak of architectural beauty and technical competence. Pottery decoration and wall paintings from this phase seem to show some Mexican influence.

For some as yet unknown reason, the Anasazi in its final phase withdrew into a very much smaller territory, where it has survived in the culture of the modern Pueblo Indians.

We will only mention briefly a fourth settled tradition of the Southwest, the Patayan, which arose about halfway through the Mogollon in the Colorado River Valley. It represents the only nonnomadic tradition of the area that lacked permanent houses and finely ground stone artifacts, although pottery was used. From this tradition may be descended the modern Yuman tribes.

Two other important traditions of the Southwest contrast with those mentioned above in that they represent a nomadic, nonagricultural way of life. The Later Western Archaic (ancestral to the modern Ute and Paiute cultures) is considered a local continuation of the Western Archaic.

The Athapaskan Tradition, on the other hand, is known to have been brought into the area by an influx of speakers of Athapaskan languages. These migrants came south along the Continental Divide from Canada, though whether on the eastern or the western side is open to question. Their descendants are the modern Navajo and Apache. Both these traditions become more prominent in the archaeological record at about the time when Pueblo influence was on the wane.

Research Problems

Why did the Patayan not take up permanent architecture? Did the Hohokam arrive in the area from Mexico, and much later than is generally supposed, taking over a previously existing tradition called the Ootam? What motivated the transition to agriculture? Why did some take up farming and others not? Did the early Anasazi, during their westward expansion, adopt the idea of pit houses and pottery from the Mogollon? Was it climate, threat of invasion, or some other factor that led to the final retreat of the Pueblo Tradition? Is the flowering of the katchina cult, as shown in rock art, the result of direct borrowing by the Anasazi from the Mogollon or of Mogollon influence on the Anasazi?

FIGURE 7

The information recorded on this and following charts is frequently the subject of heated academic debate, especially as regards time periods. Accordingly, these charts should be treated with the greatest caution except as the most general kind of signposts to further study. Nevertheless, the authors felt it would be unnecessarily stuffy to omit charts of this kind altogether.

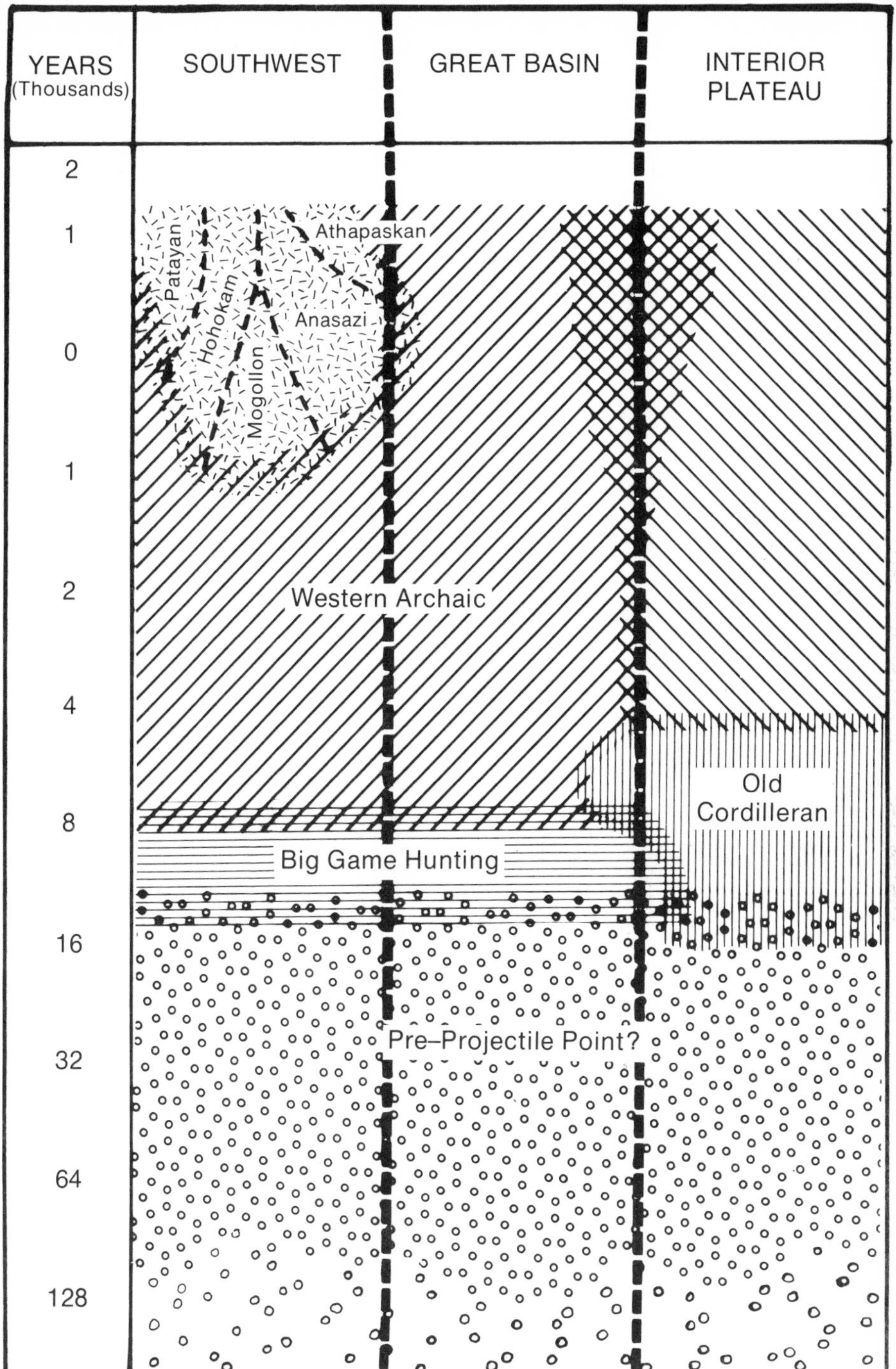
YEARS
(Thousands)
SOUTHWEST
GREAT BASIN
INTERIOR
PLATEAU
2
1
0
1
2
4
8
16
32
64
128
Patayan
Hohokam
Mogollon
Athapaskan
Anasazi
Western Archaic
Old
Cordilleran
Big Game Hunting
Pre-Projectile Point?

FIGURE 7

THE GREAT BASIN

An area lying between the Southwest and central California, and extending as far north as southern Oregon, is known as the Great Basin. Rivers and streams flow from its mountainous perimeter toward its center but are to a large extent swallowed up in geological sinks. The present climate is arid, ranging into desert conditions in some areas, and rainfall is scanty. However, in early postglacial times the region received much more moisture and was the site of several large lakes which supported a variety of game.

The Big Game Hunting Tradition is known in the Great Basin in general from fluted points found on the surface but not in association with extinct game. In the northernmost regions the Old Cordilleran Tradition appears to be represented by several finds, but there is doubt as to their significance and identification.

It seems that some of the Paleo-Indian peoples settled around the margins of the early lakes and established what is now known as the Western Pluvial Lakes Tradition. Artifacts seem to be suitable for the hunting of deer, antelope, bighorn sheep, fish, and small game. Atlatl darts came into use, as did basketry and the mano/millingstone combination. Intricately woven netting has been found in dry caves, indicating that weaving was highly developed. Bone tools are commonly associated with the tradition, and the presence of shells from the Pacific indicates possible trade contacts.

A climatic period of high temperatures followed. The lakes dried up or shrank radically. Parts of the area may then have been virtually uninhabited for as long as two thousand years. Still later, temperatures moderated. A modification of the Western Pluvial Lakes Tradition reappeared in a form suited to exploitation of a wide variety of resources—lakes, mountains, and plains. Technologically, there was little change from earlier forms. (We do not know whether or where a transitional phase existed.) However, this later development is referred to as the Western Archaic. It is very similar to the Western Archaic already described for the Southwest. (Some writers call it the Desert Tradition). With only minor changes, this tradition persisted right into historic times in most of the Great Basin, the exception being the eastern sections. It was not until the latest phase of the Western Archaic that the bow and arrow were introduced, as is shown by the smaller size of projectile points. Bedrock mortars (bowl-shaped depressions ground directly into bedrock) are found on the eastern slopes of the Sierras, and pottery also made an appearance in the region at that time.

The eastern part of the Great Basin was influenced by the Pueblo Tradition during the period of its greatest expansion out of the Southwest. The influence is indicated by the presence of agriculture and Pueblo style pottery. Some writers refer to this development as the Fremont Culture and several other names have also been applied to it. The Paiute and Shoshone peoples of the Great Basin may be the modern inheritors of the Western Archaic.

Research Problems

In view of the fact that Great Basin traditions indicate a way of life that was intimately dependent on interaction with a rather harsh environment, are there any broader inferences we can draw concerning the relationships among social structures, cultural development, and man's use of resources? Does environment really determine cultural change, as some researchers maintain? If so, which environmental factors are the pivotal ones for motivating change? Is it true, as has been hypothesized, that zones in the Great Basin in which animal and plant resources occur always contain sites designed specifically to exploit those resources? Just what the heck were those chipped stone crescents of the Western Pluvial Lakes Tradition *really* used for? (See page 256 and Figure 24, page 257.)

THE INTERIOR PLATEAU

This is a comparatively small but rugged area that stretches from the eastern slopes of the Cascade Mountains to the Flathead River in western Montana, south to southern Idaho, and north to the big bend of the Fraser River in British Columbia. Altitudes are high and the modern climate is characterized by harsh winters and cool, semialpine summers. However, game such as mule deer, bighorn sheep, mountain goats, elk, and moose are even now well established in remoter areas, and the great rivers and glacial lakes are rich in salmon and trout.

Archaeologists are only now beginning to understand the development of the Interior Plateau in prehistoric times. For this reason, its various archaeological traditions are most often termed Early, Middle, and Late, though some authorities also say Paleo-Indian, Archaic, and post-Archaic. Still others deal exclusively in archaeological *phases,* as displayed in individual sites. In short, the terminology is confused.

The Interior Plateau is the presumed homeland of what we have earlier called the Old Cordilleran Tradition, whose sites are found in valleys where rivers such as the Columbia and the Fraser break through the mountains on their way to the Pacific. It appears, therefore, that the users of Old Cordilleran tools chose the most favorable sites of the region for the purpose of exploiting the excellent seasonal fishing. In some parts of the area, however, the picture is complicated because points have been found that are remi-

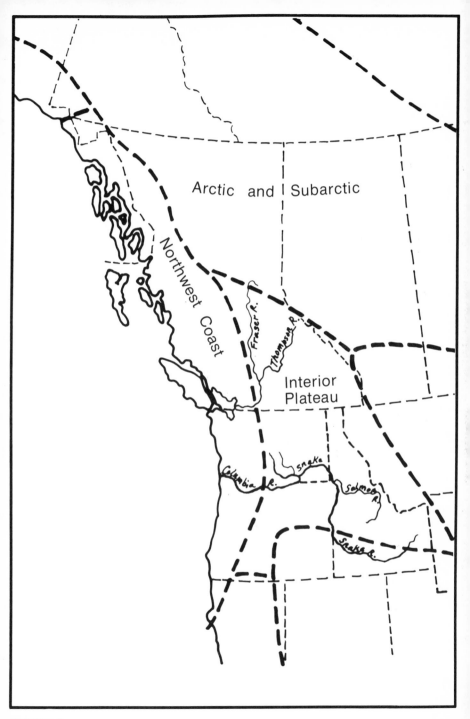

Arctic and Subarctic

Northwest Coast

Fraser R.

Thompson R.

Interior
Plateau

Columbia R.

Snake

Salmon R.

Snake R.

FIGURE 8

niscent of those of the Big Game Hunting Tradition as it occurs in the northern Great Plains.

Following the Old Cordilleran (or, according to the schema outlined above, during the early Middle Tradition), we find a developing use of stemmed and notched points, ground stone implements of the mano and millingstone type, and other stone tools somewhat like those of the Western Archaic Tradition of the nearby Great Basin (see above). Ground stone working techniques may, indeed, have been introduced into the Interior Plateau from the Great Basin, supposing that the latter's inhabitants moved elsewhere when the pluvial lakes dried up. The presence of L-shaped bone awls (tools used for weaving plant materials) may indicate the advent of basketry at this time.

A greater diversity of artifacts now appears throughout the area. Northward, stemmed and notched points were also in use, but they were accompanied by quite a different assemblage of artifacts, including ground stone mortars and pestles, ground stone pipes and tablets, stone mauls, and carved stone figurines in human and animal form. Toward the end of the Middle Tradition, a more uniform state of affairs seems to have prevailed. In both north and south are found finely ground and polished stone implements, deep-bowled mortars, atlatl weights, two-holed stone gorgets, and ground slate knives. There is considerable evidence of trade or other relations with the Northwest Coast, particularly in the introduction of the three-pronged salmon spear and the toggle harpoon (see Figure 28, page 263), which had already been known on the west coast for a considerable time.

The advent of the Late Tradition is marked by the appearance of those small triangular or leaf-shaped points that signal the use of the bow and arrow. Stonework became even more finely detailed, and types of decoration indicate further trade or contact with the traditions of the

Northwest Coast. It is worth noting here that the Interior Plateau (together with the Northwest Coast and much of California) was exceptional in having neither pottery nor agriculture in prehistoric times.

Research Problems

Is the Interior Plateau really best considered as a separate area, or should it be divided up among the neighboring areas, which seem to have influenced it so greatly? Would the true situation be better reflected by combining the Interior Plateau with the Great Basin in an "Intermontane Tradition" running from British Columbia to Mexico? What is the origin of the sophisticated artifact styles of the Late Tradition? Did traditions arise in the Plateau before being transmitted to the Northwest Coast, or was the direction of transmission reversed? Is the fact that the majority of sites so far studied have been located beside rivers a result of the prehistoric settlement pattern, or are there other types of sites still waiting to be discovered? Why the change from the mano and millingstone combination (used elsewhere primarily for grinding seeds) to the mortar and pestle (used elsewhere to pound foods such as acorns)? What brought about the change in house styles from round to rectangular during the Late Tradition?

THE NORTHWEST COAST

This area is a long narrow strip running along the Pacific coast from the Alaska Panhandle through British Columbia, Washington, and Oregon to the vicinity of Trinidad Bay in northern California. Inland, it is bounded by the western slopes of the Sierras, the Cascade Range, and the Canadian Rockies. Food resources of precolonial times were rich and varied, especially as regards fish and other marine species such as whales, seals, and shellfish. A heavy annual rainfall feeds the thick forest that characterizes much of the area, and even as far north as Alaska the climate is moderated by the influence of the Japan Current.

As we saw in the preceding section, there is some evidence to support the view that the traditions of the Northwest Coast are descended from those of the Interior Plateau, since Old Cordilleran point types seem to evolve into those found west of the mountains. If this view is correct, of course, it would support the theory that the first Americans arrived on the continent via the famous "corridor" through central Canada and the Great Plains.

On the other hand, certain aspects of the tradition have been thought to show closer links with Asia than the "corridor theory" would allow, and it may be that man first arrived on the Pacific coast by a more direct shoreline route from northwest Alaska—a route perhaps now submerged. This possibility would explain the material evidence, cited in the section on the Interior Plateau, that elements of fishing technology were carried east from the coast into the interior.

At present, archaeologists do not designate developments on the Northwest Coast in terms of changing traditions such as Paleo-Indian, Archaic, and so on. Rather, the region is believed to have experienced a steady evolution from Old Cordilleran to early historic times without any major cultural upheavals. Within this steady evolution, however, is included an assemblage of artifacts that is rich, subtle, colorful, and artistically impressive.

In its earliest phase, the tradition looks like an adaptation of the Old Cordilleran to the demands of ocean fishing and of hunting large marine mammals. Later, it moved steadily toward even better exploitation of marine resources and improved techniques of woodworking for both utilitarian and decorative purposes. Earlier sites exhibit an emphasis

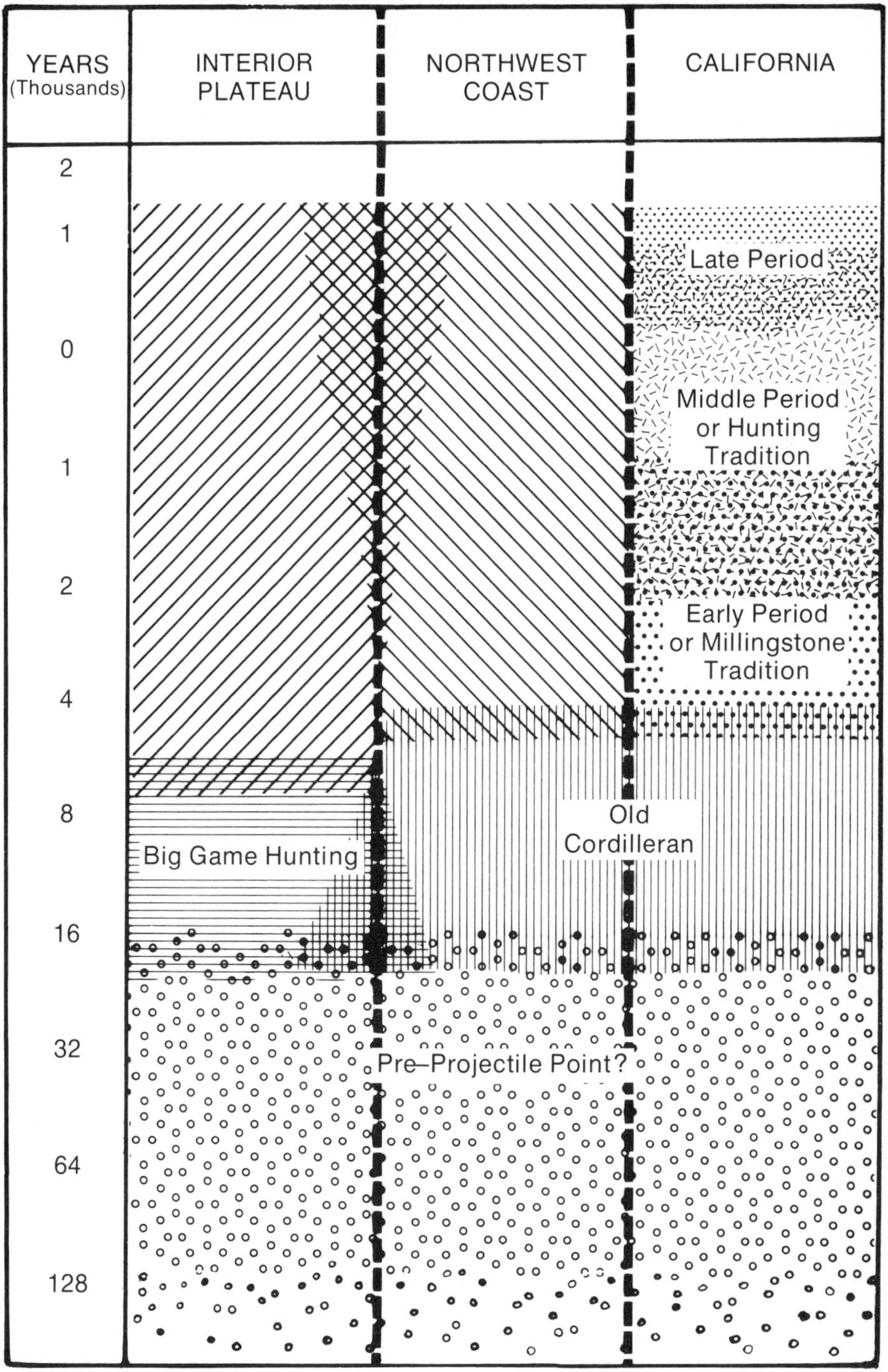
YEARS (Thousands)
INTERIOR PLATEAU
NORTHWEST COAST
CALIFORNIA
2
1
0
1
2
4
8
16
32
64
128
Late Period
Middle Period or Hunting Tradition
Early Period or Millingstone Tradition
Old Cordilleran
Big Game Hunting
Pre–Projectile Point?

FIGURE 9

on ground slate artifacts and barbed harpoons, while in later ones toggle harpoons are prominent and ground slate disappears. In sculpture, also, slate and stone tend to give way to wood.

The period just before and just after European contact saw a remarkable flowering of material culture, which displayed a strong Asian influence in many of its forms and design elements. Although agriculture and pottery were apparently never used in the region, the standard of living seems to have equaled or exceeded that of many early farming communities in both the New and the Old World. In short, the later phases of the Northwest Coast Tradition were among the most elaborate to be found in North America, ranking with the Mississippian and the Pueblo. Coastal villages of the time impressed explorers with their large, rectangular dwelling houses, imposing totem poles, decorated house fronts, and dugout canoes capable of carrying dozens of passengers. Shaped copper placques were one of the most valued forms of wealth, although materials used for handicrafts were restricted to wood, shell, bone, and so on.

Research Problems

To what, if any, outside influences do we owe the flowering of Northwest Coast art and material culture? What was the origin of the area's complex political and social organization? What was the relationship of the area to the Interior Plateau—i.e., which came first and who influenced whom? What are the links to either Eskimo or northeast Asian traditions? Is there in truth such a thing as the Old Cordilleran Tradition? If so, did it originate inland or on the coast? Why do certain peoples of the Northwest Coast speak languages unrelated to those of their neighbors but related to some that occur in California and the Southwest?

CALIFORNIA

Relatively small but very important, the archaeological area called California is not identical with the state of California but comprises the territory lying on the west side of the Sierras and south of Trinidad Bay. On the south it extends into the Mexican state of Baja California. The region thus contains both the major part of California's coastline and its fertile central valley—a considerable range of climate and terrain, from cool coastal forests in the north to the western Mojave Desert in the south. Conditions generally have been very favorable for human occupation throughout the area's history and prehistory. Food sources such as shellfish, nuts, wild fruits, and game were plentiful in pre-contact times, and there were few extremes of temperature to contend with.

The question of the antiquity of man in California is one of the most controversial in North American prehistory. Dates as early as one hundred thousand years ago have been seriously advanced for occupation by pebble tool users, and some rather questionable carbon-14 dates from an island in the Santa Barbara Channel would suggest a time between thirty thousand and ten thousand years ago. More solid evidence from the central coast indicates at least nine thousand years of human occupation.

Our picture of what is elsewhere referred to as the Paleo-Indian Tradition is clouded here by the apparent coexistence of points like those of the Old Cordilleran and its typical modifications, with fluted points of the Clovis type and stone crescents similar to those of the Big Game Hunting Tradition of the Great Basin.

We have already described the two principal theories of the dispersal of early peoples over the continent, one postulating a corridor between ice masses that led to the Great

Plains area, another suggesting that an alternative, if not the only, early route led down the Pacific coast at a time when the sea level was as much as three hundred feet lower than it is at present. If the latter were indeed the case, it would then be reasonable to suppose that the telltale early sites are presently submerged somewhere off the shores of California, Oregon, and Washington. It is to be hoped that underwater archaeology now going on in the Santa Barbara Channel may help to resolve the controversy.

Following the early Paleo-Indian remains, whether Old Cordilleran or Big Game Hunting, archaeologists find the Millingstone Tradition, which is also called the Early Period and corresponds roughly to the Later Paleo traditions of other areas. As the name implies, the Millingstone Tradition was characterized by the widespread use of ground stone implements such as the mano and millingstone. Along the coast the chief food resource seems to have been shellfish, and very large shell heaps are found. However, there was no absolute dependence on this item of diet, and versatility seems to be the best word to characterize the Millingstone way of life. In the interior, river fishing may have played the dominant role, supplemented by the gathering of nuts and seeds. It is possible that basketry began to develop during the later days of the Millingstone Tradition, but there is some disagreement on this point.

The Hunting Tradition (also called the Middle Period and not to be confused with the much earlier Big Game Hunting Tradition) is marked by increasing decoration and elaboration of artifacts and also by more imaginative use of materials. One example is the so-called basket mortar, a relatively shallow stone mortar with a woven rim designed, it is supposed, to reduce the labor of pecking and grinding deep stone mortars for the processing of acorns. Numerous finds of bone awls (for weaving plant materials) support the idea that basketry was not only known but in fairly wide use at this period. The beautifully curved, almost spiral shell fishhook was invented and is found in midden heaps along with a large increase in the remains of deep-water ocean fish such as are not found in tidal pools. This combination is a nice example of the expansion of food resources by technology: better fishhooks lead to catching more fish. Steatite, an easily worked and polished gray or greenish mineral native to parts of the region, was extensively quarried and used for articles both practical and decorative. Bone whistles appeared. The tradition takes its name from the apparent increase in the hunting of large game such as deer and elk at this time. Some experts attribute this development to the arrival in the area of new groups of hunting peoples from an unspecified locale. Evidence of greater emphasis on hunting is the proliferation of points suitable for use with the atlatl.

Next arose a series of regional specializations most often referred to as the Late Period. Here we find a notably increasing fineness in artifact workmanship. Favorite materials were the iridescent abalone and other shells, which were carved, inlaid, inset, and used in a multitude of decorative forms. Even though there is no evidence of agriculture in the region (agriculture being generally regarded as *the* prerequisite for leisure time in which to develop "high civilization"), it seems that the benefits of climate and natural resources had made possible in California an adaptation to the environment so finely tuned that a true cultural flowering was possible, as on the Northwest Coast, without agriculture. On the other hand, recent evidence indicates that the practice of burning brush in order to create new growth attractive to game was an important adjunct to hunting and food gathering practices and may perhaps be considered a precursor to agriculture.

Among material accomplishments of the Late Period is the building of plank canoes (as opposed to dugouts), the only vessels of this type known to have been made in the New World before European contact. On a more mundane but nonetheless archaeologically useful level, projectile points became smaller, indicating use of the bow and arrow. Another interesting feature is the existence of a rather complex economic system, revealed by the strings of shell disc beads that constituted the local currency. This was a genuine monetary system, in which the "coinage" had a symbolic rather than an intrinsic value, and not a system of barter. It was subject to many of the problems of inflation and devaluation suffered by modern economic systems, as recent studies have shown.

Research Problems

How early is early in California? Is the answer to this question to be found in submerged sites offshore? How does it happen that five of the six language bases that occur in North America were in use in California at the time of European contact? Does that fact imply that California was a main access route from Asia, the original linguistic "melting pot," or only a backwater? Is there any connection between the spiral abalone fishhook of the region and its nearest similar neighbor, which is found in Polynesia? Was the Hunting Tradition brought into the area by outsiders or did it evolve locally? Why did the peoples of California not use pottery (with a few very minor exceptions) or agriculture, although there is ample evidence of trade and other contacts with neighboring peoples who did? Were the techniques of stone grinding and basketry developed in California and introduced into the Great Basin, or was it the other way around? What is the significance of deliberate burning for the development of early agricultural practices? Why did food resources apparently shift from easily gathered grasses to bitter acorns that had to be leached before they could be eaten, and what was the relationship of this change to the shift from millingstones to mortars? What caused the rise of complex social and political organizations in an essentially hunting and gathering group of societies? What is the relationship of the vast trade networks to the social and political complexity of the area?

THE GREAT PLAINS

This is a large but ill-defined area of grassland and prairie, running roughly from southern Alberta and Saskatchewan to central Texas, and from the eastern slopes of the Rocky Mountains to about the longitude of Missouri, but excluding the Great Lakes. The eastern boundary of the Plains is particularly hard to establish, since archaeological transitions into the Eastern Woodlands area are as gradual as the geographical ones. Winters are cold, summers are hot, and winds are high here, now as in prehistoric times. However, the vast herds of buffalo (American bison) and pronghorn antelope that once sustained the Native American population have all but vanished.

As early as glacial times, the area was a hunter's paradise, and it is appropriate that the Big Game Hunting Tradition should have persisted longest on the Great Plains. This tradition is particularly marked in the northwestern prairies, where large kill sites have been found, seeming to indicate cooperation between sizable groups of hunters. The usual sequence of Clovis to Folsom points (which is sometimes called the Plano Tradition by specialists in this area) gives way eventually to more specialized types combining Paleo-Indian and Archaic features, such as Plainview, Hell Gap, and Scotts Bluff, although in at least one case Clovis points appear to be followed directly by Hell Gap points without transitional forms. These traditions die out at about the time of the postglacial warming period,

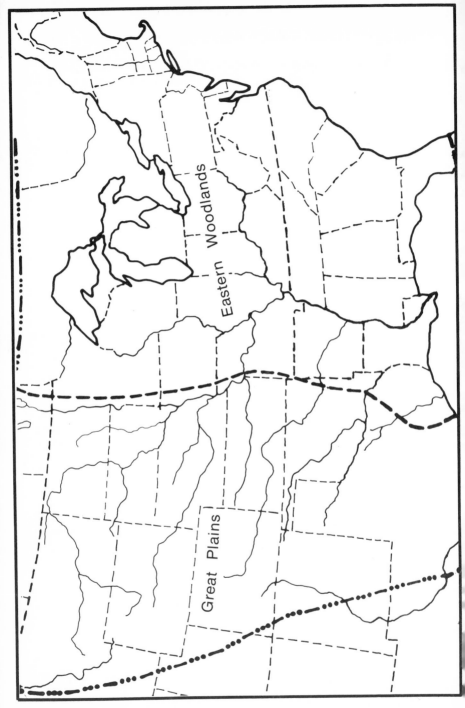

FIGURE 10

perhaps because of the extinction or migration of game such as mammoths, camels, and horses that formerly roamed the prairies.

The Plains Archaic Tradition eventually took over from Big Game Hunting, appearing first in the eastern part of the Plains. Characteristic implements are those used for hunting and butchering, as well as for grinding seeds (mano and millingstone). Point types indicate use of the atlatl. In the eastern part of the Plains artifact types are clearly influenced by those of the Eastern Archaic (see Eastern Woodlands, below), whereas traits of the Western Archaic (see the Southwest, above) are more prominent in the west. The Archaic Tradition appears relatively late in the central part of the region.

Next in succession, the Woodlands Tradition introduced pottery, agriculture, and the bow and arrow. The nature of these developments in the eastern Plains is decidedly colored by the great and dominant traditions of the Eastern Woodlands area (see Hopewell and Adena in that section), while Woodlands traits are much less visible in the southwestern part of the area and least visible in the northwest Plains, where pottery was simple and agriculture almost nonexistent. Indeed, in the northwest the only important sign of Woodlands influence is in the change from atlatl darts to arrow points.

As agriculture began to play a role in the life of the Plains, especially in the east, another tradition, called Plains Village, came into being. It was characterized by rather extensive permanent villages, favored sites being bluffs overlooking planted fields in the river bottoms.

No discussion of the Great Plains can ignore the impact of the modern horse, an escapee from the camps of Spanish explorers. (The native North American species of horses were never domesticated and had been extinct for thousands of years by the period of which we are speaking.)

Certain Plains peoples greeted the horse as joyfully as a long-lost brother, and that is exactly the way the animal is described in various myths and folktales. Some peoples, such as the Crow and the Blackfeet, simply incorporated the horse into a way of life that was essentially little changed from the Archaic. Others, like the Sioux and Cheyenne, who had been practicing agriculture on the eastern Plains, abandoned their fields and took up the life of nomads, following on horseback the vast herds of buffalo. In both cases, the horsemen caused considerable disruption among their former neighbors, many of whom packed up and moved away from the horse-borne raiders. Nevertheless, some peoples of the Plains Village Tradition, such as the Mandan of the Dakotas, managed to hold their own right into historic times.

Research Problems

What is the relationship between the period of high temperatures that followed the retreat of the glaciers and the impulse that led to the development of the Plains Archaic Tradition? Was it the Great Basin or the Eastern Woodlands that supplied the major influence on the Plains Archaic? What is the relationship in time between the appearance of pottery and that of agriculture? Are the burial mounds of the Plains related in any way to those of the east —Adena, Hopewell, and Mississippian traditions? Is the fact that the cultivated plants of the Plains developed into hardier strains than the related crops of other areas a result of spontaneous natural selection in a harsh local climate or of deliberate efforts on the part of early farmers? What accounts for the decision of some peoples to give up agriculture after the advent of the horse and why did others continue to farm? Is the introduction of the horse the sole factor that accounts for the extensive movements of population that took place at the time? Do the varied rock art styles of the Plains reflect the geographic origins of groups that moved into the area after adopting an equestrian way of life?

THE EASTERN WOODLANDS

This is an enormous and quite varied area, stretching from Florida to Labrador in the east and having a rather uncertain western boundary somewhere along the line between east Texas and southern Manitoba. It is watered by many large rivers, including the continent's largest, the Mississippi. These rivers, together with the Great Lakes and innumerable smaller lakes, served in prehistoric times as navigable highways, facilitating travel and communication and perhaps contributing to a certain cultural uniformity throughout the region. The term "woodlands" in the area's title is a key one, since the land was largely covered with thick forest, ranging from deciduous to evergreen in accordance with conditions of climate and altitude. The modern climate is warm in the south, cool in the north, but moist throughout. As a result of this moisture, and often of soil acidity, conditions are generally unfavorable for the preservation of artifacts made of organic materials.

Paleo-Indian or Big Game Hunting Tradition points have been found in a generous number of sites in the Eastern Woodlands. It is hypothesized that the tradition was brought into the area by hunters from the west, who were following the woolly mammoth (a beast of the open grasslands) during a period when the Great Plains extended farther east than they do today. The tradition may then have been adapted to the pursuit of the mastodon, a forest browser. However, archaeologists are by no means certain of this sequence of events because fluted points have almost always been found on the surface in this area, thus

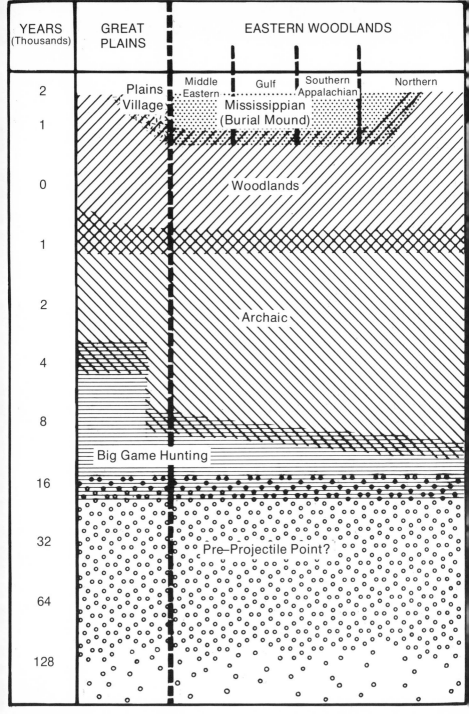

FIGURE 11

making dating very difficult. At the end of the Paleo Period (as eastern specialists generally call it), diverse local traditions began to appear, showing several variations on the fluted point.

Next in sequence is found the Eastern Archaic Tradition. The main development here seems to be further specialization, with the aim of getting the most out of the local forest environment. There is evidence that the dominant way of life was that of forest nomads following a seasonal round so as to enjoy, for example, berries in summer, nuts in fall, deer in winter, fish in spring. The atlatl dart and polished stone tools were introduced but, by contrast with the Western Archaic, little basketry or weaving has been found.

In the later Archaic, stone tools became larger, and crude pottery made its first appearance. A less nomadic way of life may have developed—evidence being the large shell mounds found at some sites, which imply rather long periods of continuous occupation. As is characteristic of the Archaic in general, in both the east and the west, there is an increase in the overall variety of cultural materials, perhaps as a result of diversifying ways of life.

Toward the end of this period, differences in artifacts, site types, and so forth become so pronounced that it is no longer reasonable to treat the area as a whole. From the late Archaic onward, therefore, it is usual for archaeologists to divide the next tradition, called Woodlands, into four subtraditions. These are the Middle Eastern Subtradition (a rather confusing term, that), the Northern Subtradition, the Southern Appalachian Subtradition, and the Gulf Subtradition.

The area dominated by the Middle Eastern Subtradition is the mainly deciduous forest that runs south from the Ohio River Valley through Kentucky to central Mississippi, Alabama, and Georgia, and as far east as the Piedmonts in the Carolinas. Here there appears to be a focus on the use of acorns as food, and occupation sites feature storage pits, indicating a largely, but perhaps not entirely, sedentary way of life.

The home of the Northern Subtradition is to be found roughly in the area north of Kentucky, and stretches as far west as Minnesota, as far north as southern Ontario and Nova Scotia, and all the way to the Atlantic on the east. The area is dominated by forests of evergreen or mixed character and the prevalence of evergreens was probably even greater in pre-contact times. In its earliest phase, the subtradition shows some rather striking features. One is the existence of the so-called Old Copper Culture in Minnesota, Wisconsin, and northern Michigan. Here we find the first signs of early metalworking in North America. The raw material came from local deposits of pure, easily shaped and melted native copper. The whole region also shows a distinctive uniformity in pottery types and in burial practices—particularly in respect to the custom of including quantities of red ochre in the grave and of providing grave goods that had been ceremonially "killed." ("Killing" in this context means the deliberate breaking of an otherwise perfect artifact before it is placed in a grave.)

Later in the Northern Subtradition of the Woodlands Tradition there appear two developments that, while they may have been lightly foreshadowed by previous events, were nevertheless impressive and unique. They are known by the names Adena and Hopewell. The Adena originated earlier and disappeared sooner than the Hopewell, the former having arisen in the Ohio River Valley, and the latter having occupied at its greatest extent a much larger area, comprising not only the Ohio region but also Illinois, Michigan, Iowa, Missouri, and even northeastern Oklahoma. The most striking characteristic of these developments is their emphasis on the construction of large earthworks and mounds, some in the shape of effigies and some apparently used as the sites of public functions. A basic form of agriculture also came into use with the Adena and Hopewell, although the planting of maize and beans only supplemented, rather than replaced, the traditional hunting and gathering of wild foods.

Adena and Hopewell artifacts are very rich in decoration and detail, featuring in particular effigy pipes and effigy pottery in animal, insect, and floral form. As is usual in the post-Archaic traditions, the bow and arrow came into use at this time. A commonly found artifact is a pierced placque of bone, ground stone, or shell which may be an archer's wrist guard, although some authorities list it as a gorget. Copper articles are found, and by coincidence it is Hopewellian use of copper that has given us knowledge of contemporary textiles as well. The reason is that samples of cloth have been preserved by contact with copper, or rather with the salts formed by its corrosion. Thus we know that the dyer's art had advanced to include resist dyeing, in which a pattern is made on cloth with a resistant substance and dye is then applied to the background. The technique resembles that of Asian and Polynesian batik work. Both Adena and Hopewellian arts evolved toward abstraction, as evidenced by flat silhouette figures of unknown function cut from mica or copper, and also by stone tablets inscribed with figures. Stone technology had reached an extremely high level and featured quantities of very good quality obsidian (imported) as well as advanced grinding and polishing techniques. This use of exotic materials, apparently traded in from areas as distant as the Rocky Mountains and the Southwest, is characteristic of Adena and Hopewell, and many researchers believe some form of influence from Mexico was important in precipitating their development.

Both Adena and Hopewell appear to have reached their climaxes without making the transition to true, systematic agriculture. Evidence of eventual cultural change can be seen in deteriorating workmanship of artifacts and a return to cruder methods of mound construction.

Hopewellian influences were very pervasive in the remoter territories of the Northern Subtradition, although designs are seen to become less sophisticated with distance from the cultural center. In some locations, such as south central Canada, objects of Hopewellian types continued to be made right into historic times. The habit of making burial mounds extended even beyond the bounds of the Northern Subtradition—one more evidence of the strength and persistence of this influence. Some authorities associate the decline of Adena and Hopewell with the breakdown of the trade networks referred to above, but whether as cause or as effect is uncertain.

South and east of the areas we have been discussing, in northern Florida and southern Georgia and Alabama, lies the area of the Southern Appalachian Subtradition. The climate here is subtropical and the terrain gentle. There is a great deal of coastline.

Woodlands Tradition attributes seem to appear here without much outside influence. That is, they arise directly out of the features of the Archaic Tradition that were already present in the area. Early pottery in the Southern Appalachian was tempered with broken pottery sherds, while in later pieces sand was used. Typical pottery was stamped with designs made by tools manufactured expressly for the purpose. In the beginning, designs covered the whole body of the pot; later styles had a patterned body with an elaborately decorated rim. Popular designs included interweavings, spirals, and checkerboards. In contrast to the nearby Middle Eastern Subtradition, the acorn was not the principal food source here, although oaks of various species are plentiful, and agriculture seems not to have come into use until relatively late. The major agricultural influence apparently came from the Mississippian Tradition (see below).

In later Woodlands phases, the evidence makes it clear that the area was extensively influenced by the Northern, Middle Eastern, and Gulf subtraditions, as shown by the occasional construction of temple mounds, the introduction of foreign pottery styles, and other signs. In fact, the custom of borrowing from neighbors was so well entrenched in the Southern Appalachian that burial customs never settled into one pattern at all, but favored now this method, now that one, apparently as the fashion or fancy struck. At the same time, the principal characteristic of the subtradition is its continuity of development from Archaic through Woodlands, indicating an absence of disruptive events like invasions and migrations of population.

West of the Southern Appalachian Subtradition lies the home of the Gulf Subtradition, which is found on a strip extending along the Gulf coast of Alabama west of Mobile Bay, through Mississippi, Louisiana, and Texas, as far south as Galveston. Northward, it stretches as far as central Arkansas, and in its later phases its influences appear as far east as northern Florida.

As with the Southern Appalachian, the Gulf Subtradition does not display any decisive break with the past following the Archaic. Rather, there is a steady evolution toward use of the bow and arrow and other typical Woodlands developments. In the lower Mississippi, the most striking sign of a change is in the appearance of burial mounds, which were, however, less sophisticated in construction than the Adena and Hopewell mounds being made at the same period. There are signs of stylistic influences from northern Mexico in the area at this time, especially in pottery design, and the custom apparently grew up of making pottery in two distinct forms—one for everyday use and one designed exclusively for funeral gifts. At a later date, pottery was "killed" ceremonially *before* firing, as may be seen from the condition of the sherds. Copper articles are sometimes found, although it is not known whether these originated in the area of the Old Copper Culture to the north or in Central America. (There is little native copper in the Gulf region.)

As time went on, the forms and functions of the mounds underwent certain changes. The earliest Gulf mounds were used for group burials only, in contrast to Adena/Hopewell mounds, which included single burials as well. Later Gulf mounds became true temple mounds, having structures on top and no associated burials. In their latest form, the mounds were rectangular rather than round, so that they resemble, and are possibly the inspiration for, the rectangular mounds of the Mississippian Tradition we are about to discuss.

Here we encounter a break in the general sequence of archaeological development in North America as we have described it so far (that is, Paleo-Indian, Archaic, post-Archaic). Not precisely within the geographical area of any of the four subtraditions we have just discussed, but extending in several directions from the central Mississippi Valley as far as the tip of Lake Michigan, the upper Ohio Valley, the Tennessee River Valley, and the upper Chattahoochee, a fifth distinct tradition is found to overlie the remains of the three subtraditions in the southern part of the Eastern Woodlands. It is called the Mississippian Tradition, and its isolated outposts are to be found even well beyond the area just outlined.

One theory has it that the core area of the Mississippian is to be found in the neighborhood of the famous Cahokia site in East St. Louis, Missouri, which may at its zenith have been the most densely populated locality in prehistoric North America. Be that as it may, a glance at a map will show that the Mississippian tended to follow major river valleys in its distribution. The reason may have been that, in its efforts to produce the required amounts of maize, its economy was heavily dependent on the rich alluvial soils deposited by annual floods. The growing of maize depletes the soil, and in spite of the natural enrichment of the fields by the yearly floods, demand eventually outran the production capacity of this type of agriculture. Archaeologists hypothesize that a search for fresh river bottoms to farm was the reason for a late outward diffusion of Mississippian peoples. Thus Mississippian influences were eventually spread far beyond the tradition's original home territory, though their effect on local populations naturally became weaker with distance until, in the area north of the Great Lakes, for example, it was quite diluted.

Although it most certainly drew inspiration from the kinds of agricultural practices already in use in the Middle Eastern Subtradition of its home area, the Mississippian developed a much more intensive form of cultivation, involving considerable land clearing and the use of improved varieties of cultivated plants. The resultant increase in food production probably brought about a growth in population that was manifested in the establishment of large settled towns. Mississippian artifacts seem to display stylistic ties to those of Mexico, so that scholars have suggested there was a renewal of contacts with that area such as the one that may have precipitated the rise of Adena and Hopewell. However, a difficulty is that the recorded number of authentic imported Mexican artifacts or exact replications of site types in the Mississippian Tradition is zero, so that we are left uncertain about the period, means of transmission, and exact geographical origin of the influence in question.

Typical earlier Mississippian sites are large, well-constructed temple mounds enclosed in palisades with a cluster of small villages in the surrounding area. Other structures appear to serve principally as fortifications. Pottery for funerary use was often of the effigy type (typically in plant or animal form) and is quite distinct from the everyday ware. Both funerary and everyday styles are much more elaborately decorated than the pottery of preceding Woodlands traditions, with the further characteristic of having handles and other applied decorations. The commonest material for tempering is crushed shell, and this is to be contrasted with the late Woodlands use of vegetable fiber.

In later Mississippian sites, a degree of local specialization may be seen. Artifact forms, for instance, become integrated with those of preexisting Woodlands types and certain variations in settlement patterns appear. One of these is the temple mound associated with several small permanent villages strung out along a river valley, instead of gathered together around a palisade, as is more typical.

As a final chapter in the story of the Mississippian Tradition, we must look at the meteoric rise, spread, and decline of what is known as the Southern Cult, a phenomenon found as far west as Spiro, Oklahoma, and as far east as Etowah, Georgia. The Southern Cult is generally viewed as a religious movement that arose during the later phases of the Mississippian Tradition. Traces of it are found in some, but not all, of the largest Mississippian sites, where it can be identified chiefly by certain distinctive design elements engraved on artifacts of shell, copper, and other materials. These designs indicate, in the main, a preoccupation with the symbolism of death and the sun, as well as some less easily interpreted motifs such as the hand with an eye inscribed on its palm. Some researchers have pointed to the style of these art works as an indication of a Mexican origin, but others, with equal force, have pointed out that the content seems to derive from North American mythological and cultural elements. This matter of origins is as yet unresolved, as is the question of the cult's mode of diffusion.

FIGURE 12

Design motifs of the Southern Cult

The Mississippian Tradition as a whole apparently flourished right up to the time of the first European contacts (the explorations of De Soto), but the Southern Cult is now thought to have died out sometime before that. A modern remnant of the cult may perhaps be found in the Green Corn Ceremony of the Creeks.

Research Problems

Did the climatic change that took place between Paleo-Indian and Woodlands times have the effect of forcing the population into agriculture because of changes in food resources? Did the use of shellfish as food during the Archaic lead to a more settled way of life, or was it the other way around? Was pottery brought to the Eastern Woodlands by migrations from north and west, or was it invented in the region independently? Why does typical pottery have conical bases? Is the fact that later Archaic materials are so similar throughout the area a result of diffusion from one center, or of a long period of undisturbed joint development? Just how important to the local economy was agriculture during the late Archaic and early Woodlands traditions? In the Middle Eastern Subtradition, what is the role of the harvesting of acorns? Is it possible that the development of the Northern Subtradition was influenced by peoples migrating from the north? Are the elements of the Adena/Hopewell/Mississippian traditions that are found in the outlying areas of the Eastern Woodlands traces of cultural borrowing or of imposition by outside forces—that is, wars or invasions? Which came first, pottery or agriculture? Why did the extensive trade networks of the Adena and Hopewell traditions, which ranged as far afield as the Rocky Mountains, cease to function? Was that breakdown of trade a cause or an effect of the general decline that eventually led to their disappearance? Was some change in the economic base (food supply) an additional factor? How *exactly* are the Adena/Hopewell/Mississippian/Southern Cult traditions related to those of Mexico and Central America? What sorts of contacts were made, how, and how often? Which, precisely, were the centers of this Mexican/Central American influence? Was resist dyeing invented in the Hopewellian context or introduced from elsewhere, such as Central America? (Was it even invented in the Americas at all?) Is there any evidence to support the idea that the Southern Cult originated *before* the overall Mississippian Tradition? Was the cult dispersed by individuals (traders, evangelists, etc.) or by movements of whole peoples?

THE ARCTIC AND SUBARCTIC

The location of this area is refreshingly easy to describe: it is north of everything else. In a belt from the Atlantic to the Pacific, it cuts across the continent on a curving line just above Lake Superior. Yet it would, of course, be a mistake to think of the region as an arctic wilderness. It contains a considerable variety of terrain, from frozen tundra in the farthest north through evergreen forest, mighty mountains, and numerous lakes and rivers. Winters are uniformly severe, but the region is even now rich in game, including seal and walrus on the coasts and moose, caribou, musk ox, elk, and bear in the interior. Cold weather breeds thick fur, and the area was a rich source of otter, mink, beaver, fox, bear, and other pelts in both prehistoric and historic times. At all periods, the coastlines have been more fully populated than the inland regions.

Geographically, the area falls into two subdivisions, the Arctic and the Subarctic.

The eastern Subarctic region comprises roughly the area east of James Bay and north of Nova Scotia. Eastern Woodlands traits can be found in somewhat diluted form here throughout the prehistoric period, although there are also indications of trade or commerce with the peoples of the Arctic and the western Subarctic. Some scholars, indeed, have argued that this area ought really to be included with the Eastern Woodlands, and certainly the archaeological sequences are similar except that the most recent tradition to appear in the eastern Subarctic is the Archaic rather than the post-Archaic Woodlands Tradition.

In the western part of both the Arctic and the Subarctic the situation is rather different. Paleo-Indian points of the Old Cordilleran and Big Game Hunting traditions and their "descendants" have been found, as well as traces of what may be the elusive "pebble tool tradition" referred to

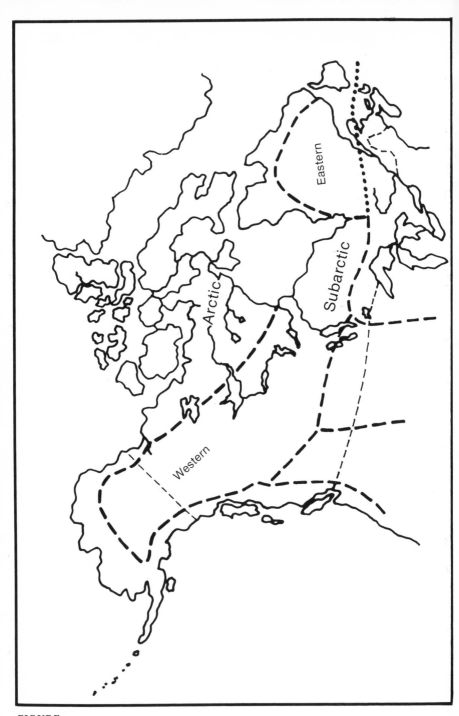

FIGURE 13

earlier in this chapter. It is a matter of debate whether this diversity indicates that the area was a primary migration route from Asia or that these traditions were brought in indirectly from the Great Plains area. (No Paleo-Indian Tradition has yet been reported from the eastern Arctic.) Spear points of the thrusting type are found in forms very similar to those of the Plano Tradition of the Great Plains.

Out of the Paleo-Indian Tradition arose the Northwest Micro-blade Tradition in the western part of the far north. As its name implies, this tradition is characterized by rather small tools that have the form of blades—single flakes longer than they are wide, with parallel edges. Stemmed and notched projectile points are also found, which may indicate the use of throwing spears. The major characteristic of this way of life appears to be hunting in deep forest.

The next development occurs only in the Arctic, where cold northern seas are the dominant environmental factor. It is called the Arctic Small Tool Tradition and may have been brought in by a new influx of migrants from Asia. Here tools become finer in workmanship, as is perhaps reflected by the fact that burins are typically found to have been hafted, implying a greater control in work such as the incising of bone. Classical types of tools such as "scrapers" come into use. The Arctic Small Tool Tradition seems to have moved east across the Arctic, eventually reaching Greenland, though at a considerably later date than that of its first appearance in the west.

Meanwhile, in the western Subarctic, the Northwest Micro-blade Tradition continued undisturbed for some time until superseded by the Denetasiro Tradition. This was a hunting tradition of the deep forests, whose modern representatives, the Athapaskan peoples of the area, flourished until historic times. The emphasis here is on bone and antler tools rather than stone, although polished stone adzes and other woodworking implements are well repre-

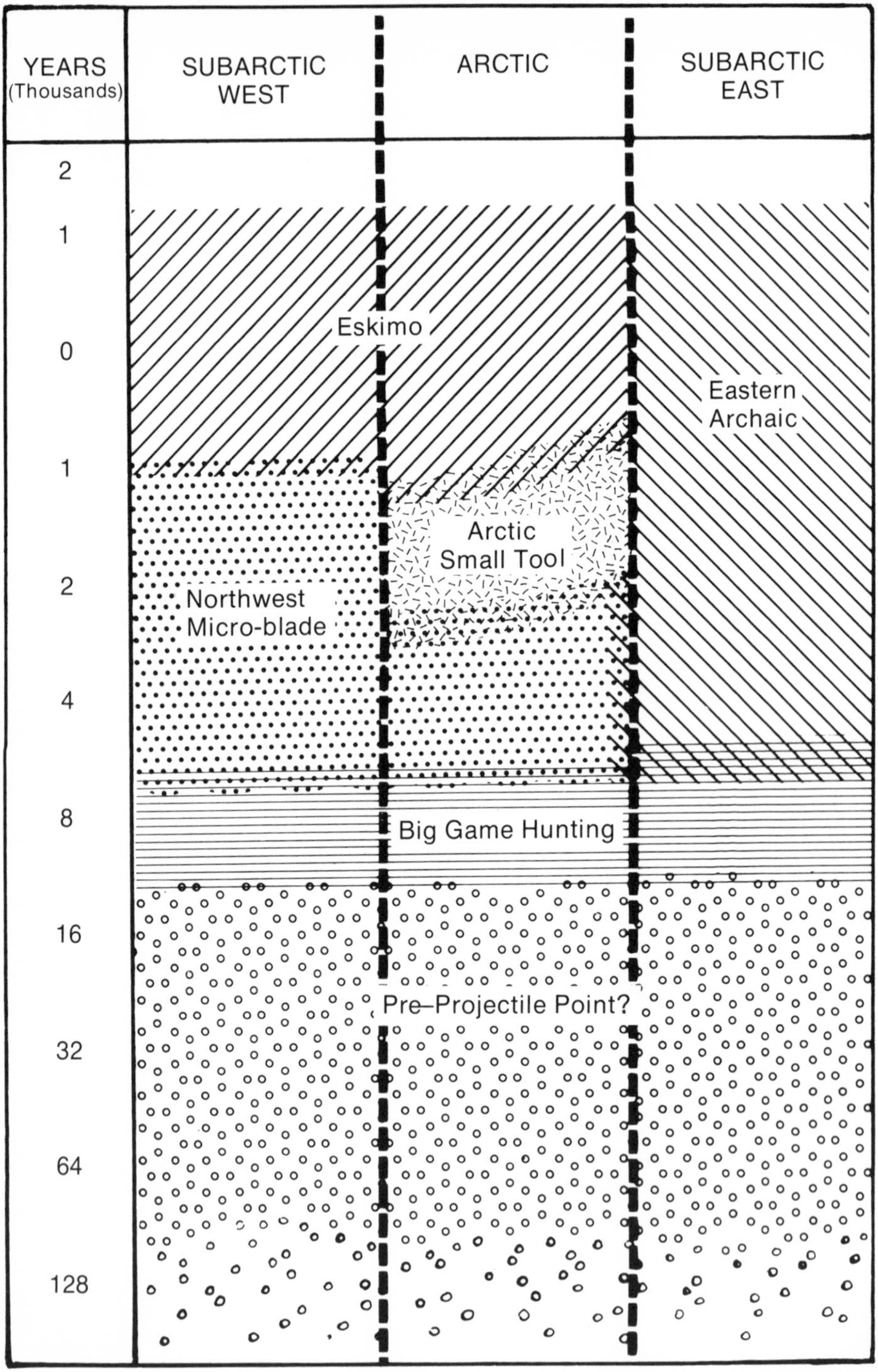
YEARS
(Thousands)
SUBARCTIC WEST
ARCTIC
SUBARCTIC EAST
2
1
0
1
2
4
8
16
32
64
128
Eskimo
Eastern Archaic
Arctic Small Tool
Northwest Micro-blade
Big Game Hunting
Pre–Projectile Point?

FIGURE 14

sented. Points are corner- or side-notched and later of small triangular types, possibly for use with the bow and arrow. Copper points are also found. The tradition appears to be one of seminomadic hunters, fishermen, and trappers.

At about the same time as the Denetasiro Tradition there appear in the Arctic the first signs of the Eskimo Tradition. Many scholars consider that the Eskimo were the last arrivals in the long migrations from Asia, reaching North America only at this relatively late date, although others contend that the tradition grew out of elements already present in the Arctic Small Tool Tradition. Quite clearly, the Eskimo Tradition represents a highly specialized adaptation to conditions that many other peoples would find intolerable. The Eskimo appear to have been the first to populate the extreme north of the continent, and it was they who brought the skills connected with the hunting of seal, walrus, and whale to their zenith. Bone and, especially, ivory carving were done with exceptional delicacy and, in the later periods, realism. The fact that the Eskimo also used pottery, whereas their immediate neighbors did not, is thought by some to mean that theirs was the only migration to take place after the introduction of pottery to Siberia. Understandably, the harpoon is the typical hunting weapon of the tradition, but the bow and arrow were also known, at least in later phases.

Research Problems

Did the fluted point tradition originate in the far north, or was it carried back to the region from the south? The same question may be asked concerning the Old Cordilleran. How many waves of migration entered North America from Asia (Siberia), and how may their impact and sequence be determined? What are the relationships of the Northwest Micro-blade and Arctic Small Tool traditions to the mesolithic and neolithic traditions of eastern Asia? Did the Eskimo use of pottery derive from Asian importation, influences from the Eastern Woodlands, or independent invention? Did the Eskimo themselves arrive or evolve?

Before we go on to aspects of site survey, we should note that even now we have not covered every last inch of North America's archaeology. There are two areas, southern Texas and southern Florida, that are not treated in the discussion above. The reason is that these two regions are more closely related, respectively, to northeast Mexico and to the Caribbean Islands than they are to North America proper. Readers who reside in these parts of Texas and Florida are referred to sources concerned with those areas.

Finally, we want to propose some general questions that apply to the entire continent rather than to any specific area. Though they are broad in scope, any individual archaeologist may be in a position to make finds that will be important for their solutions, and that archaeologist might as well be you.

Why do the presumed Central American and Mexican influences on the traditions, particularly, of the Southwest and the Mississippi/Ohio region manifest themselves so differently, or are the differences less real than apparent? Are there any North American parallels to the preoccupation with astronomy that can be demonstrated in many parts of Central America at about the time of these influences? What would have happened if the white man had never colonized, or even discovered, North America? What would have happened if a Central American Alexander or Genghis Khan had conquered large parts of North America before European contact? Why don't people always rush to adopt so-called cultural improvements from their neighbors? Is agriculture really *easier* than hunting and gathering? If not, what forces people to settle down and plant crops?

5
Starting at the Top

You read, read, read and think, think, think until one day a small inner voice tells you you are ready to go on a survey. Off you go, then, but first do read the next few paragraphs of good advice. They constitute a stitch in time, and the nine stitches they save you could even be in your own skin.

First, a word about archaeological courtesy. Rule Number One is: *Always be sure you have the permission of the landowner before you survey.* In this way you may avoid being warned off with a shotgun or wandering into the field with the bull in it. Besides, unless you have planned your survey on public land, there are laws against trespassing and not everyone, unfortunately, loves an archaeologist.

The best approach is usually to knock at the landowner's door (a few days ahead of time if possible) and give a brief, clear explanation of your interest in the property. Avoid giving the impression that what you are looking for is valuable in any but the scientific sense, or you may be taken for a pothunter. It will not hurt to stress the fact that you will not pick wild flowers, light fires, leave rubbish, or otherwise misuse the permission to survey. Many people are pleased at the idea that there might be interesting archaeological remains on their land, and you may even be offered helpful pointers such as, "Try the north corner of that field. The

tractor keeps turning up arrowheads there." If this is not
a convenient time of year, ask whether you can come back
later. A farmer who doesn't want his young crops trampled
may be perfectly willing to have you survey after the har-
vest, or just after plowing. In fact, nothing turns up a nicer
assortment of artifacts than a recent shallow plowing (although some modern deep cultivators are the bane of archaeologists, as they disturb the soil layering and jumble
together early and late deposits). In any case, a field with
standing crops should never be walked over without specific permission, and is often too thickly grown to be surveyed anyway.

Bear in mind that if permission is refused, you must
respect the owner's wishes or risk arrest, according to most
state and provincial law. One of the authors was once
forced to watch helplessly as bulldozers pushed several
acres of deep midden, marking a probable village site with
a nine-thousand-year history, over a California cliff into the
ocean. The owner had "no use for a pack of archaeologists,
or Indians either," and the law supported him. (But see
Appendix I for more information about U.S. and Canadian
law as it applies to archaeological preservation.)

For the town dweller, a note about gates: On someone
else's land *never* leave an open gate closed or a closed gate
open. This is only common sense, and besides, nothing
turns an otherwise cooperative rancher, farmer, or stock-
breeder into a hater of archaeologists more quickly than
the sight of several head of good animals making off down
a dangerous road or, conversely, huddling hopefully
against a closed gate that should have led to fodder, water,
or the home barn.

In spite of these warnings, experience shows that the
majority of private landowners are happy to allow surveyors on their land, perhaps for the small price of having a
look at their finds. (In some states or provinces, however,

artifacts legally belong to the landowner and can only be removed by permission. Check with your State Archaeologist or provincial archaeological agency if you are in doubt about local laws. See Appendix IV for addresses.)

Rule Number Two for surveyors is: *Don't disappear.* Decide beforehand where you are going and make sure you tell someone before you set out. Archaeologists may find "lost civilizations," but who is to find lost archaeologists? For both pleasure and safety, it is a good idea to take a friend along if possible. Whether your companion is a fellow archaeologist or merely an interested observer, two people are much safer than one in case of accident, and two can carry more than one. (Don't forget that if you find anything you will have more to carry on the way home. Bags of stone tools are *heavy.*) If you must go alone, make doubly sure you leave word of your route and destination.

The equipment you will need to carry on a survey is not very elaborate, but it is important. Problems are as likely to arise from taking too many needless gadgets as from leaving necessities behind. The following is a list of basics needed by almost any surveyor:

1. A clipboard or something similar to write on.
2. Several site report forms. You can copy the one included in this book (see page 125) or use the official site report form of your local archaeological society.
3. Lead pencils or some other waterproof writing implement.
4. The U.S. or Canadian Geological Survey map of your target area, either the 7.5-minute series (1 inch equals 2,000 feet) or the 15-minute series (1 inch equals 1 mile, approximately). A possible alternative is the U.S. Forest Service map if the area is on State

Forest land. To order maps by mail, see addresses in Appendix V. Also in Appendix V will be found sources for aerial photographs and satellite data. These are not always available, but can be useful, especially when the area to be surveyed is large.

5. A compass. This is needed not merely to keep you from getting lost; it is vital for taking map bearings in order to record the locations of the sites you find. Compasses may be expensive, but they need not be. Army surplus stores often carry used military compasses that are more than adequate for your purpose. One of the authors still uses a compass issued to her father during World War I. Boy Scout "Pathfinder" compasses may also be used. (Consult a standard scouting manual for technique, which is a little different from the one described in this chapter.) In all cases, the best compass model is one with a straight edge for drawing bearing lines. Obviously, the more elaborate compasses, with finer scales on their dials, will give more accurate results. A really cheap compass with only the four cardinal points marked is no good at all. (See Appendix V for possible sources of compasses and other supplies.)

6. Measuring tapes. The best are steel or reinforced cloth because they wear better. One 2-meter tape (about 6 feet) and one 30-meter tape (about 100 feet) are ideal. Note that in archaeology, as in all scientific measurement, the metric system is used.

7. A small trowel, not a garden trowel but a

triangular-bladed mason's trowel. This can be purchased in most hardware stores. You are not going to dig, of course, you are only going to clear away dirt from objects such as partially buried hearths or bedrock mortars.

8. Small cloth or plastic bags (sandwich size) for collecting surface artifacts and samples of shell, soil, or whatever.

9. Labels or tags for the bags.

10. First aid kit (including snakebite supplies where needed) and survival equipment such as matches and a pocketknife.

11. Light pack or knapsack for carrying your gear.

12. And, if you are going to be gone long, a canteen and a picnic lunch.

This second list includes items that are helpful in certain cases but not strictly necessary.

13. A light camera with black and white film, and with color film if you expect to encounter pictographs.

14. Gloves for dealing with brambles, cacti, nettles, etc.

15. Suntan lotion and/or insect repellent.

16. Binoculars. These may be useful if you want to examine distant hillsides for rock shelters or locate landmarks for map bearings.

17. The U.S. Geological Survey's Ortho-quad map of the area. Ortho-quads are aerial photographs printed to the same scale as the 7.5-minute survey map. When used together the two can give much more useful information than either alone. However, Ortho-

quads are relatively expensive and are not
available for every part of the continent. See
Appendix V for the address of the U.S. Geological Survey (USGS).
18. Specialized materials, as needed, such as
those described in the section on rock art in
chapter 3.

Taken together, the items from both lists will probably
be too much for one person to carry—another reason for
taking a friend or fellow surveyor along.

So here you are, faced with your first survey area—the
Old Jones Place, soon to be converted into a ten-acre turkey farm. What now?

The ideal thing, of course, would be for you to scrutinize
every single square yard of your territory, and you should
try to approximate this goal as closely as possible. Looking
carefully at the ground on each side of you as you walk, you
can probably examine a swath of land about ten to twenty
feet wide, and if you wanted to do an utterly systematic job
of covering some large, flat area like a football field, you
could probably walk back and forth across it at twenty-foot
intervals. Real life seldom cooperates with such systematic
plans, however. For one thing, you cannot walk in rigid
straight lines down cliff sides, through quicksand, across
most kinds of green cropland, or into bramble thickets. For
another thing, there are many kinds of conditions—most
obviously thick vegetation or leaf mold—under which you
can't see the soil surface no matter how hard you look.

In approaching any actual piece of land, you will have to
make compromises based on your background knowledge
and a reasonable regard for your own safety. While not
neglecting the unlikely places (remember where the entrance to Tut-ankh-Amen's tomb was found), you will learn

to concentrate especially hard on what reason and intuition tell you just have to be the likely areas, whether they be those beside fresh water, near natural resources, or simply particularly favorable potential campsites. You are looking not only for the kinds of remanent materials discussed in chapter 2, but for other, more subtle signs of disturbance of the natural landscape—mounds of soil or rock that have no obvious geological explanation, changes in coloration of the earth that may indicate the presence of midden material or a history of fire. Banks, hilltops, cliff tops, or even large boulders can be useful vantage points from which to spot faint traces of historic period wagon tracks and building foundations or prehistoric irrigation ditches and defensive palisades.

Another resource for the conservation archaeologist, who tries to practice "archaeology without shovels," is any bank or hole in the ground. Anything from a railroad cutting to a gopher hole may give you a fine opportunity to find out what may lie beneath the ground surface. From this point of view, foxes, woodchucks, rabbits, pack rats, muskrats, prairie dogs, and other burrowing animals are definitely the archaeologist's friends, providing sneak previews of what might be found during excavation. The most profitable approach is to examine the mound of earth at the hole's entrance, looking particularly for remanent materials, as soil coloration is not likely to show up in a pile of scrabbled dirt. One word of warning: Snakes and other venomous creatures have been known to occupy convenient holes after their builders have moved out (or been eaten), and even a gopher will fight back if cornered. So before you disturb any animal burrow it is prudent to make some warning noises and probe the entrance gingerly with a stick.

It is somewhat embarrassing to have to admit at this point that it is not always possible to conduct a survey

without digging. We have put so much emphasis on the
nondestructive approach to archaeological survey that it
would be much more convenient to ignore the fact that in
some areas of the continent, most conspicuously in the
Eastern Woodlands and the Northwest, it is unlikely that
you will find out enough from surface remains to make any
competent judgment about the presence of sites beneath
the surface. A number of factors—heavy undergrowth,
damp climate, rapid accumulation of leaf mold—are responsible for this condition, but the result is that a survey
in these areas will probably require a technique called
shovel testing.

Shovel testing lets the surveyor look below the surface of
the ground for some of the more general signs of occupation, such as change in soil color or buried layers of shell
or bone. It is not primarily designed to locate artifacts,
although of course the occasional artifact may turn up. It
is thus a more limited kind of test pit, which is a very small
excavation conducted on a known site under certain conditions so that the archaeologist can make an informed decision about whether a threatened site merits preservation or
salvage. The hows and whens of shovel testing will be gone
into in chapter 11, where test pits are discussed in detail.
It is still true, though, that in the large majority of cases a
pair of feet and good eyes are the surveyor's essential tools
and the shovel may be left behind.

In making a site survey, there are three really important
procedural considerations. The first is to be as thorough as
possible. Keep going back until you are reasonably sure
you have found everything there is to find, even if you do
not know exactly how to interpret each dark patch of soil
or pile of stones. The second thing is to *record* the results
of your survey, whether they are negative or positive. In
other words, it is just as important to note the areas where
you found nothing as it is to pinpoint the locations of actual

sites found. And a third necessity is to be absolutely accurate about which parts of the property you really did survey and which parts you may have left out because of time, weather, or plain exhaustion. If it was just too hot for you to check the other side of the ridge, or you left the rock ledge alone because it was rattlesnake season, say so in your field notes. Eventually this information, perhaps no more than a paragraph or two, should be attached to your preliminary site report (which we will be discussing below) and forwarded to the proper authorities. Even if you survey the whole property and find nothing, a short report to that effect should be sent to the same places as the site report (again, see below). Knowing exactly what has and what has not been surveyed in the area can be very helpful to a professional who is planning an extensive survey or research project, and archaeology cannot afford to waste effort in pointless duplication when there is so much work to be done and such a shortage of trained people to do it.

Don't be pessimistic about surveying in general, however. Eventually, whether on the Old Jones Place or elsewhere, you will come across unmistakable evidence of historic or prehistoric activity. After you get through congratulating yourself, what should you do next? A pothunter would stop right there, grab a shovel, and destroy the site with the enthusiasm of a terrier digging for a rat. For you, however, the job has just begun.

First, you will need to get an idea of the extent of the site area. Some sites are much larger than they might at first appear. If, and only if, the site is in danger of destruction, gather samples of artifact types from the surface, as well as other cultural debris such as bone, shell, charcoal, or ochre and similar raw materials. Each bag should be carefully labeled with the date collected, the collector's name, the site name, and site number, if known. (See pages 123 and 129 for information about site numbering.) In addition, if the site is larger than a few square yards, it will be helpful for further research if you divide it into rough squares or quadrants and keep a separate bag of material for each quadrant. Thus a sample label might read: M. Roberts, Watson's Farm, site 4 SLO 1000, shell fragments, surface coll., SE quad., 11/17/77.

It is neither possible nor desirable to pick up every artifact or piece of chipping waste you can find. It is far more important to get a general picture of the site. Is it uniform, or does it seem to be divided into areas for various activities such as cooking, processing, and manufacturing? If the site is historic, are there signs of outbuildings, fence rows, cultivation, wagon tracks? Are there any significant "features" on the surface? A feature, in the terms of an archaeological survey, is a sign of cultural material that is buried in or is part of the soil surface. The most usual examples from prehistoric sites are hearths. These must be carefully distinguished from campers' or picnickers' fireplaces, which are typically much less elaborate. A genuine prehistoric hearth is most probably marked by discoloration of the soil (blackening from charcoal, reddening from heat action). *In addition,* hearths most often consist of platforms of fire-cracked rock. A suspected hearth, tipi ring, or other feature may be verified by exposing it carefully with the trowel if it is partially buried. In the case of larger hearths especially, it is not necessary to reveal the whole feature. Better conservation practice is simply to confirm that a hearth is really present and get a general idea of its size and shape.

The next step is to locate the site accurately on your Geological Survey map. If this is not done, the site is lost for the purposes of the archaeological record. Scientifically, it might as well not exist.

The procedure for mapping is as follows. First, find the general area of the site on the map and note the major landmarks (mountain peaks, water towers, bridges, buildings, etc.) that seem to be near it. Match up one landmark from the map with what you can actually see from the site and, using the sighting device on your compass, take a bearing on it. This means that you look at your landmark through the compass sight or along the arrow and rotate the compass dial until its indicator is lined up with magnetic north, as represented by the swinging needle. Many compasses have a knob you can use to "freeze" this reading while you record it. The bearing, in any case, is simply the number of degrees clockwise around the dial from magnetic north to the sighting device. (If you find this confusing, look at Figure 15.)

It is important to choose landmarks for your bearings that are as permanent as possible. Survey maps show an amazing amount of detail, but mountain peaks are more permanent than houses, which are in turn more permanent than patches of brushwood.

Of course, you may not have much choice of landmarks, because the people who left the sites were not concerned with the convenience of archaeologists, and frequently chose to live in dense forests, canyons, or other places with poor visibility. Still, you must not make the mistake of one beginning archaeologist, who took painstaking bearings on several cars parked along a roadway. To be useful at all, a landmark must be *on the map.*

If the site offers absolutely no reasonable landmarks, you will have to walk to some spot from which you *can* take bearings, and do your mapping from there. You can then take one additional bearing back toward the site and pace off (or, preferably, measure) the distance. In either case, all your information should be recorded immediately on the site report form. (See below for instructions on completing a sample form.) *Do not* jot bearings on odd pieces of paper, or you will have a nervous breakdown trying to remember which bearings go with which of the several sites you found.

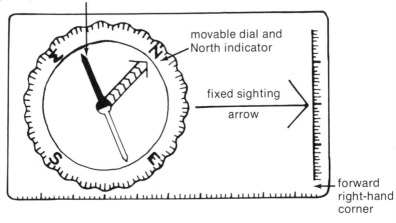

swinging compass needle

movable dial and
North indicator

fixed sighting
arrow

forward
right-hand
corner

*Typical compass of the type suggested for use in archaeological
survey*

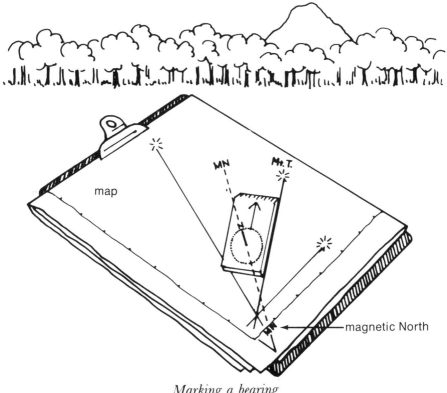

map

MN

Mt. T.

MN

magnetic North

Marking a bearing

FIGURE 15

Three or (to be safe) four bearings should be taken for each site, and it is desirable to plot them on your USGS map as soon as they are recorded. This will save you from making errors and having to come back and redo things, but it is not always possible in bad weather.

In order to plot the bearings you have taken, first orient your map so that its north arrow is actually lined up with magnetic north as shown by the compass. To do this you must lay the map flat; your clipboard is a handy surface. Place the compass on the map. Its swinging needle will of course point to magnetic north. Turn the compass's movable dial so that its north indicator is also aligned north, covering the compass needle. Thus the map's north arrow, the compass needle, and the compass indicator all point north.

Now locate on your map one of the points on which you took bearings. For example, suppose Mt. Tepesquet lies 10 degrees from your site. The steps for plotting that bearing are given below. (Refer to Figure 15.)

1. Orient your map as described above.

2. Rotate the movable dial of your compass until the number of the bearing (10 degrees) lies at the base of the fixed sighting arrow.

3. Place the compass on the map again, with the forward right-hand corner on the point on which the bearing was taken.

4. Slowly pivot the compass on its forward right-hand corner until the north-pointing compass needle is under the movable dial's north indicator.

5. Now draw a line down the right-hand edge of the compass as far as is necessary to reach the approximate area of the site.

6. Do this for all four bearings and behold—if you have done everything correctly, the four lines will intersect at a point on the map which is your site location. This process

is called quadrangulation for four bearings, or triangulation for three. There is a curious satisfaction in looking at a map and saying, "See that? That's where I am."

If time and weather allow, the preliminary site report form should also be filled out on the spot, in order to avoid inaccuracy and confusion later. A good site report takes account of conditions or features that may be relevant only to a particular area, and no one has yet been able to devise a simple, universal form. We have included a useful and fairly generalized example (see page 125) derived from the form used by the San Luis Obispo County Archaeological Society in California, and will give detailed notes on how to fill it out. Nevertheless, you should be aware that site report forms vary widely in amount of detail and degree of complexity.

First put your initials and an arbitrary number of your choice in the upper right-hand corner. The most obvious numbering system is simply to number the sites in order (so that site 16, for example, is the sixteenth site you have discovered in your survey). In any case, the number is temporary and will be replaced by an official site number later. (See page 129.) Now proceed with the numbered items.

1. *Location Description:* Record the name of the USGS or other map used, including the scale (7.5 minutes or 15 minutes) and the UTMG coordinates of the site. See Appendix VI for instructions on how to determine these coordinates from USGS maps. Canada uses a slightly different coordinate system. The Archaeological Survey of Canada can provide the necessary information. For the address, see Appendix IV.

Contour Interval is an approximation of the altitude of the site, as read from the numbered contour lines on the map. The legend of each map explains the method used for marking contours—that is, whether they represent ten-, twenty-, or fifty-foot intervals, or whatever.

Bearings: Record your four compass bearings. Always specify that you used magnetic north, rather than true north.

2. *Site Description:* Fully describe the nature of the site and its setting. For example: "Bedrock mortars (8) on rock outcrop near edge of cultivated field." Indicate whether you took photographs. Prints of any pictures should be attached to the report before it is filed.

3. *Owner or Tenant* (if known): This information can be used by later archaeologists who may wish to ask permission to visit the site.

4. *Area:* Approximate east-west and north-south dimensions of the site, in meters.

5. *Vegetation:* Record the type of vegetation community surrounding the site—for instance, oak scrub, pine barren, peat marsh, mixed deciduous forest, alpine meadow, chaparral. Continent-wide, the possible types of vegetation are much too numerous and complex to discuss here. However, the problem is more limited in any one region. Local agricultural colleges and state or provincial agricultural stations or forestry services can refer you to material that describes types of vegetation communities in your area.

6. *Water:* Record the direction, distance, and nature of the nearest fresh water supply. For

PRELIMINARY SITE REPORT

1. Location Description

   Map _____ UTMG _____

   Contour Interval _____

   Bearings

   a) _____ b) _____

   c) _____ d) _____

2. Site Description _____

   _____

   _____

   Photos? B&W _____ Color _____

3. Owner or Tenant _____

4. Area _____ 5. Vegetation _____

6. Water _____

7. Site Soil _____ 8. Surrounding Soil _____

9. Erosion _____ 10. Cultivation _____

11. Destruction? _____

12. Features _____

    _____

13. Artifacts _____

    _____

14. Remarks _____

    _____

15. Date _____ 16. By _____

17. Sketch map of site access. For detailed site map, see over.

prehistoric sites, man-made reservoirs don't count. For example: "Unnamed small creek, 55 meters due east. Probably dry in summer."

7. *Site Soil:* Fully describe the site soil—for instance: "Sandy loam with shell-bearing midden." Fortunately, soil types are universal enough to be briefly categorized. See Appendix VII.

8. *Surrounding Soil:* Describe if different from above.

9. *Erosion:* Describe any erosion that has occurred: gully wash, wind action, sea action, etc.

10. *Cultivation:* Is the land in active use now? (Yes or no.) What is the crop being grown?

11. *Destruction?* Describe natural or man-made conditions that might destroy the site.

12. *Features:* List surface features, as defined above. Don't forget to include midden heaps.

13. *Artifacts:* List all artifacts collected by quadrant (see page 119), and be as specific as possible. For example: "Chert blades, 4; fire-cracked rock, 4; quartz point, 1; pottery sherds, 11; atlatl weight, 1; chipping waste, 1 bag; incised bone fragment, 1." If you are comfortable in your knowledge of the local point types, as you should be by now, note the type. If you know of individuals who possess collections previously made on the site, mention the location of these collections as well.

14. *Remarks:* Include any additional information not previously called for, such as your

suggestions for further work. This space can also be used to say which parts of the site were *not* surveyed, due to problems of time, weather, or permission. This information can be a help to you or another archaeologist when the site is revisited.

15. *Date:* Give date when form was filled out.
16. *By:* Give your full name and address.
17. *Sketch map and detailed map:* You will need two maps on your site report form. The first is an informal sketch showing ways to get to the site, including access roads, trails, or simply the most convenient route across country (avoiding swamps, cliffs, or other hazards). On the back of the form there should be a more detailed plan of the site, showing features as you observed them. Were the artifacts concentrated in one area? Were there any middens? Where are the tipi ring stones, bedrock mortars, hearths, pieces of rock art, house pits in relation to the rest of the site? Key in with letters or numbers the locations where artifacts were picked up, and don't forget to indicate which way is north.

This completes the preliminary site report form, but not the survey report, unless the site you found was an isolated accident. More usually, the discovery of a site will be only one of the results of a more extensive survey. Even if you did not find any other sites, the full report should contain an overview of the survey as a whole, explaining exactly where, within the bounds of the survey, you looked and found nothing, and also where, if anywhere, you were unable to look. The logic of this necessity has been described above. The most convenient form for this overall survey

report is often a sketch map showing (1) the relative posi-
tions of any sites found, (2) the total area surveyed (perhaps shown by shading in), and (3) any areas not surveyed.
A few paragraphs of description is often all that need ac-
company this report, although you may wish to offer your
own interpretations of the area and its patterns of site location. The survey report is a legitimate place to speculate on
why the sites are placed the way they are, or even on why
an apparently favorable location appears not to have the
sites one might have expected. This is the point where all
your background research will pay off—nothing is more fun
than launching into free but informed speculation with no
one to raise small-minded objections, and many major discoveries started life as tremulous little suggestions.

Now that you have gone to all this trouble, you certainly
don't want it to be wasted. Yet who else is interested in your
survey or site report, and even more important, who needs
it? The first answer to both questions is: in the United
States, the State Historic Preservation Officer and the State
Archaeologist; in Canada, the Provincial Archaeologist. (A
list of the addresses of these officials, as of 1977, will be
found in Appendix IV.) In the United States, State Historic
Preservation Officers (SHPOs) and State Archaeologists
have slightly different functions (one office being supported by the federal government, the other by the state),
but both have a legitimate interest in maintaining up-to-
date files of known historic and prehistoric sites within their
territories. These files and those of the Canadian equiva-
lents are used by academic researchers and by professional
archaeologists contracting for legally mandated survey or
excavation work, so it is important that the information be
as complete as possible.

In addition, if your site is on land owned by the U.S.
National Park Service or Forest Service, a copy of your

report should also go to the appropriate regional office, as listed in Appendix IV.

It is probably the State or Provincial Archaeologist who will assign a permanent number to your site and notify you of it, although in some cases this process is administered through local archaeological societies. Every site needs a reference number, just as every library book needs a call number—so that you can find it when you want it. However, although the Smithsonian Institution has established a uniform site-numbering system for the United States, not all states have adopted it. Some county archaeological societies even use their own private (and sometimes peculiar) systems. The point is that the site must have a number, and the State Archaeologist (who needs your report anyway) can either give you a number or tell you where to get one.

You may also find it desirable to send a copy of your report to the local archaeological society for the information of its members. Think twice before you do this, however. It is a sad fact that in certain regions archaeological societies have degenerated into little more than pothunting clubs, and though the majority are as competent, sincere, and responsible as one could wish, it takes experience to tell the difference. Before you join or correspond with a society, it is a good precaution to ask around. If you find that members are very secretive about site locations, even within the society, or if you hear tales of competitive disputes about who gets to dig where, then the group should be viewed with suspicion. One society in the Midwest has reputedly even posted an armed guard on its excavation site in order to keep the members from stealing one another's artifacts. Keep well away from such a disgraceful situation if you encounter one. Bad archaeology destroys sites just as effectively as bulldozers.

On the other hand, once you find evidence that a society is genuinely interested in conservation archaeology (and a great many are), a membership can be both helpful and enjoyable. An archaeological society offers facilities for research and experiment, the chance to swap archaeological chitchat, and, most important of all, a chance to learn from the experience of others. After all, no book can teach you everything you need to know about a complex subject like archaeology. At some point you will want personal contact with others working in the field, and joining a society is a good way to begin. Whether or not you become a member, a *good* archaeological society will benefit from receiving a copy of your survey report.

The same may be true of a college or university department of archaeology or anthropology, especially if it is located nearby and/or is known to be interested in North American fieldwork. Paradoxically, many of the largest and best-known academic institutions specialize in the cultures of the ancient Near East, the Mediterranean, and other remote areas, while the smaller schools are frequently more knowledgeable about their own backyards. They are the ones who will probably be grateful for copies of your survey reports.

We have been addressing the question, "Who needs your data?" It implies another one, namely, "Who *doesn't* need your data?" More accurately, "Who should be prevented from getting it?" As a conservation archaeologist, you have a duty to protect the sites you find from bad archaeological societies, parties of pothunters, casual souvenir collectors, pranksters with faked artifacts, and, in fact, everybody who does not have a specific interest either in preserving the site or in studying it seriously.

A great problem for the archaeologist is the well-meaning but too factual newspaper story. One of the authors was once forced to camp out on a site to protect it after an overenthusiastic reporter had printed its exact location, which happened to be near a main road. The moral is not that you must slink around like an atomic spy and worry about whether you will talk in your sleep, but only that you must exercise discretion. If you want to write up your finds or let yourself be interviewed for a local newspaper, go right ahead—just make sure you keep the details of site locations to yourself.

It is not always immediately obvious how archaeologists manage to go from a collection of site maps and a few artifacts (mostly broken) to conclusions about cultural processes, lifeways, and economic or technological developments. Yet most archaeologists would probably agree that the real fun of their profession or avocation is not in writing tiny numbers on hundreds of tiny sherds or thumbing through a stack of field notes but in trying to fit all those fragments into a larger, more informative picture.

What are the principles of archaeological reasoning? In other words, what do you expect to get from your data? We have already mentioned archaeology's basic organizing principle: "Deeper is older." However, stratigraphy is not the only basis of archaeological reasoning, and stratigraphy alone will never get you from the single tile or pebble to the whole mosaic.

Since a site is a three-dimensional entity (and conservation archaeology seeks to avoid disturbing the stratigraphy unless a site's destruction is inevitable), it is important to look at its artifacts, features, and so on horizontally as well as vertically. That is, the *distribution* of remains within each level of a site or on the surface is just as revealing as the depths at which they are found. In any reasonably large site, a surface examination is likely to show that the site is not uniform. Hearths may be clustered in one area, while chipping waste, midden, or ground stone tools are in another. The site is probably divided into specialized areas devoted to particular activities such as woodworking, cooking, fish processing, or stone tool making. From data such as these the archaeologist builds a hypothesis or model concerning the probable nature and uses of the site—what the inhabitants did with their time, perhaps the season of the year when the site was occupied. But as with all scientific reasoning, the investigators must remain open-minded about their hypotheses, rather than becoming wedded to them and looking only for confirmatory data.

It is often as useful to note what is *not* found at the site as what is. A relative scarcity of fish remains as opposed to deer bones might suggest that a riverside camp was occupied in fall, when, in many regions, migratory fish are scarce but deer are plentiful. A preponderance of scrapers over axes and adzes might mean that leatherworking was a more important activity than woodworking, and so on. A prehistoric site is no more likely to be the same in every part than is a modern home, with its kitchen, garage, playroom, bathrooms, tool shed, and so on. Exciting and interesting patterns may show up when you go over your records later, if you have been careful in your surface collection, cataloging each find and recording what part of the site it came from in addition to mapping features. (Cataloging procedures are discussed in chapter 6.) Are the hearths all on the downwind side of the hill? Do all the colonial root cellars face south? Are the obsidian tools most often found with a certain type of pottery? Make a note of it. Think about it. Archaeology is really the search for patterns in seemingly unrelated sets of data.

Another characteristic of archaeological thinking is that one tends to reason outward in concentric circles—from the tool to the site, from the site to the region, from the region to the culture. Thus it is not only the intra-site situation, discussed above, that is of interest, but the inter-site situation as well. The more sites you become really familiar with (from the ground up—or, as it were, down), the more those patterns are going to jump out at you.

Archaeologists apply very sophisticated techniques of statistical analysis to such things as the correlation of site density with soil type or stream size, and anyone interested in such matters may wish to consult *Mathematics and Computers in Archaeology* by Doran and Hodson (see Appendix II), but even those of unmathematical bent may make observations that lead to hypotheses for further testing and eventually to new knowledge about vanished ways of life. "All the sites with imported quartzite tools lie along the Still River watershed. Hmmm . . ." "Black on white pottery seems to appear earlier in the west than in the east. Hmmm . . ." "The sites with the so-called atlatl weights only have small arrow points and large quantities of bird bones. Hmmm . . ." If you listen to that "hmmm," it can lead you to hypotheses about the migration of peoples, the spread of cultural traits, the effects of changing environment, the nature of outside influences, and much, much more. And even if most of your hypotheses fail to stand up to further testing (and many will), they will at least point the way to others, perhaps more durable.

6
Getting It All Together

It seems that a large proportion of the human race has an inextinguishable urge to collect things, from matchbooks to china zebras to emeralds. Many distinguished archaeologists began as collectors, if not as pothunters, and the authors cannot find it in their hearts to condemn collecting altogether. Indeed, this chapter is predicated on the assumption that at some time or other the active conservation archaeologist will come into possession of some artifacts.

However, before you collect, even from the surface, you should be aware of the responsibilities involved in collecting and the very valid arguments against it.

We hope we have already said enough on the subject of collecting subsurface objects outside the framework of a scientific excavation to warn off any responsible person. The wanton destruction of data is simply too great to tolerate. Yet one might reasonably think that collecting objects found on the surface could not disturb the soil layering of the site as a whole and would therefore be permissible. Unfortunately, this turns out not to be the case. Dr. Laurel Casjens, in an unpublished paper delivered before a meeting of the Coalition for Archaeology in Massachusetts, recently described a study based on findings in Ruby Valley,

Nevada, that clearly showed the kind of distortion of data the professional archaeologist may encounter when doing a detailed analysis of surface material from an area that has been exposed to extensive surface collection. The trouble is that the collector's natural instinct is to pick up the "best" artifacts—that is, the largest, handsomest, or least damaged items—or else to collect from the most easily accessible parts of the site. As a result, a systematic study may lead to false conclusions about the types of activity carried on in one part of the site as opposed to another, or the relative frequencies of materials from two or more traditions. It's like making a survey of the contents of a box of chocolates when someone has gone through and eaten all the ones with soft centers.

Naturally, these objections become somewhat less strenuous when the site is in danger of destruction without excavation. You will have to use your good judgment about whether to collect, but remember: When in doubt, don't.

In actual practice, many archaeologists find themselves in possession of random batches of artifacts before they get serious about archaeology. These objects will someday be the nucleus of your personal archaeological collection— assuming you decide collecting is warranted—but they are not now a collection. They are a jumble, a hodgepodge, a gallimaufry, an omnium-gatherum. They will be of no use to archaeology until they have been *cataloged.*

The purpose of an artifact catalog is fairly simple. It should give a complete, factual, precise picture of what each object looks like, what its purpose is thought to have been, when it was found, and above all *where* it was found. The reason a catalog is needed is twofold. First, it provides a succinct and portable guide that may be lent to other archaeologists for study. More important, artifact collections themselves have a way of becoming mislaid or jumbled. They are lost in shipment, borrowed and never returned, sold to antiquities dealers. One rather extensive collection from upstate New York was "donated" to the town dump by the collector's mother while he was away at college because she "thought he didn't have any more use for those old stones he used to play with." The catalog is archaeology's insurance against such accidents.

Many academic departments, archaeological societies, and state survey teams have created for themselves catalog forms of considerable complexity. Some assign numbered codes to stone tools or pottery on the basis of Professor Somebody's typology for South Central Somewhere. Others provide codes for computerization. Both systems rely on such assumptions as that any tool whose edges meet at an angle of more than so-many degrees shall be called a scraper, any point over so-many centimeters long shall be called a spear point, etc. Not only are attributions like this factually doubtful; as we pointed out in chapter 2, archaeologists are very far from being agreed about them. Until these problems are resolved, it will be best for the independent beginning archaeologist to stick to the simplest possible form. However, catalog forms naturally tend to become more elaborate as the collector acquires broader knowledge or more specialized interests.

Page 139 shows a simple type of catalog page that can be used either for the gleanings of a single area survey or for more casual occasional finds. (In the latter case, where there are only a few items per site, do not fill in a site number at the top of the page but enter that information under Location instead, whether it is an official site number or merely a description. The date cataloged will then go under Remarks.)

One difference between the casual collection and the thorough survey collection is that on a survey you will have collected materials that are not, strictly speaking, artifacts, such as midden samples, charcoal, fire-cracked rock, and so on. These should also be cataloged, though it is usually sufficient to list them by the bagful rather than by the piece, and they need not be individually numbered.

There are some basic data that should appear on the first page of the catalog so that, like all good reference books, it will be self-explanatory. You should specify what system of site numbering you are following—that of the official state archaeological survey or some other system, including your own. You should also say whether you are using any particular method of assigning names to artifact types, bearing in mind that one man's scraper is another man's knife blade.

Let us now look at the individual catalog entries.

Collection of: Name of the owner of the collection.

Date: When cataloged, not when found.

Site Name and Number: See the discussion of site numbering on page 129. The common name of the site may also go here. For example: "Old Hargraves house," "Tom Sanchez's back lot."

Number: The number you have assigned to this particular artifact. For items from the same site, it is usual and logical to give a prefix that is either the site number or (if that is too long) a number derived from it. Artifact 4SLO 1000–11 is thus the eleventh item cataloged from site 4 SLO 1000 in San Luis Obispo County, California.

These numbers should also be lettered onto each artifact *as it is being cataloged.* If you put this task off till the end of the write-up, you can easily become confused and be forced to do your measurements over. (The authors speak from experience.) Worse still, the job may not get done at all, and since the artifacts are no longer in their original bag, there is no way of being sure which is which.

The most reliable method of labeling is to use india ink and a very fine nib pen (Hunt No. 102 or a 00 size Rapidograph, for example). The numbering must be very small and neat so that it is legible but does not obscure features of the artifact. When the material is too dark for black ink to show up, you may use either silver or white ink (not always satisfactory, depending on the brand). As an alternative, you may paint on a small white background for the lettering with airplane paint or some other opaque, waterproof paint that will accept india ink. Items too fragile or too small to label may have tags tied to them or be placed in glass or plastic medicine containers, which are then marked.

Description: Be as specific as possible. "Pottery sherd, Anasazi (Basket-maker) style; black geometric motif" is better than "sherd" if you are confident of your facts. But don't guess. Even experts can't know everything.

Location: "Surface" is usually enough for the purposes of this book. Also give the name of the quadrant (see page 119). For items found in a test pit (see chapter 11) give the number or location of the pit as shown on your pit report.

Level: Use only if item was found in a test pit or (rarely) had been exposed by construction or had partially eroded out of a bank. Give depth in centimeters or meters.

Material: Again, be specific when possible. If wood, can you tell what kind? If shell, can you tell what species? And so on.

CATALOG

Collection of _____ Date _____

Site Name and Number _____

Number	Description	Location	Level	Material	Dimensions	Weight	Box or Shelf Number	Remarks

Dimensions: Self-explanatory, but don't forget to use metrics.

Weight: Ditto. You will need a small laboratory balance for this purpose. They are available by mail order from scientific supply houses. (Edmund Scientific Company has one for $17.50. See Appendix V for address.) An alternative is a postal scale, but then you may have to convert from ounces to grams.

Box or Shelf Number: This tells you where the piece is to be found in whatever storage area you have set aside.

Remarks: Especially appropriate are notes on the object's condition, such as "In two pieces," "Badly chipped," "Point missing." Also include detailed descriptions of any decoration.

Some people like to make outline drawings of each artifact and append them to the catalog. This is all right if the drawings are done freehand, but only relatively expert artists can draw accurately enough to make satisfactory records by this method. Another frequently used approach is to draw around the actual edge of the artifact with a pen or pencil held upright. The trouble with direct outlining of this kind is that it can abrade and otherwise damage the sharp edges of stone tools, with the result that any lithic specialist who examines them later under the microscope will find false evidence of wear (see pages 166–67 for a discussion of the methods and value of lithic analysis).

As an alternative method of recording, the authors recommend the use of a photocopy machine. Simply place an artifact or artifacts where you would normally place a document to be copied, and what you will get will be an accurate outline of each artifact (but not a three-dimensional photograph).

The type of catalog form shown on page 139 should fill the needs of most private collectors, as opposed to study institutions, and may be used for items collected almost anywhere, even underwater. You are welcome to photocopy it directly from this book, or it may be easier and cheaper to make your own and run it off on a mimeograph or ditto machine. (You will certainly get larger pages that way.) A hole punch and a loose-leaf notebook are the only other things you need in order to establish your catalog.

Now a word about displaying your collection. Though a series of numbered shoe boxes is a perfectly satisfactory place for artifacts, many collectors like to put their treasures where they can be admired. There is no reason why a properly cataloged collection should not be attractively housed—in anything from an antique china closet to velvet-lined jewelry boxes, according to the collector's taste—as long as the pieces are (1) accessible and (2) not permanently fixed to boards or other mountings. A really scientific collection is laid out site by site, culture by culture, period by period, or in some other systematic way, but it may be some time before your collection is large enough for this kind of treatment.

If you find cataloging your own collection interesting and informative, you may want to go on to catalog private collections belonging to others. In almost every community there are individuals who, in a lifetime of farming, forestry, or just walking, have accumulated artifacts and perhaps done a little reading, but who would not call themselves archaeologists. These collections are often fascinating, but because the owners haven't the time or inclination to catalog them, the vital facts about their origins can last only as long as one person's memory. Fortunately, the collectors are often delighted to have a knowledgeable volunteer offer to do the cataloging. However, there are a few special problems involved in this kind of project.

Foremost is the difficulty of making a catalog from oral information. There is a definite art to getting someone to remember accurately the locations of finds that may go back over a period of several decades. (For further remarks on interviewing, see chapter 10.) It will probably be necessary to sit down with the owner and go through the collection piece by piece, or at least batch by batch. Some collectors remember with uncanny accuracy exactly where and how each of their treasures was found, but not everyone is so gifted, and it is up to you, the cataloger, to judge how reliable your informant is. Obviously, "down somewhere around Millerville" is not a very satisfactory entry to put under Location. However, you will probably get nowhere if you insist on the same degree of precision you would expect of yourself on a survey. A reasonable criterion is, "Given this information, do I think I could find the site myself in half a day's surveying?" Walking over the territory where the collection was made in the company of its owner may be an invaluable aid to the memory. Even if you are in doubt about the origin of an artifact, however, you may still catalog it. "From somewhere in Alberta" or "traded to me by a guy in Ohio" is better than nothing as a description.

Clearly, it is much less important to determine *when* an artifact was collected. Even a time span of fifty years makes little difference, archaeologically speaking.

You may find that it is necessary to exercise tact when identifying artifacts. Some collectors are very knowledgeable, but there are others who will assure you solemnly, even fervently, that sherds of modern Mexican earthenware or portions of colonial millstones are of Native American origin, or that "swamp iron" nodules, "Apache tears," or fossils are man-made artifacts. You may even be presented with alleged North American relics of Druids, Irish monks,

Romans, Phoenicians, megalithic Britons, Egyptians, Libyans, Incas, Atlanteans, extraterrestrials, or the Lost Tribes of Israel. The only thing you can do is listen politely and draw your own conclusions. Genuinely unusual or puzzling objects can of course be referred to a museum or university for identification, with the owner's permission.

Finally, cataloging someone else's collection may differ from cataloging your own because private collectors sometimes do not want their artifacts "messed up" with numbers, and the cataloger must of course respect the owner's wishes. In a small collection there may not be much difficulty if the written descriptions are detailed, but in a larger collection the problem is much magnified. One substitute for labeling, though a laborious one, is to photograph each artifact in sequence and either put the artifact number on each photograph or attach the photographs to the appropriate spaces in the catalog. This is expensive and time-consuming, but it does make it possible for later researchers to be reasonably sure which artifact is which. Less expensive is drawing or photocopying as described on page 140.

It may help to persuade the owner that labeling is important (and yourself that cataloging is worth the trouble) if you point out that local catalogs are one of the primary resources of visiting professionals. Any archaeologist setting out to do a major excavation or definitive study in an unfamiliar area will routinely inquire about local artifact collections and will frequently spend time inspecting them as a preliminary to further research. And, as we have said, an uncataloged collection (or an unlabeled one) is really not much use to anyone not already familiar with it.

For related reasons, you should always keep a copy of any catalog you make. Doing so enhances the scope of your own reference material (it is, in effect, your fee for the work you did) and helps to insure that the catalog will be available to other researchers. Duplication is especially important if the collection's owner should move away, die, or accidentally destroy the original catalog.

We have now raised a rather frequently asked question concerning private collections, namely, what should become of them eventually? Unless someone in the family shares the collector's enthusiasm, most private collections end up getting thrown away, sold, or at best dumped in the attic. It is decidedly unfortunate that this is so, and you will want to take steps to see that it does not happen to your own collection or that of anyone whom you may be in a position to advise.

Here again, discretion is called for, since not every collection is worth preserving for eternity. While you are educating yourself about artifact types of your area, it may, nevertheless, be very much worth your while to catalog a collection that is neither particularly complete nor particularly unusual. You will have to use your judgment about the value of collections.

The authors feel that the best recipients for private archaeological collections are small colleges with departments of anthropology, small local historical or archaeological museums, and state or county archaeological societies. (The three are often interconnected.) A very distant last place is held by big city or university museums, for two reasons. Such institutions are almost invariably overendowed with duplicate items they can never hope to have space to display, so that they routinely turn down this type of bequest when it is offered. Furthermore, sending a collection to a large museum takes it out of the local area where it was gathered, which is the only place where it stands much chance of being displayed, studied, or appreciated. Though collectors often covet the prestige of donating to an internationally known institution, the fact is they will most often be doing a much greater service to archaeology and the community by making sure the collection stays in the area where it was found. (See chapter 12 for a discussion of who owns archaeology.)

7
Historic Archaeology— From Humpty Dumpty to Sherlock Holmes

This is the place where we try to repair the implicit injustice that any modern book on field archaeology perpetrates against specialists in historic archaeology and allied branches of the art. We have already explained that historic archaeologists use much the same approaches and methods as prehistoric archaeologists, but with the addition of historic (that is, written) sources of information to their arsenal. Yet if historic archaeologists merely substituted, say, the study of nail types for the study of stone tool types, there would be little cause for remark. The trouble is that even among other (prehistoric or classical) archaeologists, the idea that archaeology deals with *ancient* civilizations, *primitive* peoples, *early* man is so deeply ingrained that historic archaeologists seem to go around with slightly hunted expressions and are frequently found in corners and corridors at archaeological conferences, where they hold informal grievance meetings over the shameful way the program committee has neglected their specialty. Only recently have the annual meetings of the Society for Historic Archaeology, the Society for Industrial Archaeology, and similar groups offered a chance for these disgruntled souls to turn the tables and program whole days of discussion in which the terms "chipping waste," "ritual object," "hunter-gatherer subsistence," and so on do not occur. (Addresses of these societies are in Appendix IV.)

Part of the problem in appreciating the significance of historic archaeology arises from etymology. *Archaeology* proclaims itself to be the study of things *archaic*, and in that sense historic archaeology is admittedly poorly named. We have said before that historic archaeology concerns itself with the material remains of human activity during the historic period. In North America that means roughly from 1492 on. What has not, perhaps, been sufficiently emphasized is that the word "historic" is here meant to be understood as extending right up to the present. A pair of historic archaeologists we know are fond of pointing out that even the table setting for your last night's dinner is potentially significant for the archaeologist. If the planet Earth were to be quick-frozen at 7 P.M. eastern standard time today, future archaeologists might learn a good deal about you from the arrangement of utensils on your dinner table —data concerning your economic or social status and details such as what types of foods you were planning to eat and how many were in the family. The situation would in fact be much like that in the famous cases of Pompeii and Herculaneum, where whole cross sections of Roman life were "frozen," not by ice but by an eruption of volcanic ash, pumice, and mud, thus giving us today a degree of insight into everyday life that could not be duplicated by excavating any number of temples, imperial tombs, or stadia.

Historic archaeologists have actually been at work for decades on projects concerned with events as recent as the twentieth century, sometimes with surprising and timely results. Since, when one thinks of it, so much of prehistoric archaeology is concerned with the analysis of midden heaps, shell mounds, and so on, there is a certain logic in

Dr. William Rathjie's decision to study the garbage dump of Tucson, Arizona. Working in the 1970s during the all too recent and memorable economic slump, Rathjie found, rather surprisingly, that waste in an urban American community actually increased as financial times got tougher. Findings seemed to support the view that rumors of economic disaster encouraged people to buy more food than they could use immediately or store adequately, thus resulting in more spoilage. Even as an isolated piece of data, this is enough to give any economic planner food (as it were) for thought, and if further studies were to confirm the conclusion, it could have some long-term philosophical and practical effects on the way governments think about shortages. We give this example in order to put to rest the insidious notion that archaeology does not deal with the "real world," as it is sometimes called by engineers and government officials who resent the necessity for figuring archaeology into their construction budgets.

Historic archaeology has in fact come a long way in the few decades of its existence. The first excavations were undertaken almost exclusively on sites of known historic importance and were aimed mainly at gathering data that would aid in accurate restoration. The classic example of that kind of archaeology (in North America, at least) took place in Williamsburg, Virginia, a spot already rich in aboveground historic homes and public buildings, well known to even the most casual student of colonial history.

Archaeology in which restoration is the main aim might be termed Humpty Dumpty archaeology, since it seeks to find the pieces of the past and put them back together again. It was not long, however, before historic archaeology branched out into more ambitious studies. Insofar as one event can ever be said to precipitate this kind of change, it was probably James Deetz's publication in 1966 of a paper describing the social and stylistic patterns that can be derived from a detailed study of the carvings on New England gravestones.* Deetz's work opened the eyes of professionals and armchair archaeologists alike to the richness of North America's historic remains and their susceptibility to treatment in a problem-oriented archaeological rather than a purely historical way. From there it was a short but important step to asking general questions about the historic period, such as, "Why do cultures change?" "What is the effect of technological innovation, of population pressure, of alterations in the ethnic background of immigrants?" "How do alien cultures interact when they are thrown together in a new land?" Thus historic archaeology followed prehistoric archaeology in becoming problem-oriented like Sherlock Holmes, rather than thing-oriented like the restorers and collectors of bits of Humpty Dumpty. (This is not to speak slightingly of legitimate restoration, of course. It is only to point out that archaeology offers more than one avenue of exploration.)

Already, historic archaeology has spawned its first subspecialty, industrial archaeology. (And can we envision a time when there will be atomic archaeology, plastic archaeology, even space archaeology?) Though they still deal with the historic period, industrial archaeologists concern themselves specifically with the industrial revolution, now only about two hundred years old. Remarkable as it may seem, modern historians are not very well supplied with records concerning the development of manufacturing processes or the details of early products such as vacuum tubes, locomotives, and electronic computers. To be sure, the original inventions are detailed in the records of the U.S. Patent Office and the pages of early encyclopedias, but

*James Deetz, "Death's Heads, Cherubs, and Willow Trees: Experimental Archaeology in Colonial Cemeteries," *American Antiquity* 31 (1966): 502–10.

subsequent models and innovations leading to improved performance often fell victim to the well-known American mania for being up-to-date. Manufacturing prototypes, together with their operating manuals and production specifications, went to the junk heap almost as fast as they were developed. Moreover, as markets changed in response to improved transportation, westward exploration, and new power sources, old factories were unceremoniously converted from one use to another without the slightest concern for record keeping. Nothing must stand in the way of Progress! The anomalous result is that we may know more about, say, the design and use of horse-drawn plows in twelfth-century France than about the characteristics of the earliest American harrows.

Taken together, historic and industrial archaeology must be admitted to be at a rather early stage of development, if only because they have been the beneficiaries of fewer man-hours of labor. There would be no point in trying to organize an outline of historical and industrial findings, even on so limited a scale as that attempted in our prehistoric Uncyclopedia (chapter 4). However, it is certainly possible to talk about the general kinds of fieldwork and research questions that have received major attention in recent years.

One of the most conspicuous and accessible types of historic site is undoubtedly the bottle dump. Often these mounds of pretty colored glass are barely covered by wind-blown soil (in the Southwest) or fallen leaves (farther north), and unfortunately this makes them easy prey for collectors. It will probably take years and years of public education before those innocent souls who like to see the light shining through a windowful of green and amber and amethyst bottles will recognize that what they are doing is not resurrecting worthless trash but destroying potentially important archaeological data. Schoolteachers have even been known to take their classes out for a nice day's dig at a local bottle dump under the mistaken impression that nobody cares. "Why, that stuff isn't *old!*" they explain in justification. No wonder historic archaeologists sometimes seem to be a little bit paranoid.

In spite of untrained interference with bottle dumps, studies have already yielded some interesting facts about the ethnic makeup of various communities and settlements. One might almost paraphrase chef Brillat-Savarin's famous statement concerning food and say, "Tell me what you drink and I will tell you what you are." Dumps around early British and French military forts in the Great Lakes region have been given particular attention and have provided much information about the social differences between men and officers and also about the impact on soldiers' drinking habits of changing sources of supply and advances in glass technology.

The manufacturing towns of New England have been the focus of industrial archaeologists, since it was there that the first American factories were built. Recent work on "ideal" workers' communities of the nineteenth century, such as Lowell, Massachusetts, have told historians a lot of things they didn't know about the "enlightened" working conditions and "benevolent" employers of the day. Quantitative analyses have also reached the (to the casual observer) surprising conclusion that whereas steam power was the great motive force behind industrial development in Britain, it was water power that played the decisive role on this side of the Atlantic.

Another area of study, and one that has no regional limitations, is that of the interaction between Native American and European cultures as they came into inevitable conflict. In the north and west, the remains of fur trading posts reveal much about the role of native guides and Indian allies in the struggle for power between various national trading interests. One well-documented site is the Hudson's Bay Company post accidentally exposed by the lowering of Lake Roosevelt during the construction of Washington State's Grand Coulee Dam.

Ordinarily the results of this kind of study are predictable and depressingly one-sided, as Native American cultures are shown to have been destroyed or displaced by that of the white settlers. However, at least one California investigation showed the tables to have been partially turned by the Indians, who apparently "converted" in great numbers annually at the beginning of the lean season for hunting, allowing the missionary fathers to feed them for exactly as long as it took the game to come back.

In all areas, historic restoration has continued to be done on a larger or smaller scale. After all, restoration is attractive, visible, and a good way of educating the public to the goals of archaeology, whether historic or prehistoric. For these reasons, it is often easier to get money for restoration projects than for "pure research," though how one can have good restoration without research or why research should be required to generate even the most dazzling and educational public displays is a question best asked of the grant-givers rather than the archaeologists. Major restorations that have been done with the aid of specifically archaeological techniques include not only Colonial Williamsburg, but California's San Buenaventura Mission, and also Fort Clatsop, which stands on the site of the Lewis and Clark expedition's encampment at the mouth of the Columbia River in Oregon. A center for research into the techniques and theory of historic archaeology has developed around the ongoing restoration of Plimouth Plantation near Plymouth, Massachusetts, under the direction of Dr. James Deetz.

It would be possible to go on for pages, mentioning a study here, a restoration there, without adding greatly to

your basic understanding of the patterns that must, presumably, underlie historic site formation and culture
change. Though prehistorians have long been able to speak
(not always in perfect unison, it is true) about generalizations concerning hunting and gathering societies, life-
styles of early agriculturists, the social institutions of nomadic herders, and so on, it is only very recently that
historic archaeology in North America has begun to provide itself with a similar theoretical framework. With the
recent publication of Stanley South's book *Method and Theory in Historical Archaeology* (see Appendix II for details),
some extremely interesting hypotheses have been made
concerning patterns of artifact distribution at various
stages in the continent's settlement. Though the book is
highly technical and is definitely not for the beginner in
statistics and probability theory, let alone archaeology,
South's analyses of what he calls the Brunswick Pattern of
Refuse Disposal, the Carolina Artifact Pattern, and the
Frontier Artifact Pattern will probably offer opportunities
for testing in the field and argument in the classroom for
a good while to come.

Aside from the intrinsic interest of its material, there are
two great contributions that historic archaeology is in a
position to make to the subject in general. First is the social
and educational aspect of encouraging members of ethnic
minorities to concern themselves with, or, better, participate in, the archaeological investigation of their own pasts
in North America. Native Americans have sometimes argued, with a degree of justice, that archaeologists are exclusively concerned with the exploitation of aboriginal cultures. "Go dig up your own ancestors," they say, and this
is now being done. Much more positive than the making of
a rhetorical point, however, is the excitement that can be
generated in the local community when Cape Verdians,
Chicanos, black Americans, or other minorities rediscover

the value of their own pasts. Canada has pioneered in the conscious effort to bolster ethnic consciousness through archaeology, specifically in its extensive work on sites relating to early French settlement.

The other potential contribution of historic archaeology is in the theoretical realm. The exciting thing is that by its very nature historic archaeology affords researchers the opportunity to verify in the historic record the findings they make in the field. For decades, archaeologists have been basing conclusions about once-living societies on the evidence they derive from nonliving remains. Now it ought to be possible to cross-check archaeology's basic hypotheses by matching the results of excavation against the evidence provided by written records and even living representatives of the cultures that left the remains.

Certainly, some of these possibilities will be realized as the need for historic preservation and conservation becomes increasingly apparent. We hope that the large losses of historic sites to construction and neglect will move the government agencies charged with preserving North America's cultural heritage, as well as archaeologists themselves, to place a greater emphasis on historic archaeology.

8
Do-It-Yourself Artifacts

Archaeologists call it replication. It means making or using an artifact in a way as close as possible to the way the original owners made or used it. In a sense, replication is an extension of the work of cataloging and report writing. It expands the knowledge you can gain from finding and analyzing artifacts. For example, you cannot test the firing power and accuracy of an ancient bow (even assuming you had one) without the risk of breaking it, and you cannot pour water into an irreplaceable Pomo basket to see whether it really is watertight, as ethnographic sources alleged. The logical thing to do is to make your own bow or basket and test it. Projects like these are not only fascinating and challenging from a technological point of view— they can also produce very exciting experimental results.

Probably the most famous examples of modern replication are the voyages of Thor Heyerdahl on the balsa raft *Kon Tiki* and the reed boat *Ra II*. Even those who do not accept Heyerdahl's contention that there was important cultural contact by sea between the Mediterranean and the east coast of South America and between Peru and Polynesia concede that the voyages demonstrate a previously unproven capacity for long-range sea travel in boats

Thor Heyerdahl's voyage in the reed boat Ra II *was an exciting piece of living replication—perhaps a little more exciting than some of us would care for.*

that make the flimsy little *Mayflower* look like the aircraft carrier *Forrestal.*

There are two types of replication in archaeology, which may be called living and experimental. The purpose of living replication is largely to gain personal satisfaction and insight by empathizing with another way of life. Once you have built your own wickiup and lived in it for a season, or gone ice fishing with your own bone fishhook, your appreciation of the skills and difficulties involved takes a quantum jump forward. If you have tried to select a favorable campsite for even a modern canvas or nylon tent, let alone a tipi, in a variety of weathers and terrains, you will have learned a great many things that ethnological literature will not teach you—from how to make the sun act as your alarm clock to what to do when a gopher gets under your blanket. A two-hundred-page book on floodplains is a lot less impressive than waking up in six inches of water because you pitched your tent too close to a flat-bedded stream.

Probably the most widely practiced form of replication is the making of stone tools, often called flint knapping although true flint is not found in North America. Figure 16 (below) and the photographs on pages 159–61 show some steps in the manufacture of a stone point. Note that the drawing shows two types of flaking, called percussion and pressure. Some tools were made by percussion, some by pressure flaking, and some by a combination.

What follows is not a complete and comprehensive set of directions for stone tool manufacture. The process is complex, and there are, moreover, many possible approaches. For the best detailed information, the authors recommend the several publications of Don W. Crabtree, not available

Pressure flaking

Direct percussion

FIGURE 16

in book form but scattered through a number of journals, including especially *Tebiwa,* the journal of the Idaho Archaeological Society. However, the following notes will give you enough information to make a start and find out whether you want to go on to more advanced studies.

Start with a good-sized chunk or slab of conchoidally fracturing stone—chert and obsidian are the best. Try to find a piece without visible veins, cracks, or impurities. Slag glass is also excellent for the purpose. In the last century, certain American Indian groups thought so highly of glass for chipping that they knocked over telegraph poles in order to remove the glass insulators. Whenever you chip, or watch someone else chip, *it is essential to wear safety glasses or industrial goggles* to protect your eyes from splinters. The edges of chipped stone are razor sharp; if you are a right-handed chipper, protect your left hand with a stout leather glove or piece of leather. Take a while at the beginning to become familiar with your material in terms of density, hardness, and uniformity. Many knappers gently strike the piece with a hammerstone and evaluate the quality of the stone by the clarity of tone produced. In order to perform true replication, hammering (percussion flaking) should be done with another stone, pressure flaking with a piece of antler or bone. If you cannot get the latter, a piece of aluminum rod does very well and is often preferred by professional (nonreplicative) flint knappers.

When you are fairly confident of the amount of pressure or strength of hammer stroke needed to detach a flake, you can begin worrying about the size, shape, and location of the flake. Your first objective is to produce a simple, edged tool such as a chopper or scraper. Do not try to start with a beautiful side-notched point, or you will ruin a lot of good material and probably end up throwing this book out the window. A good (but not the only) technique is to detach flakes from alternate sides of the edge you are working on.

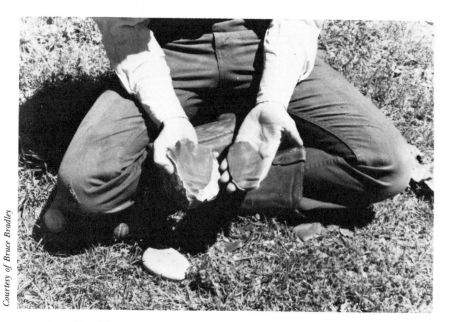

Courtesy of Bruce Bradley

Bruce Bradley replicates a projectile point. First the flake blank, a big chunk knocked from an even bigger chunk.

Your first edges will probably be blunt, but you will improve. When you feel ready to go on to points, you might try starting at the tip and working down each edge alternately. It *can* be done. Many amateur flint knappers have become so expert that they can whack out a point in five or ten minutes while taking a stroll or a coffee break. If you get that good, it would be an interesting project to replicate all the point types found in your local area.

Once you have taken up replicating stone tools, other activities naturally suggest themselves. You may experiment with hafting, the art of fastening a tool to a handle or shaft. A study of the literature will suggest appropriate materials and methods, and it can be enlightening to exper-

Percussion flaking gives the blank its general form . . .

. . . and then a little refinement.

Pressure flaking thins and finishes the edge.

All at a glance: The stages of manufacture from flake blank (left) to finished point (right) and (above) the tools used—stone, antler, and leather palm protector. In this case, the workman's glasses protected his eyes.

iment with them. Try to discover which kinds of bindings (deer sinew, rawhide, plant fiber, for example) are strongest, easiest to work with, most water-resistant. Which adhesives, such as natural asphaltum, tree gums, plant saps, are most appropriate? A material that is perfectly suitable for fastening an arrow point may be quite useless for a fishing spear. Keep a record of your findings, especially if they conflict with generally accepted ideas on ancient practice.

Another large area that is fruitful for living replication is that of crafts, from colonial candle making, dyeing, weaving, or woodworking to Native American beadwork (using glass trade beads or beads manufactured from shell, bone, or stone), leatherwork, and pottery making. Bear in mind that if you are doing replication rather than mere hobbywork you will need to gather, process, or manufacture as many of your own tools and materials as possible—plants for dye, minerals for paint, clay for pottery, and so on. There are many excellent books on the techniques of early American and American Indian crafts, but the majority deal with store-bought materials. Since you are after an understanding of the conditions and requirements of early workers, you need to know (among other things) how much labor was involved in making a given product, and thus the value that might have been placed on it. You are *not* interested in finding the quickest way to produce an attractive gift for Aunt Minnie.

Remember, too, that Native Americans and many colonial craftspeople worked without printed patterns. This was quite a feat of memory, as well as of manual skill. For example, to produce a simple "Morning Star" design on a bead loom, you must use the following sequence, row by row (the row is fourteen beads wide): (1) 14 black; (2) 3 black, 8 white, 3 black; (3) 4 black, 6 white, 4 black; (4) 1 black, 1 white, 3 black, 4 white, 3 black, 1 white, 1 black;

(5) 1 black, 2 white, 3 black, 2 white, 3 black, 2 white, 1 black; (6) 1 black, 12 white, 1 black; and repeat in the order 6, 5, 4, 3, 2, 1. One beginner compared it to doing trigonometry without any trigonometry tables. The comparison becomes more apt, and one's respect for early craftspeople grows, in direct proportion to the complexity of the design.

A visit to any major ethnographic museum will show you that some of the most magnificent American Indian decorative work was done with porcupine quill embroidery. (Many of the designs were later adapted for beadwork with imported materials.) A very ambitious replicative project might be done with this art form, but only by an accomplished handworker who was lucky enough to have available a supply of porcupine quills. This is not impossible, as porcupines are still regularly shot as "varmints" in parts of the north and northwest. However, the authors are not going to offer suggestions for dequilling a porcupine, as they have never tried it. The only clue we can give you is to say that the quills were pounded flat and dyed with vegetable dyes before being worked into leather as a kind of embroidery. For obvious reasons, ordinary craft books stress beadwork and ignore quillwork. However, the U.S. Department of the Interior's series on Indian handcrafts contains a pamphlet by Carrie A. Lyford with enough information to fascinate and stimulate would-be quillworkers. (See Appendix II.)

One replicative area that may sound tempting is foodstuffs. Certainly there are many tasty items on the list of early native foods, including oysters, venison, abalone, corn, beans, squash, nuts, berries, and wild turkey. However, you are likely to encounter three problems. First is that of availability. Unless you are a licensed and skillful hunter and are hunting in the legal season, game is hard to come by. As for cultivated crops, their names may be the same, but modern hybrid varieties are often unrecognizably different from their native forebears. Then there is the problem of palatability. Native American diet included many items most of us are culturally prejudiced against eating—grasshoppers, snakes, caterpillars, seal blubber, and the contents of a deer's or buffalo's stomach, to name only a few. Finally, and most importantly, there is the problem of safety. Early accounts give long lists of plants gathered by Native Americans for food, but they almost always are vague or overgeneral in their nomenclature. Even when there is no doubt which plant is meant, identification is sometimes difficult for the nonspecialist. The edible camas *(Camassia quamash)* is too easily confused with the death camas (various species of *Zigadenus),* and yampa *(Perideridia gairdneri)* with the deadly water hemlock *(Cicuta douglasii).* Even staple items of food sometimes require processing to make them safe to eat. An example is acorns, which must be leached to remove the tannic acid. For these reasons, prehistoric foods and cooking methods should not be replicated unless you have access to a professional ethnobotanist (a specialist in human use of plants).

There are, however, almost unlimited nonfood uses of plants to investigate, including early agricultural methods if you live in a rural area. How much food could a family or village raise on a field of a certain size, using the methods of the time and unimproved seed stocks? What is on record on the subjects of crop rotation, land clearing, fertilization? Do the methods really work as described? How soon are the fields "worn out," necessitating a move to virgin land? Which kinds of bark or rushes are most useful for basket weaving? Which plant fibers can be used to make thread, cord, or rope? Are there plant saps or gums suitable for dye?

The same sort of approach can be made to fishing, whether with line, net, spear, weir, or fish trap, in warm coastal waters or through a hole in the ice. (But if you are going after game fish such as trout or salmon, find out about local fishing regulations first.)

There are undoubtedly dozens of other areas that might prove equally fruitful for living replication. What about musical instruments, boat building, snowshoe construction, leather processing, horsemanship, for example?

Experimental, or scientific, replication is not greatly different *except* in its planning and record keeping. An excellent and readable book on the progress of scientific replication to date is *Archaeology by Experiment* by John Coles (see Appendix II), although the majority of its examples are taken from European archaeology and are not directly applicable to North American situations.

Coles mentions what must have been one of the earliest (and most self-interested) archaeological or anthropological experiments on record. Spanish explorers in Florida became uneasy about the effectiveness of their famous armor against Native American weaponry. They set up a dummy wearing two sets of chain mail and promised freedom to one of their native prisoners if he could pierce the target. Using a stone-tipped reed arrow and his own bow, the man calmly took a position 150 feet from the target and shot clean through it. The Spaniards were at least realistic in their evaluation of this result. They took off their hot and cumbersome mail and replaced it with padded jackets for the duration of their stay in the New World.

That anecdote points up the main difference between the two types of replication, which is not so much in procedure as in attitude. The Spaniards were not interested in understanding American Indian life (except insofar as understanding allowed them to dominate their "enemies"). They only wanted to reach certain concrete conclusions about the opposing weapons technology. It will not do, however, to make too much of this distinction, as understanding and analysis are seldom entirely separable. Yet we may say that scientific replication has as its first goal the collecting of data that will confirm or deny some hypothesis.

If, instead of living for a summer in the wickiup mentioned earlier, you were to build two or more wickiups with different materials or according to different methods garnered from the ethnographic literature, and then make periodic observations as to which structure was more weathertight, more durable, or sturdier, that would be scientific replication.

In this type of replication, you have the same obligation to keep precise records and follow good scientific procedure as you would have on a site survey or in cataloging.

Since there is no end to the possibilities for experiments, we will simply end this chapter by taking a brief look at the nature and value of some of the recent developments in the field.

One exceedingly interesting area of study has been dubbed lithic analysis, or just plain lithics. It is the study of stone tools in terms of the physical characteristics of their materials, the techniques of their manufacture, and especially the way they become worn through use (use-wear analysis). The goal of use-wear analysis is to allow the archaeologist to "do a Sherlock Holmes," that is, to examine a given stone tool and announce something like, "Ah, yes, Watson. I can confidently say that this tool is a scraper because the type, shape, and location of the microscopic scars along its edge are characteristic of prolonged friction on animal hide. *This* tool, however, though it may look much like the other, is unquestionably an adze used for woodworking." Needless to say, lithics has not yet achieved this degree of perfection. The mathematics involved is complex, well-controlled data are scarce, and there are some who fear that the characteristics of natural stone are so variable that it is impossible to generalize about them. Every type of stone (flint, chert, chalcedony, obsidian, quartz, etc.) has its own characteristics of brittleness and hardness. No two materials respond exactly the same way to wear, so that tests run on flint must be repeated for chert or whatever.

What some archaeologists are now doing is to classify *types* of wear on various kinds of stone (as seen through the light microscope) after samples have been used in the laboratory to work materials such as bone, wood, and leather. (This is where the replication comes in.) Thus, by much tedious testing—just try scraping a piece of antler 2,000 times with a wedge of obsidian, examining it after each 250 strokes—it may someday become possible to give meaningful functional names to tools about whose actual uses we are now merely guessing.

Another type of investigation, one that requires less manual skill, is what has been called decay analysis. We have already noted that in many cases archaeologists do not expect perishable artifacts to be found in a particular area or context because they will have been destroyed by soil conditions and/or weathering. There are also situations in archaeology where there is doubt as to whether a particular people made use of some perishable material or foodstuff at all, one side arguing, "We haven't found any so they didn't use it," the other replying, "Of course they used it, it just wasn't preserved."

Decay analysis tries to turn such problems upside down by burying materials or erecting structures and seeing just how rapidly local conditions really act on them. Obviously, such experiments are long-term undertakings—often the longer the better. Yet interesting results may be obtained in periods as short as six months, if a proper analysis is done. One of the pioneering efforts in this field was made on England's Overton Down by a committee of the British Association for the Advancement of Science in 1960. The basic project was to construct, in an authentic manner, an example of a prehistoric type of British earthwork known as a bank and ditch. Preliminary data were derived from calculating the man-hours of labor required (using both modern but unmechanized metal tools and ancient tools such as antler picks and shoulder blade shovels). However, the real meat of the experiment was to be enjoyed when the structure was finished. At carefully plotted locations inside the bank, its builders had left samples of such materials as flint, linen cloth, leather, and pottery. They had also constructed their bank in such a way that any erosion from it into the ditch could be accurately measured. The project had been planned so that sections of the bank would be excavated at specified time intervals, beginning only seven and a half months after its completion and continuing over several years.

The excavators not only found out some interesting things about the decay rates of the buried materials and the erosion rate of the earthwork, they were delighted with what they learned from the *details* of their study. One clearly demonstrated finding was that the ditch tended to erode in such a manner as to undercut its own banks. The implication was that materials like early or middle Stone Age flints (which would have been lying well *under* the surface at the time when an authentic late Stone Age or neolithic earthwork was constructed) could easily have been washed into the center of the ditch, where they might have been found by archaeologists and erroneously used to give the structure an excessively early date. This method of dating had long been in dispute. Equally enlightening were the displacements of artifacts within the bank, caused by the burrowing of moles and even by earthworms. If Overton Down had been a genuine excavation, its builders concluded, archaeologists might have been considerably misled by the fact that potsherds and so on were no longer to be found on their original levels. All in all, the Overton

Down experiment has been extremely worthwhile and may be expected to continue to produce results for many years.

Another approach to scientific replication is to look for some mystery or gap in our knowledge about local artifacts and then propose some verifiable solution. One such experiment was done by Emil W. Haury in 1931. Archaeologists had been awed and puzzled by bead necklaces found at early Pueblo Indian sites in Arizona. The beads of these necklaces were made of bone, shell, clay, or stone (mostly the last), and were strung on strings up to ten meters long, as many as fifteen thousand beads per necklace. The beads themselves were in general incredibly tiny, about the size of a standard pinhead, with holes too small for any but the finest modern steel needle to get through.

Haury had no reliable evidence as to how the Pueblo people had actually made the beads, so he approached the question from the other side. How would *he* make the beads, using what he knew of local materials and ancient tools? In particular, what could he possibly use to drill such very tiny holes? The answer he came up with was one that could only have occurred to someone with more than "book knowledge" of that part of the Southwest. It was cactus spines. Two species of cactus provided him with small, sharp, but very strong spines that made excellent drills when tried on the materials in question. Haury was able to produce beads that looked just like the original ones. Of course, as he himself pointed out, this does not prove that the Pueblo beadmakers *did* use his method, merely that they could have.

This observation in turn raises an interesting point, one that we have stressed by implication throughout this book. Certain writers like Erich Von Däniken are fond of arguing that Earth's early cultures must have been inspired by "gods from outer space" because certain structures or artifacts *could not possibly* have been made without space age technology. Such suppositions make entertaining science fiction, but they reflect a deep-seated ignorance of nonindustrial cultures. Writers like Von Däniken would not be so quick to fashion theories about men from outer space if they had more respect for the knowledge and abilities of the early peoples who in fact fashioned the structures and artifacts that are so glibly and condescendingly proclaimed "impossible for primitive tribesmen." Perhaps a few more experiments of Haury's type will help us to stop underestimating the ingenuity, dedication, and resourcefulness of ancient peoples.

9
Pots, pH, Pollen, and the Bristlecone Pine

It is one of the nice things about archaeology that, unlike many sports or other hobbies such as astronomy, skiing, photography, and golf, it requires no major investment in elaborate, ever-to-be-upgraded equipment. Many conservation archaeologists, including those of highest competence, are able to operate with little more than some maps, a good compass, a couple of meter tapes, and an inexpensive laboratory balance. Add a few specialized items such as Pliofilm for recording rock art, and the materials for cataloging, and there is no reason why your survey work should not compare favorably with that of any fully equipped expedition.

At the same time, however, archaeology as a whole has, in the last few decades, tended to move out of the field (or at least out of the trench) and into the laboratory. As archaeologists have become increasingly unwilling to destroy irreplaceable sites by unnecessary digging, they have devised compensatory ways of deriving more information from the artifacts already on hand. It is desirable for you, as a conservation archaeologist, to know about this development for three reasons. First, you need to know the significance of various laboratory tests or dating methods that may be referred to in your reading of professional literature. Next, you need to consider which tests could usefully be applied to your own finds or those you may come across in the collections of others. (Though many tests are too expensive to be applied routinely, they are still a possibility that should not be overlooked.) And finally, the archaeological laboratory is in itself a very fascinating place whose many specialties can become avocations or even careers for those with access to appropriate training and facilities.

This chapter, therefore, will highlight some (but by no means all) of the newest developments in scientific archaeology. A few of these procedures are carried out in field laboratories as well, and familiarity with them may make you particularly attractive to a field director choosing volunteer help. You should note, however, that we are not giving actual directions for performing any of these tests, because they are too complex, or too expensive, or both.

One major subdivision of scientific techniques has to do with direct chemical or biological examination of cultural materials. Petrologic analysis, for example, looks at pieces of rock (whether artifacts or raw materials not indigenous to the immediate area of the site) in an effort to determine where the rock originated. Two lumps of chert or obsidian or native copper may look much alike to the field archaeologist or even the geologist, although they come from veins hundreds or thousands of miles apart. The more distant the possible sources of such minerals, the more interesting it becomes to know where they actually came from. Whole theories of cultural diffusion, population migration, or trade route formation may stand or fall by the results of petrologic tests that assay the trace elements occurring as minor impurities in otherwise unremarkable stone. Rock from certain beds or veins is chemically "postmarked" at its point of origin as legibly as if it had been sent through the mail.

A similar analysis of trace elements may sometimes be done on metals and, surprisingly, on pottery, since pottery is made from clay and clay is a mineral substance that may be tested like any other. Paints, too, often have a mineral base (although certain early paints were vegetable and some very modern ones are acrylic). Mineral-based paints can be analyzed if it is possible to get a large enough sample without damaging the painted surface. As an example, before European contact Native Americans used red paints based on various compounds of iron, whereas the red paint introduced by the colonists looks exactly the same, but is lead-based.

The tests just described are physical or chemical in nature. Another group of laboratory procedures involves detailed examination of biological materials.

Although the field archaeologist is generally expected to do rough identification of flora and fauna (that is, plant and animal remains) found at the site, it is not always possible to do this in detail on the spot. Thus bags labeled vaguely "bird bones," "plant stalks—cattail?" and so on find their way to the laboratory for identification by the specialist. The need for this work is obvious. "Birds," for instance, may occur virtually anywhere, but if you know whether the species involved is the herring gull, the cactus wren, or the snowy owl you will have some very specific information about the climatic and ecological conditions that prevailed at the time the site was formed. Floral and faunal analysis can also give important clues to an ancient people's diet, use of raw materials, or early agricultural practices.

Laboratories competent to do biological analysis are usually found associated with major museums or universities because even the experts need what are called type collections with which they can compare their specimens. Does this cervical vertebra belong to a black-footed ferret *(Mustela nigripes)* or a common weasel *(Mustela cicognani)?* It will have to be carefully measured and compared with skeletons in the type collection, and even then there may be substantial doubt.

Some kinds of remains are too small for anything but microscopic study. They include insect parts, minute seeds, and the bones of the smallest animals. A recent development in microscopic analysis is palynology, the study of pollen grains that are sometimes preserved in acid or peaty soil. Since each family of plant produces pollen grains of a distinctive shape, a soil sample containing preserved pollen may yield an interesting picture of the wild or cultivated plants that formerly bloomed in an area, provided they were not types pollinated by the wind (which might have been brought to the site from tens or even hundreds of miles away). Such information provides clues not only to the climate of the period but to chronology as well, as climatic changes are sometimes linked to past geological events whose dates are known. However, palynology often identifies only the genus and not the species of a plant.

Fascinating results may also be gained from the analysis of human remains, especially in the relatively new field of paleopathology, which is more or less archaeological medical history. Ancient bones by themselves can provide data on dietary deficiency diseases (such as rickets) and early medical practices (such as trepanning), while more fully preserved bodies like those found in Peru, Egypt, and the bogs of northern Europe are only now beginning to be examined for clues to the history of organic and epidemic diseases, and much more.

We have not changed our view that when human bones are discovered every consideration should be given to the wishes of any possible living descendants. However, the fact remains that when no one requests reburial (and no one has in the cases mentioned above), the autopsying of early man is likely to produce significant results not only for anthropology, but perhaps for modern medicine as well.

An entirely different group of scientific/archaeological activities consists of tests performed in the course of surveying for new sites. As such, they are of particular interest to the conservation archaeologist. They are not, strictly speaking, laboratory tests, but the results obtained must be carefully analyzed before conclusions are drawn.

Most widely known is the use of a metal detector. This machine usually looks rather like an upright vacuum cleaner, although it is not so easy to use, as it must be held off the ground. In heavy brush or on a steep slope, it can quickly make you wish you had never heard of archaeology. Relatively inexpensive models of this machine (if you call $150 to $200 inexpensive) are often sold at retail for the use of amateur treasure hunters and mining prospectors, but the metal detector's use in North American archaeology is limited to historic sites and the very small number of prehistoric sites that might be expected to contain native copper or trade metal items. Metal detectors are tricky to use, as they indiscriminately register iron fence posts, old auto parts, steel cans, underground power cables, and sometimes even the metal toe plates on one's own boots.

An infinitely more sensitive, complex, and versatile (but also more cumbersome) piece of equipment is the proton magnetometer, which measures not magnetic attraction *per se* but magnetic flux. Under the right conditions it can locate not only iron and steel but also (and this is where it becomes interesting to the archaeologist) firing sites such as kilns, furnaces, hearths, and ovens, as well as refilled pits or ditches, walls, foundations, and other structures. The magnetic properties of these nonmetallic features arise from certain subtle effects produced by heat or by high humus content. Like any elaborate measuring device, the proton magnetometer requires an expert to interpret its results. Its use in North America has up to now been quite limited.

A method somewhat similar to magnetometry is the measurement of soil resistivity, or rather of distortions in soil resistivity. This method is based on the principle that most soil contains water in which are dissolved salts and organic material that will act as an electrical conductor between two or more electrodes. Dry materials, by contrast, resist current, while buried metals are superior conductors. The procedure when using a resistivity meter for archaeological survey is basically to insert a series of electrical probes into the soil and measure the resistance between them as current is applied. When measurements are taken at a series of points in straight, parallel lines, a sort of resistivity map of the area may be plotted, thus pinpointing likely places for probing or excavation. The resistivity meter is generally not so expensive to use as the proton magnetometer, and is not confused by nearby metal objects. However, current models are even less maneuverable than the magnetometer, and the two devices serve many of the same purposes.

Soil is also the focus of attention in two other procedures often used in survey work. Gardeners and farmers are generally familiar with simple tests for soil acidity or pH, and under some conditions these tests can be helpful in archaeology. The pH range of normal soil is from 4.0 to 9.0. Any reading below 7.0 (neutral) is acid and any reading above 7.0 is alkaline. It is often possible to map the limits of an extensive occupation site by measuring the pH of a large number of soil samples and observing where they tend to return to readings similar to those well away from the site. This is possible because over the long term, the dissolving or decay of normal occupation debris such as bone, shell, and charcoal tends to raise the pH of the soil in contrast to that of the surrounding area. In order to do such tests successfully, you must be a fairly accomplished soil scien-

tist, familiar with the pH changes that occur from one mi-
croenvironment to another. Pine forests, for instance, are
characteristically acid, whereas isolated limestone outcroppings or pieces of farmland where agricultural lime has
been applied may send your readings right off the scale and
make you think you've located the famous Seven Cities of
Cibola. Many state or provincial agricultural stations have
maps or other information about soil acidity patterns in the
local area. Another valuable source of soil data is the U.S.
Soil Conservation Service station in your area.

A rather similar kind of soil test is phosphate analysis.
This test relies on the fact that human waste, even when
completely decayed, increases the quantities of phosphates
in the soil. The test is more elaborate than pH tests and,
again, the normal constitution of the surrounding soils
must be accurately known before results become significant. Care must also be taken not to test soils that have ever
been exposed to commercial fertilizers or animal manures,
which contain—what else?—phosphates.

By far the most extensive, and perhaps the most interesting, topic dealt with by the archaeological laboratory is the
perennial question of dating. Although archaeology still
relies primarily on stratigraphy for dating ("deeper is
older"), and will continue to do so for the foreseeable
future, science has recently spawned some elegant and
promising methods whereby physical, chemical, or geo-
physical processes can be used as archaeological clocks.
These types of tests can tell us not only "earlier than Level
I and later than Level III," as in stratigraphy's relative
chronology, but may aspire to absolute chronology, which
says, for example, "four thousand thirty-six years, two
months, and eleven days before today." Needless to say, no
tests actually achieve this kind of accuracy, as it is a general
rule of measurement that the greater the span measured,
the greater the margin of error inherent in the process.

Nevertheless, every little bit helps when the archaeologist is faced, as so often happens, with apparent contradictions.

Probably the biggest splash in the world of twentieth-century archaeological science so far was made by the two techniques of carbon-14 (also called radiocarbon) dating and dendrochronology, or tree ring dating. The subject is complicated, and it is probably easier to start with tree rings. Dendrochronology is based on the simple observations, familiar to any forest ranger or naturalist, that trees grow outward in rings, adding a new band of wood each season, and that some (not all) species grow more in good years than in bad ones. A look at a suitable tree stump will demonstrate the phenomenon clearly, and with a little practice anyone can count back through the rings to some notable year such as "the time we had that spring blizzard" or "the great drought." It was astronomer A. E. Douglass, however, who realized that, by taking borings from very old, but still living, trees and matching the patterns of their tree rings with the patterns preserved in wood from archaeological sites, he could fit the samples with great exactitude into a time sequence that contained one absolutely fixed date—the present. Since that time, the search for venerable trees has gone steadily forward, and has come to a (perhaps temporary) halt with *Pinus longaevia* (formerly called *P. aristata*), the bristlecone pine. The oldest known individual of this species has been living and growing in California's White Mountains for 4,900 years, and by using it and specimens of ancient wood now dead, it has been possible to make a complete tree ring sequence going back 8,200 years into Earth's history. The bristlecone pine has not only pushed back the available sequence of tree rings for dendrochronological dating, however; it has also provided data indispensable for interpreting the results of carbon-14 dating.

The principle of C-14 dating is quite simple. Carbon is

the chemical basis of all the complex organic molecules
that make life possible on this planet. A "normal," stable
carbon atom has the atomic number 12, but carbon can also
exist in various unstable forms with other atomic numbers.
These are called isotopes, and one isotope of carbon-12 is
carbon-14. Like most unstable isotopes, C-14 tends to
"decay," or turn back into a more stable form (in this case
C-12) at a fixed rate. Scientists describe this change by
saying that given any known number of C-14 isotopes, it is
statistically probable that half of them will have decayed
into C-12 within a fixed period. That period is known as the
isotope's half-life. (Note that half-life only expresses a
probability, not a certainty, which means that real results
may vary.)

In most respects, however, C-14 acts exactly like C-12. It
combines with oxygen to form carbon dioxide and thus
enters into the life cycles on this planet, being utilized in
the metabolism of plants, which are then eaten by animals,
and so on. Therefore, the proportion of C-14 to C-12 in
plant and animal life is the same as it is in the atmosphere,
or about one part per million million at present. As soon
as the organism dies, however, it stops taking up C-14,
while those isotopes it already has in its tissues continue to
decay in their stately and inexorable manner. Thus it
should clearly be possible to calculate the age of any formerly living sample by the proportion of C-14 in it: the less
C-14, the more time there has been for decay and thus the
older the sample.

There is nothing wrong with this principle, and it is still
the basis for all C-14 testing today, but unfortunately
(though not unpredictably) the actual situation turned out
to be a little more complex than originally anticipated.
Atomic physicists began it by pointing out that the amount
of C-14 in the earth's atmosphere has probably not always
been what it is today. C-14 is formed in the upper atmo-

sphere when carbon atoms are exposed to cosmic radiation, and the amount of cosmic radiation reaching our atmosphere is in turn affected by the strength of the earth's magnetic field. Since it is known that there have been some considerable fluctuations in the earth's magnetic field during past ages, it began to seem that the farther back one went with C-14 dating, the greater was the chance that magnetic conditions would have altered the available amount of C-14 in unpredictable ways, increasing the margin of error on the tests beyond acceptable limits. The trouble was, there was no way of checking the C-14 dates to see how far off they were for any particular period, nor even in which direction the error lay.

Affairs had reached this impasse when dendrochronology entered the picture, and suddenly—hooray! A sample of wood could be given both a tree ring date and a C-14 date. If the two did not agree, it was fair to infer that the C-14 date was distorted because of variations in the available amount of the isotope. In this way, it has become possible over the past two decades or so to construct charts for recalibrating the raw C-14 dates so that the test can be applied with confidence to other organic materials besides wood.

That is not quite the end of the story, however. Scientists have the same right as the rest of us to change their minds, and it has recently been discovered that the original half-life used in calculating C-14 dates (5,568 years plus or minus 30 years) was in error. The new half-life, as accepted by the International Radiocarbon Dating Conference of 1962 and later years, is 5,730 years plus or minus 40 years. This has caused considerable confusion, as it is now necessary to ask, for every published C-14 date, which half-life was used and also whether it was recalibrated to conform with dendrochronological findings. Establishing a uniform system for all future C-14 dates is of course a problem for specialists, but anyone who reads archaeological literature should be aware that C-14 dates cannot always be taken at face value. (To convert a C-14 date from the old half-life figure to the new one, multiply by 1.029.)

The above summary of the nature of C-14 dating demonstrates why it is necessary to use care when collecting samples to be tested in this way. Any contamination by carbon-containing materials, which include paper, cotton wool, cloth, plastic, and the human hand, can affect the C-14 content of the sample and distort the results of the test. For that reason, the best way to pick up the sample is to use a clean metal tool. The material should be wrapped immediately in aluminum foil and put in a clean, tightly closed glass jar. Even air can carry enough carbon particles to contaminate the sample, which is why no surface deposit can be used for C-14 testing, no matter what its apparent age. Furthermore, in damp climates mold may grow on samples if they are put in containers that allow too much air space, and mold is a worse contaminator than air. The best material to collect is charcoal, since it is nearly pure carbon, but any organic substance will do, as long as it is unmistakably part of a cultural site and not an accidental intrusion. Some of the early C-14 dates gave very unreliable, not to say astounding, results because they were done on charcoal from naturally occurring forest fires or on other nonarchaeological material.

C-14 dating is one of the tests that are too expensive to be used on any but the exceptional site. (The going rate is in the neighborhood of $150 a sample.) It also has the disadvantages of destroying the sample material, which must be vaporized in the process, and of requiring trained technicians with special equipment. Nevertheless, a few archaeological societies and other groups maintain funds to provide for a limited number of C-14 tests per year, so it is by no means impossible that you will someday be involved in gathering material for the purpose.

Unlike C-14, which can be used to date a rather wide variety of materials, the next several tests we want to discuss apply exclusively to a single type of sample. If the substance in question is pottery, it may be desirable to test it for thermoluminescence. The term means the giving off of light when a material is heated. The phenomenon occurs in pottery because minute amounts of impurities (such as uranium, potassium, and thorium) in the original clay, plus natural external sources of radiation, cause the clay to act as a "trap" for certain highly charged ions whose energy is released as light when they are heated. The exact nature of these "traps" (and the electron "holes" that go with them) is a matter of scientific conjecture, and what is definitely known about the process is too complex to detail here. (This is another way of saying the authors don't really understand it themselves.) The relevant point for the conservation archaeologist is that the greater the age of the pottery, the greater its potential thermoluminescence. Furthermore, the thermoluminescent potential inherent in the clay in its natural state is destroyed when the clay is fired and becomes pottery. Therefore, we can be sure that it is the age of the pot *as pottery* that is being tested, rather than the age of the clay it was made from. The technique of measuring thermoluminescence is still in the developmental stage. There are some researchers who maintain the test will ultimately prove unreliable. (Not even its advocates have claimed for it a range of accuracy better than 3 to 10 percent.) Nevertheless, the possibilities raised are exciting, and archaeologists are keeping a hopeful eye on future developments.

Radioactive phenomena are also the basis of potassium-argon dating, referred to as K-Ar dating from the chemical symbols for the two elements. For archaeological purposes, the K-Ar method is useful for any site dating from the time of the earliest human species up to about twenty-five hundred years ago, but it is restricted to cases in which the surrounding rock is of the same or later date than the sites. At first glance, this might seem an impossible condition. The age of most rock is in the millions or billions of years, making it far older than any but the very earliest "early man" sites, such as those excavated by the Leakeys along the Great Rift Valley in Africa. There is, however, one class of rock that may easily be of recent date, up to and including five minutes ago. That is of course volcanic rock, examples of which are lava, obsidian, pumice, and tuff. Volcanic activity has taken place during geologically recent times in many areas, including the Mediterranean, Mexico, the Pacific coast of North America, Iceland, Japan, Java, and Africa. Wherever archaeological remains are found embedded in or overlain by this newly formed rock, it is theoretically possible to measure the decay of the unstable isotope K-40 into its stable decay product Ar-40, thus dating the remains by dating their geological context. Though the method is new and largely untried in archaeology, it has been successfully used for some time in geology, where the materials to be dated are much older.

A more widely applicable test in the context of North American archaeology (and that of some other areas) is based on obsidian hydration. As we know, obsidian was a highly prized tool material because of its superior flaking properties, and was widely distributed by trade far beyond the areas of its natural occurrence. It happens to be a chemical peculiarity of obsidian that any freshly fractured surface will absorb water from its surroundings in a process called hydration. The hydration layer is invisible to the naked eye, and should not be confused with natural patina or layers of chalky matrix. Hydration begins at the surface and proceeds inward along a rather sharply defined front. The deeper the hydration layer, the longer the time period since the tool was freshly made. It is possible to measure the hydration fairly directly, using a very thin section of the obsidian, cross-polarized light, an oil immersion lens, and a microscope equipped with image-splitting eyepieces. An alternative procedure uses a scanning densitometer. Both techniques give a good degree of accuracy, but the interpretation of the results is complicated by the fact that different environments offer different amounts of water for hydration. It is therefore necessary to know the past rainfall amounts for the area from which the samples are gathered before proceeding with hydration testing. Temperature of the environment and composition of the individual sample have also been listed as important variables, and each relatively small environment has its own hydration rate.

There is almost no end to the scientific developments that deserve mention in this chapter. Bored with C-14? Try archaeo-magnetic analysis, which is used to date claylike materials whose magnetic properties have been "frozen" by heat (ancient hearths or bricks, for example) through matching their magnetic orientation with previous geographic locations of the earth's ever-wandering magnetic poles. Are you a bone freak? Isoleucine racemization measures certain fixed-rate biochemical changes in mammalian bone. (And you get ten extra points for pronouncing it correctly.) Love scuba diving? In some mineral-rich areas of the sea, manganese nodules may form by accretion on the surface of submerged artifacts from shipwrecks or inundated villages, thus dating the objects by the size of the nodules.

At present, the archaeological dating game is certainly a

bewildering one. Yet archaeologists will have to continue to play it until that happy science-fictional day when some genius (possibly a reader of this book?) invents the Universal Date-o-Scope. "Got an artifact? Step right up. Put your sample in the slot and read the date. Ten cents, please."

10
Talking Archaeology

Richard Daugherty and the members of his archaeological crew were puzzled. For several seasons they had been excavating the coastal village once occupied by the Ozette people of Washington State. They had had the great good luck to find an exciting and continuous record of the lives of these daring early whale hunters, and their work had been crowned by the discovery of an entire wooden house, perfectly preserved in the debris of a mud slide that had occurred before the first arrival of the white man. The artifacts that had been found were richly varied, informative, and in some cases elegantly carved. But the archaeologists were still puzzled. What were all these short-handled, round-headed wooden paddles that kept turning up in the ruins? Much too small for use even in children's boats, the paddles were a mystery to which no one had proposed a reasonable solution.

Daugherty and his crew had been lucky in more than their finds, however. They also had the active cooperation and assistance of the Makah Indians, a local group whose membership included descendants of the original Ozette people. The Makahs not only lent the archaeologists a nearby building for their laboratory and sent their high-school-age children to help with the dig, they arranged for their elders to visit the remote and inaccessible site by helicopter. What took place then was much more than a nostalgic outing. The Makah elders knew unhesitatingly what those mysterious, centuries-old paddles were. Some of them had played a game like shuttlecock with just such paddles as children. They also gave the archaeologists much other useful information about cultural objects and customs. It was a superb example of the kind of advantages that may come about when archaeology is willing to talk, as well as survey, dig, and analyze.

Purists in the field of archaeology sometimes argue that it should be treated strictly as a science, dealing only with facts and artifacts. One school even holds that the archaeologist is to be distinguished from the prehistorian in that one gathers data, while the other interprets it. According to this view, anyone who gathers cultural information from living persons would wear still another label, that of anthropologist. In practice, such rigid academic distinctions often do more to constrict than to broaden the search for knowledge. It would certainly be too bad for beginning archaeologists to cut themselves off from talking archaeology on the basis that "archaeology isn't anthropology."

"But," you may ask, "how can I find people who have relevant information for me and how can I get them to talk?" In approaching this question, we must realize that not all Native American groups welcome the questions of curious outsiders. There is a joke to the effect that the typical Native American household consists of one or more grandparents, mother and father, four children, and an anthropologist. We can hardly blame people for wanting to protect their privacy, especially when they have been "over-anthropologized." The problem is aggravated for very visible groups such as those who occupy major reservation lands. In other words, some people just don't want to be interviewed. Another thing to remember is that, although many groups of Native Americans live in towns and cities side by side with their black, white, or Oriental neighbors, more live on small or little-known tribal lands, or are represented in the community only by craft or dance societies that keep in touch with a dispersed membership. That is, the people you want to talk to may not be easy to locate. However, an archaeologist with a genuine and informed interest in a group's cultural past may often approach such groups and receive a cordial welcome.

The relationship that results can be a genuine test of your sensitivity and open-mindedness, since many Native Americans are justifiably suspicious of curiosity seekers, outsiders, and do-gooders. Nor is there total agreement among the American Indian community on the aims and value of archaeology, as we have already said when discussing burial sites in chapter 3. Yet the rewards of a good relationship with a Native American group can be enormous. And even better, of course, is a situation in which the archaeologist is a member of the group whose past is being studied. The effect on archaeology and anthropology could only be beneficial if many more Native Americans were to become involved in these important disciplines.

If you do not already have access through personal acquaintances to the group you are interested in, the best approach is simply to write a courteous letter of inquiry to the Tribal Council or similar governing body. Most states and Canadian provinces have a Department of Indian (or Native) Affairs that can help you locate the group you want. Remember, though, that Native American cultures are enormously varied and that many individual Native Americans now reside very far from their ancestral homes. A Mohawk may be justifiably annoyed at being mistaken for a Sioux, merely because he happens to be living and working in North Dakota.

People other than Native Americans may also have valuable information for the prehistoric archaeologist. (Mind you, we do not want to fall into the fallacy of supposing that whites or blacks necessarily have an accurate view of other cultures. The problem of cultural bias is one we have already discussed in terms of evaluating early written records.) Nevertheless, much purely factual information can often be obtained from long-term residents and "old-timers." A little mental mathematics will show us that a person who was seventy-five years old in 1975, for example, may well have had parents or grandparents who witnessed aspects of Native American life that have now vanished. W. R. "Mac" McHargue, for instance, the father of one of the authors, was born in 1893. He still has very vivid memories of his childhood in south central and southwestern Montana, where *his* father was a traveling minister of the kind called a circuit rider, regularly riding or driving a route several hundred miles long in order to hold services in tiny towns that could not afford their own clergymen.

Grandfather McHargue's experiences, therefore, go back well before the time when the last of Montana's native population was finally (and some would say tragically) confined to reservation lands. Circuit riders of the time not only covered vast territories, but often took an interest, for better or worse, in converting the inhabitants of Indian villages they passed by on their routes. An inquiring archaeologist in that part of Montana could do a lot worse than to hunt up Mac McHargue or others like him and ask for their memories. Where were those encampments that Grandfather visited? Does the name Indian Fork mean that there were villages along that stream? If the local Indian group came to the town every year to sell or trade ponies and handicrafts, where did they camp? Are there any famous "painted rocks" in the area? Where was the "ring of stones on the ground" that the boy Mac came across while searching for a strayed mare? What was the best place for the kids to go when they went hunting "arrowheads"? And so on and on. Memories of days gone by are like archaeological remains themselves—a "nonrenewable resource."

Naturally, the value of personal recollections is even greater if the period you are interested in is historic. Nearly every neighborhood has its old-time residents who can recount relevant family or town history. It is a very worthwhile project to try to compile a sourcebook of oral information for the use of the historic archaeologist. The older the town, the more it has probably changed from its original layout. Try to get information about the old names of streets (often changed to honor prominent residents or national heroes) and the former locations of businesses, schools, or farms. If property has been destroyed by fires, floods, or tornadoes, try to find out what the buildings were like. Ask about the original locations of old buildings. A surprising number have been moved, whether by trucks or by oxen, from the places where they were built. Find out as much as possible about "what was there before" the new high school, the new highway, the industrial park. It is a good idea to work in conjunction with the local historical society, which can tell you what areas need investigating and will almost certainly want a copy of your finished work.

So much for the uses and goals of talking archaeology. Now a word about techniques. If you are not a speed-writer, you will probably want to buy or borrow a tape recorder, and you will need a typewriter for transcribing your material. There are ground rules for conducting a reasonable taped interview just as there are for any other activity. (Note, for instance, how your favorite radio or television talk show personality keeps the conversation going by giving just the right verbal nudge at the right time.)

1. Never just drop in on the person you wish to interview. Always make an appointment in advance and make it clear

that you have a specific purpose and area of interest. Some
people think that the elderly are always lonely and anxious
to talk to anyone who comes along. On the contrary, they
are probably as busy as you are, and they are doing *you* a
favor by donating their time.

2. Never tape-record anyone without prior permission.
To do so is not only discourteous, it is illegal.

3. Some people are very nervous about being recorded.
It may be helpful to put the machine out of sight or to begin
with a casual conversation on some unrelated topic, so that
your informant has time to get used to the machine. Most
people settle down and forget the recorder after five or ten
minutes.

4. Be alert to the existence of folklore. A good story often
gets attached to more than one set of circumstances. (In the
authors' town of Groton, Massachusetts, it is the one about
the house that was being moved and got stuck in the mud
at the corner of Main and Hollis streets. This story is told
of at least three different houses, including the one we live
in.) Of course, folklore may contain a grain of truth—just
look at Schliemann's discovery of Homeric Troy—but it is
not history and cannot be treated as history. The best evidence is always firsthand observation of the "I was there
and I saw it" variety. Hearsay evidence ("Grandma used to
say") can also be helpful, but policemen and lawyers know
how difficult to evaluate and how easily distorted it is.

5. You must give thought to verification. To put it another way, hearing is not always believing. Informants are
sometimes honestly mistaken. They may occasionally in-
vent information, either to please you, to tease you, or to
test your knowledge. A little common sense and experience
will show that some informants go in for make-believe and
some don't; some have excellent memories and some can't
remember what they had for breakfast. This is as true of the
general population as it is of the elderly. Sometimes,

though, elderly people have much clearer memories of their youth than they do of more recent times. You have to use the same basic intelligence in assessing information given you in pursuit of talking archaeology as you do in evaluating what anyone tells you in everyday life: if you have reason to doubt what you hear, check it with someone else who is in a position to know. If the two sources disagree, find a third, and maybe a fourth.

6. If you plan a sophisticated, large-scale program of interviews, you may want to work out a standard list of questions to be asked each time, which will make it much easier to collate and analyze your results. This procedure will also help you to avoid letting your own biases or preconceptions influence the way you edit your material.

From the perspective offered above, it is clear that what was formerly considered to be the separate and distinct field of ethnography is now becoming accepted as a tool of archaeology as well. This reflects some deeper changes in our basic thinking about the interrelationships among the social sciences in general. For the first few centuries of the so-called scientific and industrial age, the tendency was for research to give rise to increasing numbers of distinct -ologies, -ographies, and -istics. In the last half of the present century, however, scientists have begun to complain of the restrictions of "tunnel vision" and to praise the virtues of a "multidisciplinary approach." This point of view has had an inevitable effect on developments in archaeology. We might now say that the three sciences that study man's way of life are only divided by the fact that archaeology is concerned with the dead, anthropology with the living, and history with those, living or dead, who left written records. Put another way, archaeology is the anthropology of the dead. Like anthropology and history, it examines and tries to record the gorgeous and prodigal variety of human cultures, both past and present. However, as we have just pointed out, the three disciplines are no longer considered to be distinct and self-sufficient, and each is understood to have contributions to make to the others.

It is natural that other hybrid specialties are appearing among professionals and avocationals alike. We now have not only historic archaeology, industrial archaeology, and underwater archaeology, but the even younger field of ethno-archaeology. This new approach attempts to take information gleaned from present-day nonindustrial peoples who live by hunting and gathering, pastoralism, or simple agriculture and apply it to archaeological data from similar cultures. Ethno-archaeologists interview informants carefully and they also pay particular attention to the *remains* of the activities they observe, trying to deduce from an abandoned hut or a butchering site what the archaeological evidence will look like in a hundred or a thousand years when it *becomes* archaeology. So far, ethno-archaeology has not been able to fulfill its implicit aim of making firm generalizations about the patterns that are manifested in the conversion of debris to archaeological remains. Yet the very fact that such a field of study has arisen (a field that would have been unthinkable for previous generations of anthropologists, archaeologists, and ethnologists alike) bears witness to the possibilities inherent in talking archaeology.

II
Can You Dig It?

Having come so far in this book, you will surely have noticed that the authors are not keen on the idea of having beginning archaeologists do much digging. Problem-oriented conservation archaeology is not concerned with the mere accumulation of artifacts, but with the answers to certain narrowly framed questions concerning economies, populations, and cultural change. It is only when a site offers a high probability of helping to answer such questions that the usefulness of digging it seems to outweigh the certainty of simultaneously destroying it.

Yet it would be foolish to deny that for most of us, professionals and avocationals alike, digging holds a considerable lure. Where would Pompeii, Troy, Persepolis, Babylon, Harappa, Chichén Itzá, and Ur be without excavation? We would be more than human if we did not look forward to the thrill of discovery that may come with the next scrape of the trowel, the next flick of the brush. This chapter, therefore, will deal with some ways in which the beginner may become involved in certain types of digging—one as a more or less reluctant necessity and others as deliberate steps toward further training of the kind you cannot get from books.

As you become more and more experienced in area survey, you will quite probably encounter this situation: You
have come across an interesting and virtually undisturbed
site. You have filed your full report with the State or Provincial Archaeologist and other interested parties in the archaeological community. You also know that the site will soon
be destroyed with no way to conserve it for the future.
However, for a variety of reasons, such as lack of funds and
manpower, neither the archaeological society nor the local
college department of anthropology has shown an interest
in the site, which happens to be on private land not involved in any project using federal funds. (See Appendix I
for a summary of the archaeological law that would apply
if the site were on federal land or the proposed construction were funded by the federal government.) At this point,
you are justified in making further examination yourself so
that an informed decision may be made as to whether the
site merits protection or salvage. You decide to dig one or
more test pits. Don't forget that you must have the permission of the owner, just as you did for your survey, and that
some states and provinces require you to obtain a permit
before digging, at least on public land.

Digging a test pit is like taking your first bite of pie; it tells
you what's under the crust and whether it's good enough
to go on with. Archaeological sites are unlike pies, however, in that they are not the same all the way through.
Some may start out lemon and run through apple, pecan,
and peach before ending up chocolate. And some, of
course, turn out to be nothing but crust. In archaeology,
the thickness of the pie is also of prime importance, as in
many cases it indicates age. The number of layers is likewise of interest. And finally, the overall size of the pie must
be noted. Removing a bite-size sample is helpful in all these
areas. But like taking a bite of pie, digging a test pit is an

irreversible process. The material from the pit can never be replaced. You have eaten your bite and destroyed the original evidence from the test pit.

It is therefore clear that the fewer pits you dig, the better for the integrity of the site as a whole.

(Let us note here parenthetically that if you have read much of the literature of archaeology—and you should certainly have done so before you take on your first test pit— you will have encountered references to the digging of pits for sampling purposes. The sampling meant is statistical sampling and refers to a mathematical technique whereby archaeologists hope to get a rather precise idea of the contents of a whole site by excavating certain representative parts of it. The principle is the same as that of the pollster who hopes to learn the opinions of a whole population by interviewing only a sample of consumers or voters. Perhaps in the future we really will be able to evaluate sites by this means, at least as accurately as the researchers who tell us so confidently which brand of peanut butter or president we prefer. At present, however, the authors do not feel that statistical sampling has progressed to the point where it is simple enough for nonspecialists to use in the field. A bad sampling technique, or one that is improperly carried out, is worse than no sampling because it can mislead you about the nature of the site and disrupts part of the site area with test pits.)

Since you are going to dig only one or two test pits, you must use some care in choosing their locations. First, try to pick a place that is not covered with trees or brush. Not only do roots make the work of digging much harder, but the presence of even quite small roots complicates the job of keeping your pit's walls vertical (a necessity explained below). Very large roots may actually heave the soil and its accompanying artifacts until it is impossible to tell one level from another. This is known as disrupting the stratigraphy, or The Archaeologist's Nightmare.

Obviously, you will also prefer a spot that is not too rocky, and sandy soils are to be avoided because they are subject to cave-ins. (If you are in a glacial moraine or on a beach, of course, you are out of luck.)

Other things being equal, try to pick a place near what you think, from the surface distribution of artifacts, is the site's center. Occupation sites tend to be lens-shaped in cross section; that is, they are thicker in the center and thinner toward the edges.

Before you begin, you must assemble your equipment. In addition to the maps, meter tapes, and compass you use in surveying, you will need a shovel. One with a square back and a straight edge is best, but the folding U.S. Army item called an entrenching tool will work quite well and is inexpensive, readily available, and easy to carry. You will also want a triangular-bladed mason's trowel (*not* a garden trowel); a small, hand-held gardening fork or hoe; a large supply of artifact bags and labels; a bucket; a dustpan; a small spirit level; a plumb bob (a lead sinker or stone tied to a string); and a screen for sieving soil. (Figure 17 shows a suggested method of constructing such a screen. Quarter-inch mesh from the hardware store is usually adequate for this purpose, although on many professional digs soil is screened through a series of meshes, each finer than the last.)

Let us now speak more precisely about what a test pit can tell you and how it relates to the projected excavation. In digging a pit, you are trying to get a rough idea of what you might expect to find in the site as a whole. Just as in surface surveying you must be able to plot the site and each artifact collected on a two-dimensional map, so in digging it is necessary to be able to locate every find on a three-dimen-

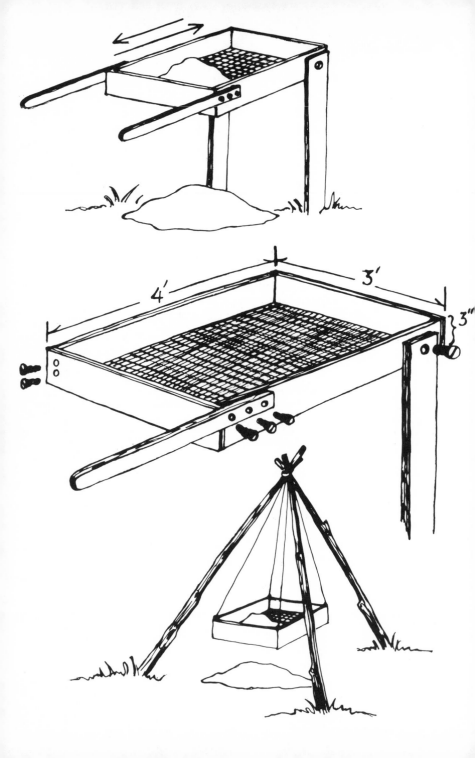

sional system that refers to the whole volume of soil excavated—length times breadth times depth. Remember that the dating of one artifact or feature with respect to another often depends solely on its relative position in the soil strata—in other words, on its context.

One common way of approaching this problem in a formal excavation is to lay out a grid over the entire site surface and then dig each square separately, recording the exact depth of each artifact and even its position in the square before it is removed. Thus a certain potsherd might be noted to have come from square E2/S16, level 4 (37 cm. depth), at a point 12 cm. from a spot 22 cm. south of the northeast corner. (This assumes that grid lines running north and south are labeled S1, S2, S3, etc., and grid lines

FIGURE 17

The simplest kind of soil screen is the one shown in the photographs on pages 214–17. It is nothing but a wooden box with the bottom made of 1/4-inch wire mesh. The variation shown here in A and B is easier on the back, and can also be used by one person alone. The dimensions shown in the diagram are about the largest practical ones. If 4 × 3 feet seems too large, make your screen 3 × 2 feet. Use good, stout wood screws and 1 × 3 lumber. The screen is stapled, tacked, or nailed to the bottom. The legs will swivel freely yet remain securely attached if the screws used to fasten them are bolted on the reverse side. (The legs can be folded for carrying.) The user holds the handles (left) like those of a wheelbarrow and shakes the screen back and forth on its legs. An alternative, shown in C, is to suspend a simple box screen from a tripod made of fallen branches. If you're working in a wooded area (and you probably are, or you wouldn't be test pitting), you can throw the sticks away when you move on, rather than carrying them around.

running east and west are labeled E1, E2, E3, etc. There are other systems.)

Now relax. You are not going to have to be all that exact about your measurements, but you must take steps not to mess things up for the excavators of the future. The first thing you have to do, therefore, is to locate the pit very accurately. The best procedure is to establish a datum point and measure the pit's position from there. A datum point is simply any permanent landscape feature that figures on the sketch map of the site appearing on the site report form. It may be a big boulder, the intersection of two stone walls, a prominent tree stump or geological formation— anything, in short, that is easy to identify and not likely to vanish for the next several decades at least.

Describe the datum point in the appropriate space on the test pit record form (see page 207) and measure distance and compass direction from the datum point to the first corner of your pit. (Call it corner A.) Then mark corners B, C, and D with stakes and record the orientation of the pit as shown on the sample form. It is helpful to connect the corner stakes with string, so that you can see the line along which you wish to dig, but be careful not to trip over the string.

The next thing you must be sure of is that you can specify precisely the volume of soil you dig. In other words, how many cubes or parts of cubes of the three-dimensional grid laid out by the imaginary future excavators have already been disturbed? This is one of the reasons why you must try to make the side walls of your pit absolutely vertical. If the walls slant outward, you have dug soil from another cube; if they slant inward, you have dug less than your designated volume.

For the above reasons, test pits are usually dug down from a surface area of either 1 × 1 or 2 × 2 meters. The second is probably preferable, as it gives you more room

to work, but it will also make you move and screen four
times as much soil, and this can be a problem if you are
working alone and are pressed for time. Very small sites
also need smaller test pits, so that the pit does not occupy
a significant percentage of the site as a whole.

Decide beforehand how you will designate each level.
The best method is to stick to natural soil levels as you find
them—topsoil, charcoal, gravel, yellow clay, or whatever, in
numbered sequence. However, when the soil is very uniform you may have to choose an arbitrary depth, such as 10
centimeters. The decision is really up to you, but 10 to 20
centimeters is usually a convenient number. Be aware that
in any excavation you must be even more alert to general
occupation debris (other than artifacts) than you are on
survey. However, as we said when discussing cataloging,
such materials need not be individually bagged, but may be
collected together in bags labeled "Level I, chipping
waste," "Level IV, charcoal," and so on. Later they will be
weighed and cataloged by weight.

You are now ready to start the actual work of excavation
—and work is the right word. Anyone who deliberately
chooses to spend hours in the hot sun or pouring rain
scraping at a hole in the ground must have not only a
strong back but, some would add, a weak mind. You see,
archaeologists do not really dig—not with shovels like sen-
sible people. That shovel is mainly for filling in afterward,
or possibly for breaking a tough root or digging a layer of
sterile soil. Archaeologists use those little mason's trowels
like the one you brought along. In fact, the first thing you
do is merely to scrape at the surface dirt with your trowel.
Scrape the soil over the whole area of the pit, and of course
collect and bag any artifacts or cultural debris you may
notice. Keep a copy of the test pit record form and the test
pit feature record form handy (see pages 205–11 for details
of filling them out). On the test pit feature record form

sketch in the space provided each artifact or feature as it is uncovered. Measure the distance from the object to the corners of the pit and record this information. (On page 211 is an example of a filled-in test pit feature record form.) A separate test pit feature record form may be required for each level of the test pit. It cannot be emphasized strongly enough that *all material should be put in labeled bags and recorded immediately.* It will inevitably become jumbled and mislaid if you get excited and leave it piled on one side. If you're going to do that, you might as well be a pothunter.

After the first layer of soil is loosened, it is screened. You can use your shovel to fill the screen, but don't actually dig with it. Remember, too, not to remove any objects, even stones, that are embedded in soil below the level you're

This part of a trench in a professional excavation shows soil profiles very clearly.

working on. (Uncover these gradually as you continue on down.) Carry the screen a reasonable distance away from the pit before using it. This makes for more labor, but it is necessary in order to keep the screened earth from falling into the pit. After the loose dirt and gravel have been shaken through the screen, larger pieces are picked over by hand. Local, unshaped rock that is not fire-cracked may be tossed away, while cultural materials are sorted into their appropriate bags. Then the whole loosening-shoveling-screening-picking-bagging process is repeated until you have reached the bottom of the first level.

At this point it is important to pay attention to the "squaring up" of your pit. Using the flat back of a trowel, shave the sides until they are as vertical as you can make them. Be sure the corners are good and square. Finally, level off the floor. Picky people may go so far as to use a spirit level for this job, and a weighted string to check the straightness of the sides, but that is not strictly necessary unless you have a very uncertain eye for angles. It is enough just to make the pit neat and square so that there is little chance of having material from one level fall into another. Even more important, "squaring up" lets you observe changes of soil color in the flat pit bottom, which may indicate the presence of ancient features such as fire pits or post molds. When the first level is completed, the others are "taken down" in the same manner.

The obvious question now is, "How far down do I go?" The answer is rather irritating: "Just far enough." In the large majority of cases, this means digging through the layer of cultural material until you reach sterile soil, that is, soil that shows no signs of human cultural remains. This, however, is another time when your study of local geology may be useful. Such phenomena as mudslides, sandstorms, flooding, or even volcanic eruptions can leave layers of sterile soil, gravel, or pumice on top of still older cultural materials. Only you can judge how far is far enough, once you have reached the first few centimeters of sterile soil. If geological factors seem to warrant it, or if the literature leads you to think the site ought to be deeper than it appears, it can certainly do no harm to go down another ten centimeters or so. Soil that looks sterile need not be screened, although it must still be removed very carefully so as not to disturb the top of the underlying cultural layer, if there is one.

On the other hand, there are cases in which you should stop digging a test pit not because you have run out of material, but because you have not. In parts of California, for example, midden is layered nine feet deep. It is pretty obvious that no one person can dig a nine-foot-deep test pit. Not only would the labor be staggering (36 cubic meters of soil for a 2 × 2 pit), but there would be severe danger of cave-ins and flooding. Furthermore, since an informal rule of thumb has it that midden of this type is formed at the rate of one foot every thousand years, cultural material of more than a meter (3.28 feet) in depth is very probably old enough to justify further excavation *by virtue of its depth alone.* The whole point of your digging a test pit was to see whether a full-scale excavation was necessary, so it would appear that the requirement had now been met. Any pit that goes as deep as 1 meter should be brought forcefully to the attention of the State or Provincial Archaeologist and other archaeological authorities without delay. It is a valuable and interesting site and some trained person should investigate it before it is destroyed.

However, in North America as a whole, only a tiny minority of test pits will have to be discontinued before cultural material runs out. In all ordinary cases, you will hit sterile soil sooner or later and decide to call it quits. You have your bags of artifacts, charcoal, chipping waste, shell, bone, or whatever, and you have your meticulously accurate map locating the pit. You have records of any features uncovered. Now, as a last step, you make a record of the pit's soil profile. This means the way the pit's sides look in cross section. A soil profile is best shown on a sketch because there is not enough contrast between most soil layers to show up well in a photograph. In the space provided on the test pit record form draw the various layers of soil you dug through, showing their relative thicknesses, and label them as accurately as the state of your knowledge will allow (see example, page 208). "Charcoal, 8 cm.," "Red clay, 32 cm.," "Water-washed stone, 10 cm.," "Lens of oyster shell, 20 × 3 cm." might be typical entries.

Before you fill in the pit, you will leave an archaeological calling card. At each bottom corner of the pit you will put a piece of non-biodegradable twentieth-century rubbish that will serve as an announcement that "Kilroy was here" to any future investigator who may not know the site has been disturbed. The calling card can be anything from an aluminum pop-top can ring to a piece of glass. This is the one case in which littering is positively desirable.

Now at last you can fill up the pit. It is good manners to bury any debris you may have generated, whether it is cut brush and branches or just plain trash.

Analysis and cataloging of finds from test pits are the same as for surface-collected materials, with the single exception that entries for pit number (if more than one) and level are made in the catalog.

There are also the test pit record, and a test pit feature record for each level on which features or artifacts are found, to be completed. To fill out the test pit record form proceed as follows:

1. *Site:* The name and/or number of the site.
2. *Date:* The date when the test pit was dug and the report filled out. (They should be the same.)
3. *Test Pit Number:* The number you assign to this particular pit, the same number that appears on your site plan.
4. *By:* Name(s) of person(s) digging the test pit and completing the form.
5. *Levels 1, 2, etc.:* The system of designating levels for this excavation. Levels may be arbitrary (for example: 0–10 cm., 10–20 cm., 20–30 cm., etc.), or they may consist of recognizable soil strata—for instance, humus, fine sand, red clay.
6. *Size Screen:* The size of the mesh in the screen used. This is normally 1/4 inch.
7. *Excavation Profiles:* The relative appearances of the various soil strata in two adjoining walls of the test pit are drawn on the squares provided. Indicate the boundaries of the levels as defined above along the edges of each drawing. The size of the pit is defined by inserting the distances between A and B and between B and C on the form. For example: A   1 meter   B. The soil strata may be drawn schematically and keyed to labels below or sketched realistically and labeled directly.
8. *Catalog Record:* If materials or artifacts were recovered, indicate that a catalog record is attached.
9. *Feature Record:* If features or artifacts were uncovered, indicate that test pit feature records are attached.

TEST PIT RECORD

1. Site _____   2. Date _____

3. Test Pit Number _____   4. By _____

5.
Level 1 _____   Level 4 _____

Level 2 _____   Level 5 _____

Level 3 _____   Level 6 _____

6. Size Screen _____

7. Excavation Profiles

A   B   B   C

8. Catalog Record _____   9. Feature Record _____

TEST PIT RECORD

1. Site **Bertrando Farm #3**

2. Date October 29, 1977

3. Test Pit Number **2**

4. By **B. Bertrando**

5.

Level 1 10 cm	Level 4
Level 2 20 cm	Level 5
Level 3 30 cm	Level 6

6. Size Screen   1/4 inch

7. Excavation Profiles

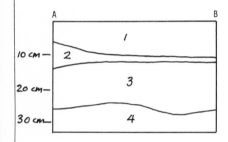
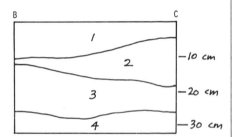

1. Dark soil with some chipping waste
2. Lens of clam, oyster, and other shell mixed with bird bone and some chipping waste
3. Orange soil with chipping waste, bird bone, and large oyster and moon snail shell
4. Light-colored soil with no obvious cultural material

8. Catalog Record **yes**

9. Feature Record **yes**

The procedure for filling out a test pit feature record (see page 210) is the same as that for the test pit record with respect to items 1 through 4. This information identifies the feature with the correct site if the records should become detached from each other. It is essential that the two be kept together because the accurate location and description of features within the site as a whole is important in the evaluation of the site in terms of its use and internal organization. The rest of the feature record is filled out as follows:

5. *Feature's Distance from Surface:* This means the distance (in centimeters) of the *top* of the feature from the soil surface, regardless of the level in which it occurs.

6. *Notes:* Insert here a general description of the feature and any aspects of it you feel may be important for establishing its relationship to the site as a whole. If you aren't sure what the feature really is, say so.

7. *Plan:* This should be an accurate sketch map of the feature and its position relative to the four lettered corners of the test pit. It is important to locate accurately the various elements of the feature. Thus a drawing of six spear points in a circle with all their points toward the center conveys much more useful information than a rough circle drawn on the plan with a note saying "Six spear points." Even better would be a photograph. Clearly, it is also necessary to make notes on the plan when needed to explain details of the feature.

8. *Profile:* Use this space to sketch a side view of the feature, or more than one view if they are significantly different.

TEST PIT FEATURE RECORD

1. Site _____   2. Date _____

3. Test Pit Number _____   4. By _____

5. Feature's Distance from Surface _____

6. Notes

7. Plan

   A   B

   C   D

8. Profile

TEST PIT FEATURE RECORD

1. Site _Bertrando Farm #3_   2. Date _October 29, 1977_

3. Test Pit Number _2_   4. By _B. Bertrando_

5. Feature's Distance from Surface _12 cm to #1 + 2   11 cm to #3_

6. Notes _Distances (features to corners):_
   1b to A = 35 cm, 1b to C = 80 cm
   2y to C = 45 cm, 2y to D = 75 cm
   3x to B = 45 cm, 3x to D = 95 cm

7. Plan

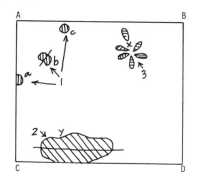

1. Possible post molds

2. Concentration of burnt earth with charred seeds and bone

3. Cluster of spear points?

8. Profile

1.   ↑
   10 cm   typical (b)
      ↓

2.   ↑
       25 cm
          ↓

By this time, you have generated a rather large package of data for this site. The completed package includes the site report with its map of access routes to the site and its detailed map of the site itself, accurately fixed by a datum point; test pit records for each pit dug; feature records for each feature discovered; and catalog forms for all the materials or artifacts recovered from the surface or the test pits. These documents, it is hoped, will provide necessary information to those who must decide what is the wisest use of the site in the face of its threatened destruction.

It is clear now that although the conservation archaeologist invariably tries to start at the top (and often does not go beyond the top at all), even under survey conditions it is not always possible to avoid disturbing subsurface soil. Test pits, as we have just seen, are dug on known sites in order to learn more about their need for preservation. Shovel testing, on the other hand, although much like test pitting in many ways, is designed to help locate sites previously unknown.

For this reason, a site surveyor who is compelled to do shovel testing proceeds somewhat differently from the test pit excavator. The question is, "When do you do shovel testing?" The answer, as you might guess, is, "As seldom as possible." Nevertheless, there are certain areas of North America in which you simply are not likely to find sites by surface survey alone. These include almost all the continent's heavily forested areas, particularly the Eastern Woodlands and the rain forests of the Northwest Coast. There and in some other regions, acid soils combine with rapidly accumulating leaf mold to make it statistically improbable that you would find a site on the surface unless you fell over it and dug it up with your chin. You can easily tell whether shovel testing is standard procedure in your area by reading survey reports in local archaeological publications. Even then, the warnings in chapter 2 about familiarizing yourself with the plants, animals, soils, geology, and previous archaeological research of your area *before* you go out to survey apply doubly and triply to shovel testing. You should certainly go along with an experienced shovel tester, either avocational or professional, before you set out yourself to convert some innocent patch of woodland into something that might be mistaken for a prairie dog town.

When necessity does force you to test below the surface as part of a survey, bear in mind that shovel testing is usually done in a much more systematic pattern than test pitting, generally being performed on some sort of grid system. The spacing of the elements of the grid is best decided on the basis of your estimate of the average minimum site size in the region. This is no more than common sense—you do not sift marbles out of sand with a grid made of chicken wire. Thus, if sites in your area are usually at least twenty-five meters in diameter, you would do your shovel testing at twenty-five-meter intervals.

A shovel test is in many ways less formal than a test pit, except for its spacing. It is not necessary, for example, to lay out your little excavation with corner stakes, datum points, and so on. Having measured off a point on your predetermined grid (you may even move a meter or so either way to avoid a tree root or boulder), you simply dig a square hole once or twice the width of your shovel blade, going down until you reach sterile soil. Naturally, you do not go at it like a terrier after a bone. You will still try to keep your side walls straight so that you can examine the soil profile, and you still screen the soil you remove, but you do not go through the routine of scraping with a trowel and plotting the location of each artifact or feature within the pit area. The object of this excavation is to find disturbances in the soil pattern that may indicate the presence of a site, not to make specific conclusions about the nature or period of the site.

Once a shovel test seems to indicate that a site is present, it is important to check your finding by making one or two other tests in the immediate area, say five or ten meters away. In this way you should be able to tell whether what you found on your first test was an accident or the mark of a genuine site. Needless to say, it is very important to locate each shovel test accurately on a map of the area surveyed.

Another technique for exploring below the ground surface, one that really boils down to a variation of shovel testing, is the use of a coring tool, a much smaller version of the huge devices used in oil prospecting and undersea explorations. (Some practitioners use a posthole digger

Photo by Michael E. Roberts

Dr. Laurel Casjens and Valerie Talmage do a shovel test. Val takes the first shovelful while Laurel records the location and its environment.

Screening soil can be hard on the back.

Find anything?

Photo by Michael E. Roberts

Soil profiles are measured before they are sketched.

A soil sample is bagged for later testing.

Photo by Michael E. Roberts

"Come, let us sit upon the ground . . ." At least half of archaeology is record keeping.

instead.) The core usually used in archaeology is about forty centimeters long and the diameter of a quarter—a hollow metal tube with a window cut out of the side to enable you to inspect the soil brought up by the core.

The advantage of using a coring tool in survey is that a core can be done much more quickly than a shovel test (a few minutes, as compared to half an hour or more). Cores may also be made at smaller intervals than shovel tests, and of course the volume of soil disturbed is considerably smaller. This might be desirable on a small but potentially important site. On the other hand, coring in hard soil requires quite a lot of muscle, to the point where only the relatively husky and youthful individual can be expected to spend a day at it.

Taking soil cores isn't easy, even on an island on a nice spring day.

Inevitably, conservation archaeologists who live in an area where subsurface testing techniques are called for will be required to become much more soil-conscious than their colleagues in other places. Being constantly called upon to evaluate the results of shovel tests or soil cores, they must become intimately (some would say too intimately) familiar with the normal soils of their region. They should also give thought to the fact that subsurface techniques lend themselves to various kinds of follow-up soil analysis. Thus many surveyors find it useful to become proficient at pH or phosphate testing, using soil samples from the survey area and the experimental procedures mentioned (but by no means fully described) in chapter 9.

The actual process of surveying for sites by shovel testing or coring is much the same as that used for aboveground survey in other circumstances. The surveyor decides beforehand on the location and direction of a series of transects laid out in parallel lines across the area to be surveyed. Instead of simply walking and looking for signs of surface occupation, as described in chapter 5, however, he or she makes shovel tests or cores at regular intervals, assessing the results for evidence of disturbance such as may indicate previous use or occupation of the land. At each test location the appropriate data are recorded. Two forms are used for this purpose—the transect record, which sets down the details of each test in the transect, and the transect profile record, which diagrams the actual soil profiles encountered in each test or core. A typical transect record is shown on page 220 and is filled out as follows:

1. *Area Surveyed:* A description of the territory examined. For example: "West bank of Punky Creek from Laurel Street to railroad bridge." There will of course be no site number, because a site is what you are looking for. The area should also be marked on a USGS quad map, but you need not be picky about establishing datum points and so on unless sites are definitely found.
2. *Date:* The date when the test or core was made and the form filled out.
3. *Recorder:* Name of the person recording the data, especially if, as sometimes happens, the person doing the digging is not also doing the recording.
4. *Shovel Test or Core Number:* The number you assign to the test or core being described. You may want to leave a line blank between

TRANSECT RECORD

1. Area Surveyed _____ 2. Date _____ 3. Recorder _____

4. ST/Core Number	5. Size	6. Depth	7. Location and Description	8. Cultural Indications	9. Soil Samples?	10. pH?	11. Phosphates?	12. Tester	13. Excavator(s)

ST/core number entries to allow more space for description.

5. *Size:* The dimensions of the shovel test pit or diameter of the core.

6. *Depth:* Distance in centimeters to the bottom of the pit or core.

7. *Location and Description:* Record the angle of slope, type of vegetation, surface features, or any other noteworthy details of the immediate test area. Use as much space as necessary.

8. *Cultural Indications:* List and describe any artifacts or cultural materials found (these will be rare). Also note any clear evidence of previous occupation in the soil, such as the presence of midden, shell, or burnt rock.

9. *Soil Samples?* If soil samples were taken for testing, indicate from which levels they came, using one line for each level.

10. and 11. *Chemical Tests:* Record the type and results of any chemical testing.

12. *Tester:* The name of the person performing the chemical tests.

13. *Excavator(s):* The name(s) of the person(s) actually digging. (More than one person may work on the same transect.)

For the transect profile record, items 1 and 2 are the same as above.

3. *Interval (m.):* The distance between cores or shovel tests along this transect (in meters).

4. *Recorder:* Name of the person recording the data.

5. *Shovel Test or Core Number:* The number of the shovel test or core, as previously recorded on

TRANSECT PROFILE RECORD

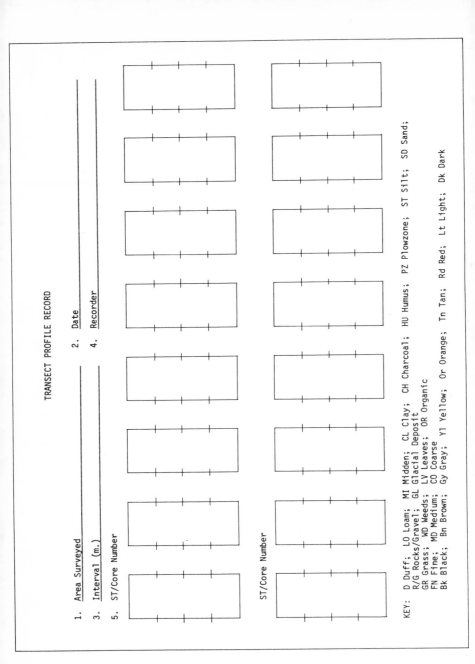

1. Area Surveyed

2. Date

3. Interval (m.)

4. Recorder

5. ST/Core Number

ST/Core Number

KEY: D Duff; LO Loam; MI Midden; CL Clay; CH Charcoal; HU Humus; PZ Plowzone; ST Silt; SD Sand;
      R/G Rocks/Gravel; GL Glacial Deposit
      GR Grass; WD Weeds; LV Leaves; OR Organic
      FN Fine; MD Medium; CO Coarse
      Bk Black; Bn Brown; Gy Gray; Yl Yellow; Or Orange; Tn Tan; Rd Red; Lt Light; Dk Dark

your map of the area being surveyed. A number is recorded over each profile box on the form and one profile is drawn in it (not four, as for a test pit). The ticks at the sides of the boxes are used to establish any convenient scale of centimeters, depending on the depth of the test. The code at the bottom of the sheet may be used to identify the soil types encountered. Figure 18 shows samples of completed profile boxes. It will be noted that the pits or cores were taken down to glacial deposits, which in the northeast, at least, are (rightly or wrongly) considered to be sterile. Observe also that Test 13 was not required to go as deep as Test 14.

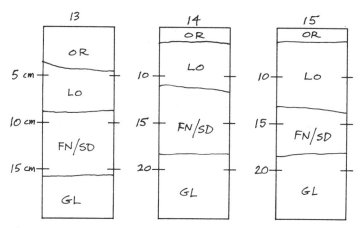

FIGURE 18
Completed profile boxes

To the same extent that shovel testing and test pitting require more background and training, and generate a greater volume of data, than does surveying, it is more important that the record of the excavations be available to other archaeologists for future reference. If you have not in the past sent copies of your survey reports to anyone but the state or provincial archaeological authorities, it is time now to make the extra effort and be sure your data go to other interested parties in academic departments or responsible archaeological societies. You may also have the opportunity to publish your findings through the archaeological society or in a regional archaeological journal. This is an excellent way of assuring that your work becomes a permanent part of the scholarly record.

There is another reason why you may want to spread your test records around as widely as possible among responsible archaeologists. If they are the basis for a decision to excavate the site fully, you have a very good chance of being invited to participate. Now as we've said, not all doctors do surgery, and not all archaeologists dig. Archaeological sites are an endangered resource and there is much useful and exciting work to be done without digging. Nevertheless, we are not trying to kid anyone into forgetting about digging. If you have already gone through the effort and hard work of study and survey, form filling and cataloging, then chances are you have been bitten by the archaeology bug and will not be satisfied until you have been on a full-scale dig at least once. You certainly understand now why it is not possible for any individual or school group to conduct a responsible dig without supervision by an experienced and qualified archaeologist, whether avocational or professional. What, then, does the beginner have to do in order to take part in a well-run, responsible dig?

There are really five possible ways to answer this question, and we have just touched on one of them: get in on the ground floor (or pit floor). Perhaps you have written the test pit or survey report that drew attention to the site and its imminent destruction. Or you may be a member of an archaeological society that decides to take on a dig and calls for volunteers. Either way, you have a very reasonable chance of being recruited on the spot when you present yourself to the dig director. This will be all the more probable if you can offer detailed local knowledge to a director who is not intimately familiar with the area. As a volunteer, you do not need to be available every day, but you must be able to promise to show up regularly after work, after school, or on weekends.

A second method, but one that is not yet widely available, is to participate in a certification program run by your local archaeological society or, in at least one case (Arkansas), by the state. For a low or minimal cost avocationals are given basic training in such areas as excavation, survey, museology, laboratory analysis, and cataloging, which then qualifies them to do more independent work. Academic credit is rarely given.

Two other possibilities, which, however, require bigger investments of money and time, are to enroll in a field school or to become a paying participant in a scientific-recreational program.

Field schools are serious academic exercises that generally take place in the summer months. They are held under the auspices of colleges or universities, museums, or archaeological societies and are often directed by highly competent professionals. Some field schools accept only full-time college students, but others are open to anyone who can demonstrate physical fitness and a knowledge of basic archaeological procedure. Some charge a fee of up to five or six hundred dollars plus room and board, while others are less expensive. Many do not accept applicants under the age of eighteen (occasionally sixteen). Field schools are also by nature ephemeral because they are dependent on the interest, professional fortunes, and funding sources of their directors. However, they generally offer high-quality training in excavation technique.

The paying-participant approach is a relatively new one that has grown up in response to increasing public interest in archaeology. Two organizations that offer such opportunities are the Explorers' Club and Earthwatch (See Appendix V for addresses). Prices for these expeditions run in the hundreds of dollars because they not only cover room, board, and tuition for you, but also help to finance the expedition leader and his staff. In this way you, as a member of the public, are underwriting the costs of scientific research. Expeditions of this type go abroad as well as to locations in North America and generally accept participants aged sixteen or over—including *way* over. They offer a unique opportunity for the nonspecialist to work with prominent scientists, and there is usually no educational requirement beyond a desire to learn and a willingness to work. The experience can be very valuable for those who can afford it. In addition, both organizations provide a

Field school participants learn professional surveying techniques as well as the mechanics of excavation and laboratory work.

limited number of scholarships to high school students and public school teachers.

These approaches are all very well, but they may not help you if you are short of money or opportunity. In the event you still want to try your hand at full-scale excavation, you are going to have to get out and beat the bushes—literally, perhaps.

The first thing is to track down your quarry. If you don't know of any archaeological activity in your area, there are still tactics you can try. One of them is to write to the Archaeological Institute of America (see Appendix IV for address) and ask for the latest edition of their annual "Fieldwork Opportunities Bulletin," which lists, among other things, digs in the United States and abroad that are accepting volunteers. The price of this publication in 1976 was $1.00. Educational and age requirements vary quite widely from project to project, so read carefully.

If the AIA listing does not solve your problem, try contacting college or university departments of anthropology or archaeology that may have an interest in your area. Publicly funded schools are a good bet, and so are any private institutions that may be located within driving distance. Local libraries usually have a reference shelf with college catalogs, which will help you by supplying addresses and telling you which schools have departments of archaeology or anthropology (not all do). If you can find out which professors are interested in North American archaeology, so much the better. They are the ones who might be likely to spend the summer digging in your area. (It is unfortunate, from our point of view, that in North America the chairpersons of departments of archaeology tend to be specialists in classical, Mesoamerican, or Near Eastern studies rather than in local areas. However, a letter to the head of a department will probably be forwarded to the appropriate person if you so request.) The things to emphasize in a letter of inquiry are (1) your serious, scholarly interest (don't come on like a pothunter) and (2) the local expertise you have to offer. The best time to write is in late winter or spring, when the next season's excavations are being planned—not in the fall, when staff and budgets for next year are always uncertain.

Larger museums with archaeological collections also fund excavations. And the office of the State or Provincial Archaeologist may help you by giving you the names and addresses of persons who have been granted permits to dig in your area. Projects involving archaeological salvage (excavation done one step ahead of the bulldozers) are especially likely to prove fruitful, as they are often hastily assembled and thus understaffed. Furthermore, salvage goes on all year round.

Still another option is to watch the newspapers carefully for reports of digs in progress. If the journalist involved is responsible, the story will not tell you exactly where the dig is located, but the name and affiliation of the director should appear. If these are still inadequate, call the paper and ask for an address.

Once you have located an active excavation site that is nearby and made contact with its director by letter or phone, you may well have solved your problem and been accepted as a volunteer. If not, however—that is, if your offer of assistance has been turned down—there is one last move you can make. It's called not taking no for an answer. Virtually every dig, unless it is on private land and surrounded by an electric fence, is prepared to welcome an occasional visitor, either casually or by appointment. There is nothing to keep you from turning up as a curious observer, and our experience suggests that an interested and well-informed person on the spot has a better chance of being invited to participate than someone who is just a voice on the telephone. There is a fine line, of course, between being persistent and being a pest. Yet most dig directors will admit that an offer of free assistance is pretty hard to turn down when it's right there in front of them. So if you really want to get on a dig—go to it, good luck, and remember, if things don't work out at first there's always next season.

12
Who Owns Archaeology?

We have seen, in discussions of pothunting, private land, and so on, that there is some disagreement about the ownership of archaeological remains. The pothunter would like "finders keepers" to be the controlling philosophy, while landowners often claim (and in law sometimes possess) the rights to anything found on their property, no matter who does the finding.

Another point of view would have it that all American Indian artifacts belong exclusively to surviving American Indian groups—with the presumed implication that remains left by early settlers belong exclusively to members of non-Indian groups such as the Mayflower Descendants. On the surface, there is some logic in this approach, but it presents considerable practical problems. Should objects excavated from New York's Ellis Island belong only to the descendants of European immigrants? Even more vexing, to whom can we give the objects excavated from California's famous missions, since the Spanish padres were celibate and presumably left no descendants? In the same way, although North American peoples had produced a dazzling variety of cultures and customs before the settlers came, it is tragic but true that not all presettlement peoples have any living descendants at all.

Partly as a response to the argument for Indian ownership of artifacts, one observer has semiseriously suggested
that under common law, all objects of Native American
manufacture actually belong to the U.S. government. The
reasoning goes like this: In colonial times, common law
provided that if a person died without making a will and
had no descendants closer than the third generation, his or
her possessions became government property. Since almost no American Indians made wills, and the existence of
descendants would be virtually impossible to prove at this
late date, courts might be forced to rule in the government's favor if a test case were ever brought.

A fifth claim would have it that archaeology belongs to
"science." Now science is an abstraction, and when trans-
lated into everyday terms it tends to mean professional
archaeologists, academic departments, and large museums, in whose care the actual artifacts are often relegated
to dusty storage bins. Naturally, this point of view is opposed by nearly everyone else, from pothunters to Native
American groups.

Rather than giving fuel to divisive squabbles, however,
the authors suggest that it is better to adopt the philosophy
that archaeology belongs to the people—to all the people,
not only of North America but ultimately of the world,
future as well as present. After all, archaeology is nothing
if it is not understanding and knowledge, and what individual or group can own knowledge?

Yet "the people" is just as much an abstraction as "science." What does this idea really mean to you, the archaeologist? First of all, it means the obligation to make known
your findings. We have already discussed in chapter 5 the
question of whom to notify *officially* of your survey and
experimental results, and we have also mentioned the possibility of publishing your findings in professional journals
and newsletters. That is not all, however. If we are really

serious in asking who owns archaeology, then "the people" will have to be defined as your neighbors and residents of local communities. They are the ones who daily walk the lands beneath which lie forgotten battlefields, villages, settlements, hunting grounds, and sacred places. Theirs is the primary right to the knowledge uncovered by archaeologists.

There are, of course, better ways to maintain this public "right to know" than by publishing lists of site locations in the newspapers. (We have already said how we feel about *that.*) But newspapers can and should be used to inform the public about archaeology in general. Reporters are often delighted to do "background" articles on topics concerning local archaeology, and they are usually sympathetic if you explain the dangers of identifying sites. A really big archaeological event, such as the full-scale salvage excavation of a future construction site by archaeological society members, might even attract a crew from the local television station, if they are notified in advance.

Another approach to informing the public, and a uniquely creative and satisfying one, is to set up a traveling archaeological display or a permanent museum. This undertaking need not be as complex as it sounds at first. In its very simplest form, an archaeological museum can be little more than an expansion of an individual's artifact collection, housed in a garage, a barn, a spare room, or perhaps in space donated by the town hall or local community college. A traveling display does not even need permanent housing, but is designed to spend a few weeks in each of several locations, such as public libraries, schools, banks, and county fairs. In most areas, a surprising number of public buildings have space for display of educational materials.

No matter how small or how large a display you plan, the important thing is to let the artifacts tell a story about the

The Hollister Adobe Indian Museum is a historic structure converted for use as an archaeological museum by members of the San Luis Obispo County Archaeological Society of California.

life of the people who made them. An elaborate geometric arrangement of 350 stone tools may be impressive or even decorative, but it tells nothing about how or when a particular tool was made, who made it, or what it was used for. A much better display would be a dozen or even half a dozen tools from roughly the same cultural grouping, with drawings and labels showing how the tools related to the culture of their makers. Our culture has taught most members of the public to classify all Indian stone tools as arrowheads, that is, weapons. People are frequently amazed to find that those "weapons" were actually used for fishing, woodworking, engraving, preparing food, leatherworking, or game hunting, and relatively rarely for war. In historic archaeology, too, a limited collection of early kitchen utensils or blacksmith's equipment will tell a better story than a hodgepodge of unrelated items.

A good display, then, is one that has something to say, not one that overwhelms with quantity. There are three basic types of display that are especially effective in presenting coherent information to the viewer:

1. Manufacturing stages of some important cultural item. On a shelf or mounting board, show the raw materials and where they come from locally, the tools used, the techniques of the craft, and an example of the finished product. The last may be a good color photograph of an object owned by a museum or American Indian group, since the beautiful and impressive items like baskets, jewelry, masks, and clothing do not often turn up in private collections. If you specify that the photographs are for a nonprofit educational display, many museums will supply them free or with only a small charge to cover the cost of reproduction.

If you are adept at replication, examples of your work may fit well into a display of this sort. You might, for example, show some authentic finished stone tools, some unflaked raw stone, and several examples of your own work in various stages from rough shaping to final finish. Don't forget to make it clear in the labels which work is yours and which is archaeological.

2. Gathering, processing, or growing of an important food item. A dried oak branch bearing acorns, a few cracked acorns, a mortar and pestle, and a pile of acorn meal, with a caption explaining how the meal was leached with water to remove the tannic acid, would make a simple but excellent example of this kind of display.

3. Dioramas. These are three-dimensional model scenes that show some aspect of early historic or prehistoric life. Your creativity and the accuracy of your research are your only limitations. A diorama uses no authentic artifacts at all. Instead, it shows scenes that may represent anything

from the construction of the Great Serpent Mound or a day in the life of the pueblo at Canyon De Chelly (pronounced De Shay) to typical autumn activities in a Seminole village or a party of Salish preparing to go on a whale hunt. Whatever subject you choose for your diorama, it should accurately represent something from your local area.

Dioramas are viewed either from the side, at about eye level, or from above. The decision probably depends on what sort of display case you can find or make. An expensive glass museum case is not necessary. Old commercial cases or glass-fronted bookcases can sometimes be converted for the purpose, or sheets of clear plastic may be glued together to cover a tabletop display. Even a large

Dr. Maurice Robbins, an avocational who is now Massachusetts State Archaeologist, explains that the dioramas in the Bronson Museum are in the ideal position because they are at eye level.

Photo by Michael E. Roberts

aquarium tank may be used, perhaps with a terrarium landscape.

Unless the case is to be placed right under a window, it will need lighting. The best type of lighting is a hidden fluorescent tube which will light the scene indirectly. Fluorescent light not only uses less electricity, it doesn't generate heat which might damage the display or even constitute a fire hazard.

A side-viewed diorama usually needs a background—a painted scene, or possibly an enlarged color photograph. For the ground surface papier-mâché or modeling clay may be used to build up realistic topography, and then painted. Small stones, sand, and gravel also give realistic textures, and there are many natural materials that, when dried and stuck into the "ground," are useful in giving the impression of low undergrowth, brush, or other vegetation. One of the best of these is sphagnum moss. Larger trees are easily made of well-branched twigs, with foliage made of torn and painted sponge, or various kinds of small branching plants such as pearly everlasting. Asparagus fern from the florist makes excellent evergreen branches when stuck into holes in a vertical twig. (Like all plant materials, asparagus fern should be varnished for preservation.) Every geographical region offers its own unique materials. Paint and glue and an imaginative eye are all you need to set your scene.

When it comes to populating your diorama, you may have more difficulty. Though one may occasionally find sets of lead soldiers (U.S. Cavalry variety) that include acceptable Indians, these are generally expensive and many are insultingly inaccurate physical representations. Of course bright orange skin colors can be repainted, but what is one to do about the almost inevitable feathered war bonnet or loincloth? Even when depicting the Plains groups, by whom these accoutrements were in fact worn on occasion, an encampment of Crows that showed nothing but adult men in war bonnets would be about as ludicrous as a twentieth-century suburban street scene where everyone from postman to housewife was attired in a tall silk hat.

If you buy ready-made figures, therefore, be prepared to make extensive alterations, which may include whittling away inappropriate accessories or headdresses, repainting, and constructing authentic clothing from scraps of leather or cloth. The alternative is to make your own figures out of modeling clay, or out of carved wood if you are a talented whittler. It is probably more respectful of the people you are portraying to use simple, even abstract, figures than to perpetuate gaudy stereotypes.

If you plan to have the sort of museum that is open to the public at specified times, and not on a by-appointment-only

Professionally made diorama showing an Indian village of the Eastern Woodlands, in the Bronson Museum, Attleboro, Massachusetts.

Photo by Michael E. Roberts

All the displays in the Hollister Adobe Indian Museum are the work of avocationals. Nearly everyone can play a useful part, whether it's designing, mounting, researching, labeling, publicizing, doing carpentry, or sweeping and dusting.

basis, there are certain steps you should think of taking. Most elementary is to have locks for display cases. It seems to be a leftover from the "hunting and gathering" stage of human development that there is always someone in any crowd who will walk off with anything that isn't nailed down. Don't put temptation in the way of the public. Likewise, you will have to consider safety and fragility. It is a rule of life that people will try to lean or sit on anything that is of remotely the right height, so provide your displays with signs saying, "Please do not lean on glass," or whatever. Better still, use extra-thick glass or Plexiglas and don't leave anything more destructible than a sixty-pound stone mortar out in the open.

In spite of having to take these protective measures, you will find that there are few things more satisfying than making your own museum. Not only do you get to meet a lot of interesting people and to feel you are contributing to the education of the public, there are sometimes more tangible signs that your work has borne fruit. The authors have known formerly hostile landowners to turn up at the museum with boxes full of artifacts to be identified and cordial invitations to "C'mon out and see where I found 'em." Even lifelong pothunters sometimes see the light when they realize there is more to Native American culture than their own thrill of possession. In the last analysis, a museum is your recognition of the concept that, ultimately, archaeology does indeed belong to the people.

Appendix I
Summary of United States and Canadian Archaeological Law

THE UNITED STATES

Activities which result in alteration of the land's surface—the drilling of test holes; construction of roads, pipelines, and electrical transmission lines; leveling of land at wellheads; the construction of flood control devices, etc.—often result in the destruction of any archaeological sites present at those locations. The lands of the nation are rich in prehistoric and historic remains, and such archaeological sites constitute a finite, nonrenewable, and rapidly vanishing resource. Under current laws, destruction of archaeological sites is specifically prohibited on all lands under federal ownership. It should also be recognized that failure to conduct location and identification surveys for land modification projects receiving federal funding or licensing results in less than full compliance with the requirements of the Antiquities Act of 1906, the National Environmental Policy Act of 1969, the National Historic Preservation Act of 1966, and Executive Order No. 11593. A brief resume of pertinent portions of the existing antiquities legislation is presented below.

The Federal Antiquities Act of 1906

That any person who shall appropriate, excavate, injure, or destroy any historic or prehistoric ruin or monument, or any object of antiquity, situated on lands owned or controlled by the Government of the

United States, without the permission of the Secretary of the Department of the Government having jurisdiction over the lands on which said antiquities are situated, shall upon conviction be fined in a sum of not more than five hundred dollars or be imprisoned for a period of not more than ninety days or shall suffer both fine and imprisonment, in the discretion of the court.

That permits for the examination of ruins, the excavation of archaeological sites, and the gathering of objects of antiquity upon the lands under their respective jurisdictions may be granted by the Secretaries of the Interior, Agriculture, and War to institutions which they may deem properly qualified to conduct such examinations, excavations, or gathering, subject to such rules and regulations as they may prescribe: *Provided,* that the examinations, excavations, and gatherings are undertaken for the benefit of reputable museums, universities, colleges, or other recognized scientific or educational institutions, with a view to increasing the knowledge of such objects, and that the gatherings shall be made for permanent preservation in public museums.

The Historic Sites Act of 1935

. . . it is hereby declared that it is a national policy to preserve for public use historic sites, buildings, and objects of national significance for the inspiration and benefit of the people of the United States.

[Among the numerous duties assigned the Secretary of the Interior and delegated to the National Park Service by this Act are the following:]

Make a survey of historic and archaeologic sites, buildings, and objects for the purpose of determining which possess exceptional value as commemorating or illustrating the history of the United States.

Restore, reconstruct, rehabilitate, preserve, and maintain historic or prehistoric sites, buildings, objects, and properties of national historical or archaeological significance and where deemed desirable establish and maintain museums in connection therewith.

The Historic Preservation Act of 1966

The Secretary of the Interior is authorized to expand and maintain a national register of districts, sites, buildings, structures, and objects significant in American history, architecture, archeology, and culture, hereinafter referred to as the National Register, and to grant funds to States for the purpose of preparing comprehensive statewide historic surveys and plans, in accordance with criteria established by the Secretary, for the preservation, acquisition, and development of such properties.

The Reservoir Salvage Act of 1960 (as amended in 1974)

That it is the purpose of this Act to further the policy set forth in the [Historic Sites Act of 1935] by specifically providing for the preservation of historical and archaeological data (including relics and specimens) which might otherwise be irreparably lost or destroyed as the result of (1) flooding, the building of access roads, the erection of workmen's communities, the relocation of railroads and highways, and other alteration of the terrain caused by the construction of a dam by any agency of the United States, or by any private person or corporation holding a license issued by any such agency or (2) any alteration of the terrain caused as a result of any Federal construction project or Federally licensed project, activity, or program.

The National Environmental Policy Act of 1969

It is the continuing policy of the Federal Government, in cooperation with State and local governments and other concerned public and private organizations, to use all practicable means and measures, including financial and technical assistance, in a manner calculated to foster and promote the general welfare, to create and maintain conditions under which man and nature can exist in productive harmony, and fulfill the social, economic, and other requirements of present and future generations of Americans.

. . . it is the continuing responsibility of the Federal Government to . . . preserve important historic cultural and natural aspects of our national heritage.

. . . all agencies of the Federal Government shall . . . include in every recommendation or report on proposals for legislation and other major Federal actions significantly affecting the quality of the human environment, a detailed statement by the responsible official on—(i) the environmental impact of the proposed action, (ii) any adverse environmental effects which cannot be avoided should the proposal be implemented, (iii) alternatives to the proposed action, (iv) the relationship between local short-term uses of man's environment and the maintenance and enhancement of long-term productivity, and (v) any irreversible and irretrievable commitment of resources which would be involved in the proposed action should it be implemented.

The President's Executive Order 11593

The heads of Federal agencies shall: . . . locate, inventory, and nominate to the Secretary of the Interior all sites, buildings, districts, and objects under their jurisdiction or control that appear to qualify for listing on the National Register of Historic Places.

CANADA

The Dominion of Canada has no unified body of archaeological law for the whole country. Instead, each province makes its own law on the subject, and there is considerable variation. In general, provincial laws are strong on preservation of known historic and prehistoric sites, but less strong on requiring archaeological survey before land-moving or construction operations are begun. See Appendix IV for addresses of agencies responsible for archaeology in the various provinces. They can supply information on applicable law for the territories they cover.

In addition, Canada has a national Archaeological Survey and a preservation agency called Heritage Canada. (Addresses in Appendix IV.) They act as clearinghouses for archaeological information on a national basis (perhaps paralleling the function of the National Register of Historic Places in the United States) and should be notified of any historic or prehistoric sites you locate. The national Archaeological Survey of Canada has a standardized reporting form it will send you for the purpose.

On the other hand, a large portion of Canada's territory (about 45 percent) is classified as Crown Lands, and these areas are protected by regulations put forth by the central government. If you want further information or permission to survey on Canadian Crown Lands, contact Heritage Canada.

Appendix II
Suggestions for Further Reading

Archaeology and Archaeological Resources. Pamphlet published by the Society for American Archaeology. Available from SAA, 1703 New Hampshire Avenue, NW, Washington, D.C. 20009.

Bibby, Geoffrey. *Testimony of the Spade.* New York: Alfred A. Knopf, 1956. Paperback edition, New York: New American Library, 1974.

Binford, Lewis R. *An Archaeological Perspective.* New York: Academic Press, 1972.

Brennan, Louis. *American Dawn: A New Model of American Prehistory.* New York: Macmillan Co., 1970.

————. *Artifacts of Prehistoric America.* Harrisburg, Pa.: Stackpole Books, 1975.

Brothwell, Don, and Higgs, Eric, eds. *Science in Archaeology.* London: Thames & Hudson, 1963.

Brown, Dee. *Bury My Heart at Wounded Knee: An Indian History of the American West.* New York: Holt, Rinehart and Winston, 1971. Paperback edition, New York: Bantam Books, 1972.

Ceram, C. W. *God, Graves and Scholars,* rev. ed. New York: Alfred A. Knopf, 1967. Paperback edition, New York: Bantam Books, 1972.

Clark, Grahame. *Archaeology and Society.* New York: Barnes & Noble, 1969. Paperback.

Coles, John. *Archaeology by Experiment.* New York: Charles Scribner's Sons, 1974.

————. *Field Archaeology in Britain.* New York: Barnes & Noble, 1972.

Coon, Carleton. *The Hunting Peoples.* Boston: Atlantic Monthly Press, 1971. Paperback edition, Boston: Little, Brown & Co., 1972.

Deuel, Leo. *Conquistadors Without Swords: Archaeologists in the Americas.* New York: Schocken Books, 1974. Paperback.

Dockstader, Frederick. *Indian Art in North America.* New York: New York Graphic Society, 1961. (Out of print.)

Doran, James E., and Hodson, Frank R. *Mathematics and Computers in Archaeology.* Cambridge, Mass.: Harvard University Press, 1975.

Feder, Norman. *American Indian Art.* New York: Henry N. Abrams, 1971.

Frison, George C. *The Casper Site: A Hell Gap Bison Kill on the High Plains.* New York: Academic Press, 1974.

Grant, Campbell. *Rock Art of the American Indian.* New York: Apollo Editions, 1972. Paperback.

Heizer, Robert F., and Graham, John A. *A Guide to Field Methods in Archaeology.* Palo Alto, Calif.: National Press, 1967. (Out of print.)

Hodges, Henry. *Artifacts: An Introduction to Early Materials and Technology.* New York: Humanities Press, 1964.

King, Thomas F. *The Citizen Activist and Cultural Resources: A Guide to Strategies.* Reprint published by and available from the New York Archaeological Council, 4242 Ridge Lea Road, Buffalo, N.Y. 14226.

King, Thomas F., et al. *Anthropology and Historic Preservation: Caring for Culture's Clutter.* New York: Academic Press, 1977.

Kirk, Ruth, with Daugherty, Richard. *Hunters of the Whale: An Adventure in Northwest Coast Archaeology.* New York: William Morrow & Co., 1974.

Kroeber, Theodora. *Ishi in Two Worlds: A Biography of the Last Wild Indian in North America.* Berkeley: University of California Press, 1962. Paperback.

Lee, Richard B., and Devore, Irven, eds. *Man the Hunter.* Chicago: Aldine Publishing Co., 1968. Paperback.

Lipe, William D. "A Conservation Model for American Archaeology." *The Kiva* 39 (1974): nos. 3–4.

Lipe, William D., and Lindsay, Alexander J., eds. *Proceedings of the 1974 Cultural Resource Management Conference.* Museum of Northern Arizona Technical Series No. 14, The Northern Arizona Society of Science and Art, Flagstaff, Arizona.

Lyford, Carrie A. *Quill and Beadwork of the Western Sioux.* Bureau of Indian Affairs, U.S. Department of the Interior, Washington, D.C.

Mallery, Garrick. *Picture-Writing of the American Indians.* 2 vols. New York: Dover Books, 1972. Paperback.

McGimsey, Charles R. III. *Public Archaeology.* New York: Seminar Press, 1972.

McManamon, Francis P. *Archeology and Public Planning.* Pamphlet published by the Massachusetts Historical Commission in 1976. Available from MHC, 294 Washington Street, Boston, Mass. 02108.

Michels, Joseph W. *Dating Methods in Archaeology.* New York: Academic Press, 1973.

Miles, Charles. *Indian and Eskimo Artifacts of North America.* New York: Bonanza Books, 1963. (Out of print.)

Pyddoke, Edward, ed. *The Scientist and Archaeology.* New York: Roy Publishers, 1963. (Out of print.)

Rahtz, Philip A. *Rescue Archaeology.* Harmondsworth, England: Penguin Books, 1974. Paperback.

Roberts, Michael E. *Handbook of Archaeological Survey.* Published by and available from the San Luis Obispo County Archaeological Society, Box 109, San Luis Obispo, Calif. 93406.

Semenov, S. A. *Prehistoric Technology.* New York: Barnes & Noble, 1976.

South, Stanley. *Method and Theory in Historical Archaeology.* New York: Academic Press, 1976.

Tamarin, Alfred. *We Have Not Vanished: Eastern Indians of the United States.* Chicago: Follett, 1974.

Tite, M. S. *Methods of Physical Examination in Archaeology.* New York: Academic Press, 1972.

Willey, Gordon R. *Introduction to American Archaeology: Volume I, North and Middle America.* Englewood Cliffs, N.J.: Prentice-Hall, 1966.

Willey, Gordon R., and Phillips, Philip. *Method and Theory in American Archaeology.* Chicago: University of Chicago Press, 1962. Paperback.

Appendix III

A Guide to Typical Prehistoric Artifacts of North America by Region

A warning about what we call typical artifacts: Like all handmade objects, prehistoric artifacts exhibit a great deal of variation; the illustrations can only show generalized types, and the examples you find in the field are likely to be thicker, thinner, lumpier, larger, smaller, sharper, blunter, or less well shaped than the pictured specimens. If an archaeologist of the future described a "Ford Car Tradition," for instance, the illustration might show only a typical Ford sedan, no coupes, no convertibles, no wagons, no pickups, no custom bodies, let alone the differences among the Tin Lizzie, Mustang, Thunderbird, Edsel, and so on.

Another thing to remember about the artifacts we have labeled typical is that they often appear in association with much more ordinary forms that could come from any area or period. The only characteristic that makes artifacts typical is that they are particularly identifiable with a particular area or time. This doesn't mean that they were the most impressive, the most attractive, or even the most numerous remains of a particular tradition.

In each regional section we have included information on rock art, not because it is necessarily typical, but because it is so visible, well known, and permanent—at least when

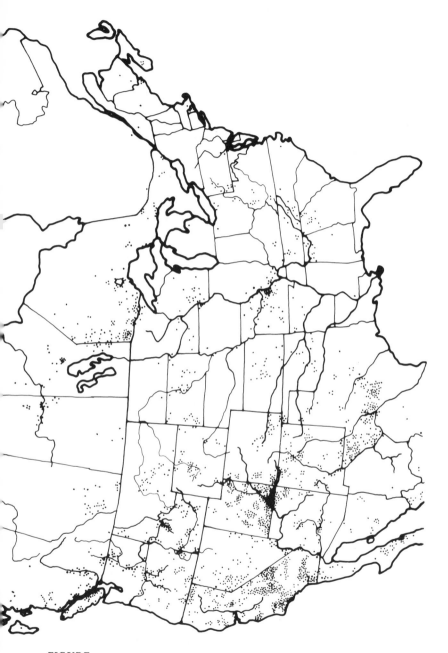

FIGURE 19

Distribution of rock art sites in the United States and Canada (after Campbell Grant)

not subjected to vandalism, weather, and the well-meaning but harmful practice of chalk outlining.

We have omitted artifacts of the Paleo-Indian period from this appendix because they have already been both described and illustrated in chapter 4. Do not forget, however, that Clovis, Sandia, Folsom, and Old Cordilleran points lurk somewhere in the background of each of the areas discussed below.

TYPICAL ARTIFACTS OF THE SOUTHWEST

1. Later Paleo-Indian or Big Game Hunting: Stone points of the western part of the area pass directly from Clovis to Archaic types. In the east are found points similar to those of the Later Paleo Tradition of the Great Plains (see below).

2. Western Archaic: Stone points, generally stemmed and notched, which were usually hafted for use as spears or atlatl darts. The mano (or grinding stone) and millingstone (or grinding surface) are typical food-processing utensils. Baskets, netting, and matting are typical *in combination with* manos and millingstones.

3. Mogollon: Pottery is plain or a polished red ware. Tubular stone pipes for smoking; balls and discs of stone of unknown purpose. Later pottery is painted red on brown.

4. Hohokam: Pottery is red on buff (sometimes red on yellow) with geometrical designs. Polished and grooved stone axes. Finely worked ground utensils of stone. Stone or clay figurines showing possible Mexican influence. Later pottery is quite large and figurines depict heads only. Etched designs on shell.

5. Anasazi

a. Basketmaker: Artifacts similar to those of the Western Archaic, but associated with house pits (indicating a seden-

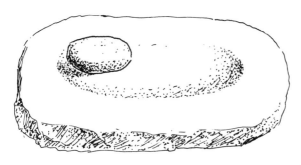

Mano and millingstone

Mogollon pot

Mogollon pipe

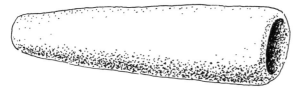

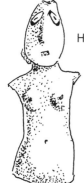

Hohokam figurine

Hohokam point

FIGURE 20
Southwest

251

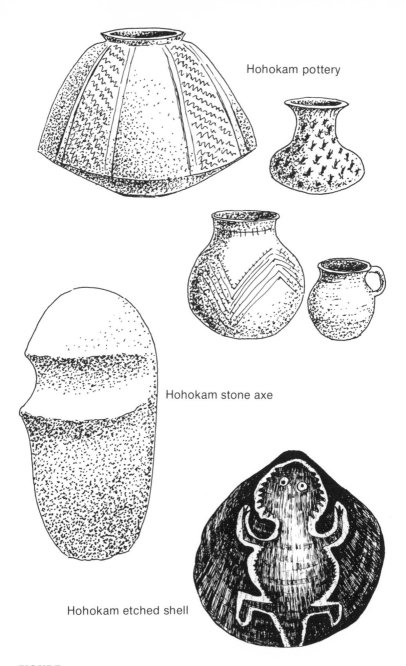

Hohokam pottery

Hohokam stone axe

Hohokam etched shell

FIGURE 21
Southwest

tary life). Pottery black on gray. Smaller points for arrows, similar to Pueblo.

b. Pueblo: Early phase pottery is either corrugated or glazed black on white. Cotton fabrics (preserved in dry caves). Basketry disappears. Pottery vessels in human or animal shape (effigy vessels), or in stirrup form, or shaped like hollow rings. May have been influenced by Mississippian Tradition (see Eastern Woodlands). Later, many-colored (polychrome) pottery and artwork in polished stone such as turquoise. Later, corrugated cooking ware dies out and painted designs on pottery and house walls become much more elaborate. In the final phase glazed pottery goes out of style, but the real test is the tradition's reduced area at this period. Points are small, stemmed and notched.

6. Patayan: Rough brown pottery, sometimes painted red. Tools are always flaked stone, never ground. Shells from Pacific coast are occasionally found.

7. Later Western Archaic: Same artifacts as Western Archaic, except that atlatl points are replaced by arrow points and there is some very crude pottery.

8. Athapaskan: Pottery with conical bases. Compare pottery of Eastern Woodlands.

Rock Art of the Southwest

Both pictographs and petroglyphs are very common throughout the region, although it is usually impossible to associate them with a particular tradition. In the northern areas, pecked human or semihuman figures may be life-size or larger, appearing most often on sandstone cliff faces. A little farther south are seen mummylike figures (having heads but no limbs). They may be either pecked or painted and the prevalent colors are red-brown and white. In the territory of the Pueblo Tradition, designs are often birds or

Anasazi pottery

Pueblo points

FIGURE 22
Southwest

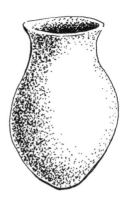

Pueblo
corrugated pot

Athapaskan
pot

FIGURE 23

Southwest

animals similar to those appearing on Pueblo pottery. Katchina masks and figures are also found. In what is now Navajo country, rock designs often resemble those of modern Navajo arts such as sand painting. To the southeast, outside the actual Pueblo area as defined by archaeology, pecked designs very much like those of the Pueblos are found on outcroppings of basaltic rock.

In contrast to the foregoing examples, rock art sites of the southernmost part of the area occur most frequently in rock shelters, where popular subjects are stylized animals and mummylike designs. The extreme Southwest exhibits an entirely different kind of art, in which figures up to 160 feet long are constructed on the ground by removing gravel to expose the light-colored soil beneath. (The technique bears a startling resemblance to that used in making the famous "lines of Nazca," which lie four thousand miles away in the uplands of Peru.)

TYPICAL ARTIFACTS OF THE GREAT BASIN

The general chronology of the Great Basin has been successfully defined by means of certain types of projectile points that have been found in association with materials datable by the carbon-14 method (see chapter 9). Thus in this particular case artifacts are typical of periods rather than merely of cultural traditions.

1. Paleo-Indian: Fluted points of the Big Game Hunting types and some willow-leaf-shaped points similar to those of the Old Cordilleran—10,000 to 7000 B.C. and probably very much earlier. See the introduction to chapter 4.

2. Western Pluvial Lakes: Black Rock point, like an unfluted Folsom point with a concave base. Chipped stone crescents that may or may not be projectile points, found in association with ancient lakes—9000 to 6500 B.C.

3. Western Archaic: Northern Side-notched points, relatively large triangular shape; notches in the sides, presumably for hafting—5000 to 2000 B.C. Humboldt points, leaf-shaped with concave or notched base—4000 to 1000 B.C. Pinto points, triangular with corner notches and concave base—3500 to 500 B.C. Elko points, similar to Pinto but generally wider—2000 to 1200 B.C. Gypsum points, triangular with pointed stem—1700 to 250 B.C. Rose Spring/Eastgate points, long and triangular with stem; Rose Spring stems are narrower at base, Eastgate stems are wider—550 B.C. to historic times. Desert Side-notched points, small triangles with notches on sides—A.D. 250 to historic times. Cottonwood points, small triangles with flat or concave base—A.D. 1200 to historic times.

Rock Art of the Great Basin

Rock art of the Great Basin is most often found on basaltic rock surfaces when the figures are pecked or scratched.

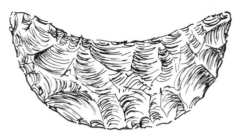

Western Pluvial Lakes
chipped stone crescent

Northern
Side-notched
point

Black Rock
point

Humboldt
point

Pinto
point

Elko point

FIGURE 24
Great Basin

Gypsum
point

Rose Spring
point

Eastgate
point

Desert
Side-notched
point

Cottonwood
point

FIGURE 25
Great Basin

Rock walls offering protection from the weather are the favored sites for pictographs. However, this may be nothing more than a reflection of the fact that painted surfaces have survived only in sheltered locations. In the northern part of the region designs are very simple, with meandering lines, zigzags, concentric circles, and some animal shapes. Southern Nevada and southeastern California contain impressive petroglyphs showing vast herds of Rocky Mountain or bighorn sheep, mounted men, and men armed with atlatls or bows and arrows, combined with more abstract designs such as are found on basketry. To the east, rock art indicates the influence of the Pueblo Tradition, with its katchinas and semihuman triangular figures.

TYPICAL ARTIFACTS OF THE INTERIOR PLATEAU

1. Paleo-Indian
a. Old Cordilleran (Early Tradition): This large, leaf-shaped unfluted point has already been described (see page 66 for drawing). Associated with Old Cordilleran points in the Interior Plateau are curious, bifacially flaked tools nearly circular in outline. Their function is unknown.
b. Big Game Hunting: Fluted points have not been found in the region. However, in a few locations points have turned up which bear a close resemblance to those that evolve directly from fluted points in other regions. Examples are the Lind Coulee point (leaf-shaped, with a very noticeable indentation at the base) and Windust (somewhat like Hell Gap). Thus there is just a suggestion that the Big Game Hunting Tradition may have existed in the region.
2. Middle Tradition: Stemmed and notched points. Ground and polished stone tools such as mauls. Stone fishing sinkers with notched sides. L-shaped bone awls.
3. Late Tradition: Points are similar in style to Middle Tradition examples, but tend to be smaller as if for use with bow and arrow; triangular; very narrow outlines are typical. Long straight stone pipes, flaring at the end.

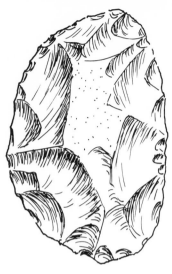

Early Tradition
circular bifacial tool

Lind
Coulee
point

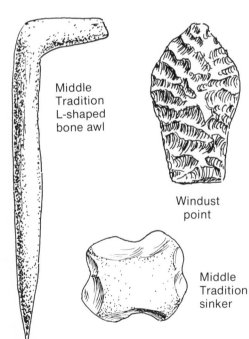

Middle
Tradition
L-shaped
bone awl

Windust
point

Middle
Tradition
sinker

Middle
Tradition
ground and
polished
stone maul

FIGURE 26
Interior Plateau

Late
Tradition
triangular
point

Late Tradition
stemmed point

Late
Tradition
stone pipe

FIGURE 27

Interior Plateau

Rock Art of the Interior Plateau

Both pecked and painted rock art are well represented in
the area, where the kind of stone that is available seems to
dictate the distribution of each type. In areas where there
is sandstone, pecking predominates, while the harder gra-
nitic rocks are more often painted. Styles tend to resemble
those of other regions on the area's borders. Thus the
influence of the Great Plains dominates in the east, that of
the Great Basin in the south, and that of the Northwest
Coast in the west.

261

In the Fraser River Canyon are found highly naturalistic renderings (both pecked and painted) of men, bighorn sheep, and other animals. Similar artwork occurs somewhat to the east, where the renderings may include horsemen. In the area of the upper Columbia River, styles become much more sophisticated and abstract, with new design elements such as humanoid figures. In the eastern part of the region, rock art shows tipis, arrows, game animals, and human figures such as might be found in the Great Plains. A favored site is large rock outcroppings overlooking lakes. Southward, designs of circles, dots, and bighorn sheep are reminiscent of those in the Great Basin.

Because the Interior Plateau receives relatively little rainfall, modern man has constructed a number of large dams there. These have inundated many rock art sites, which tend to be located near prehistoric village sites of fishing camps beside rivers.

TYPICAL ARTIFACTS OF THE NORTHWEST COAST

Old Cordilleran points have been described elsewhere. Because there is really no well-defined sequence of traditions in the area, there is, as it were, little for artifacts to be typical *of.* However, it is possible to follow the usual evolution of point types from large un-tanged heads of thrusting spears through the increasingly small stemmed, notched, or flared points used for throwing spears, atlatl darts, and finally arrow points and thus make a relative estimate of the age of the site. A further indication is the presence of ground slate artifacts and barbed harpoons in earlier sites and toggle harpoons in later ones. Available evidence indicates that decoration became progressively finer with time, culminating in the masks, totem poles, and carved wooden or bone articles produced during a cultural flowering of a relatively late period.

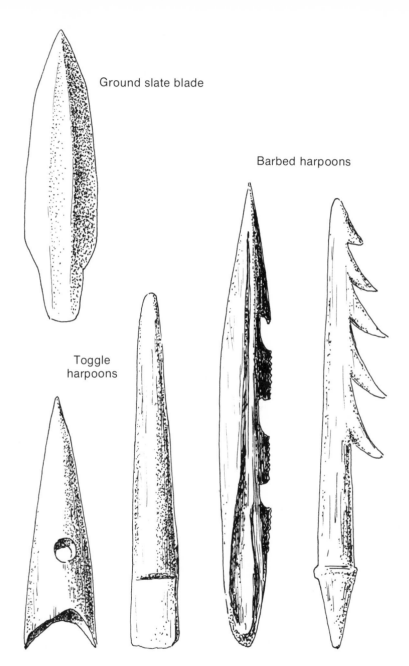

Ground slate blade

Barbed harpoons

Toggle
harpoons

FIGURE 28
Northwest Coast

263

Rock Art of the Northwest Coast

Both pictographs and petroglyphs occur. The latter are most often found on beach boulders and represent totemic and clan symbols of tribal groups in the area. Further inland are found painted versions of typical Northwest Coast motifs of the late period, similar to those found on masks, totem poles, wooden articles, and so on. They include canoes, salmon, killer whales, deer, a two-headed critter with a serpentine body, and various imaginary monsters. In some areas both art forms appear, and the petroglyphs are generally considered to be the older type.

Bird design

Carved mask

Killer whale design

FIGURE 29
Northwest Coast

TYPICAL ARTIFACTS OF CALIFORNIA

1. Later Paleo-Indian, Millingstone, or Early Period: The situation here is similar to that of the Interior Plateau, namely, that some areas show Clovis/Folsom points while others appear to feature points of the Old Cordilleran. Successors of both traditions are found in the Millingstone or Early Period along with crude manos and millingstones. (In California and the Southwest, millingstones are often called metates—meh-TAH-tehs.) Also typical are beads of olivella shell with the spire cut off, bone awls, large triangular points, "cogstones" of unknown function, and stone crescents comparable to those of the Great Basin (see Figure 24, page 257).

2. Hunting Tradition or Middle Period: Mortars and pestles of ground stone (not necessarily of the bedrock type); expanded-base drills. Shell and stone disc beads. Leaf-shaped points or points with narrow stems. Single-pipe bone whistles (compare below). Circular abalone shell fishhooks. Basket mortars (relatively shallow stone mortars with remains of black asphaltum around the edge where baskets were attached).

3. Late Period: Exotic abalone shell decorations. Shell disc beads become smaller. Bone whistles of several pipes lashed together in the style of a Pan pipe. On the coast, points are small, willow-leaf-shaped or with concave bases, while inland stemmed and notched points with deeply serrated edges are found. Carved steatite effigies, elaborate stone bowls and pestles. Finely done basketry.

Rock Art of California

California's rock art is among the richest and most complex in the world, let alone North America. In terms of abstraction alone, it is almost impossible to describe accu-

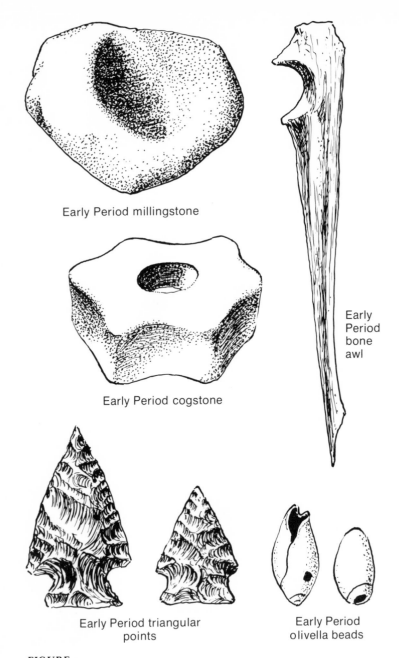

Early Period millingstone

Early Period cogstone

Early
Period
bone
awl

Early Period triangular
points

Early Period
olivella beads

FIGURE 30
California

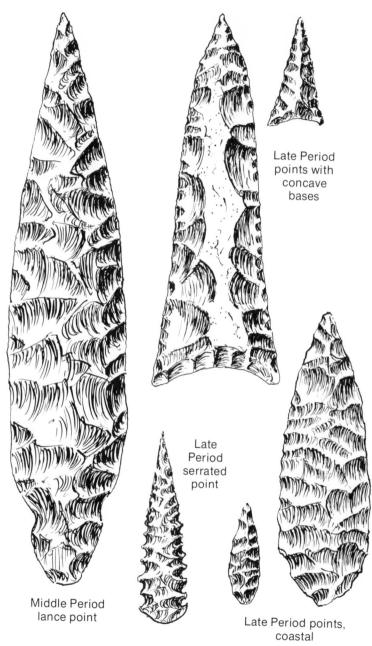

Late Period
points with
concave
bases

Late
Period
serrated
point

Middle Period
lance point

Late Period points,
coastal

FIGURE 31
California

267

Late Period basket (may be post-contact)

Late Period
Pan pipe

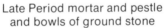

Late Period mortar and pestle
and bowls of ground stone

FIGURE 32
California

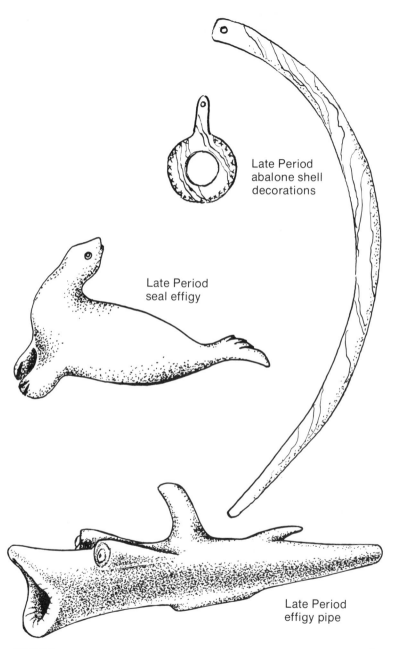

Late Period
abalone shell
decorations

Late Period
seal effigy

Late Period
effigy pipe

FIGURE 33
California

269

rately, since one man's "salamander between two electric hot-plates" is another's "one-eyed man carrying two bongo drums" and neither has any connection with the artist's original intention. Colors are diverse, including black, white, gray, red ochre, yellow ochre, and sepentine green. Pictographs are more generally found west of the Sierras and south of the San Joaquin Valley, while petroglyphs predominate in the rest of the region. Among the latter, circles, rakes, and bear and bird tracks, as well as pit and groove designs, occur in areas north of San Francisco, where painting is extremely rare. Favored sites in this area are isolated boulders on the slopes of the Sierras. Pit and groove designs are also found in the southern part of the state, where they often appear on outcrops of serpentine.

However, the real glory of California rock art is found in that central part of the area formerly occupied by the Chumash Indians. There, on cliff faces and inside rock shelters, are to be found bewildering and awesome paintings of up to six colors and as long as a hundred feet. Common motifs are the circle and all its variations—wheels, spokes, rays, and spirals—and the rattlesnake, sometimes reduced to a string of linked diamonds. In addition there are endless abstract renderings of human figures, lizards, bears, whales, frogs, and other creatures, as well as phantasmagorical visions of little men with rakes for hands, insects, birds of prey, bug-eyed monsters, hands, and arrows. The paintings are bright, sharp, intricate, technically competent. We have almost no clues to their meaning or purpose, except that in a few cases there seem to be clear references to constellations, comets, or other celestial objects. These latter may someday help to date the Chumash pictographs, at least, but we know almost nothing at present about their age. It is generally agreed, however, that they cannot be extremely ancient or they would not appear so fresh and bright (at least in those cases where they have not been scrawled over or shot at by vandals). One of the paintings unquestionably shows a ship with masts and another depicts men on horseback, so that both must be of the early historic period.

Elsewhere, for example on the islands of the Santa Barbara Channel and in the coastal parts of Chumash territory, paintings and petroglyphs are more realistic and emphasize a variety of marine creatures such as the whale, swordfish, and porpoise. Southward of this area, complex maze designs are found pecked onto rock outcroppings.

TYPICAL ARTIFACTS OF THE GREAT PLAINS

1. Later Paleo-Indian or Plano: Local forms that evolved after Clovis and Folsom points disappeared include the so-called Cody knife, an indescribable triangular object (see Figure 34). More conventional point types include Midland and Plainview, similar to Folsom but without the fluting. Midland points have a somewhat bigger "bite" taken out of the base. Agate Basin, Hell Gap, and Scotts Bluff points are all generally lance-shaped. Scotts Bluff points have "shoulders," whereas Hell Gap points have an obvious stem and Agate Basin points are tapered. Meserve and Dalton points are triangular, with possible short flutings extending from the base. The lower third of the Dalton point has a curious "fishtail" shape.

2. Plains Archaic: Some McKean points are lance-shaped; other typical forms are stemmed or notched for use with the atlatl, but have not been reliably divided into named types. Manos and millingstones are often found associated.

3. Woodlands: Artifacts of the Archaic types persist, but are now combined with round- or conical-based pots, similar to those of the Eastern Woodlands. (Pottery may have arrived in the region before agriculture.) Hoes made from

Cody knife

Midland
point

Plainview
point

Agate Basin
point

Hell Gap
point

Scotts
Bluff
point

FIGURE 34
Great Plains

Meserve
point

McKean
point

Plains Village
bone fishhook

Dalton point

Hoe head made of buffalo
shoulder blade,
Woodlands

Plains Village pot

FIGURE 35
Great Plains

273

the shoulder blades of the buffalo indicate agricultural activity.

4. Plains Village: Round-based pottery. Bone fishhooks in riverside sites.

Rock Art of the Great Plains

By their very nature, plains are flat or rolling land not very well supplied with the kinds of cliff faces or boulders that invite rock art. Where available, however, both sandstone bluffs and "glacial erratics" (boulders left by the retreating ice masses) have been used for the purpose. In the northern part of the area, and often in association with buffalo jumps, are found pictographs in black and red, showing an assortment of realistic and abstract human and animal figures. On the sandstone cliffs along the Missouri River there are carved (and, rarely, painted) designs very like those known from the painted buffalo robes of many Plains Indian groups. Montana, Wyoming, and the Dakotas display men holding round shields, also a variety of game animals and horsemen, both carved and painted. In central Wyoming occurs a complex of carvings showing humanoid figures in fantastic headdresses, abstract bighorn sheep, and other designs. The style is reminiscent of petroglyphs that are found in both central California and the Great Basin. Art of the eastern Plains reflects the styles of the Eastern Woodlands, especially in footprints and handprints, turkey tracks, bear tracks, etc. Curiously, the same sort of rock art appears in an isolated area of northeastern Nebraska. In this case, the explanation is known. The artists were members of the Winnebago tribal group who were exiled there by the U.S. government after being dispossessed from their ancestral territories in Wisconsin.

TYPICAL ARTIFACTS OF THE EASTERN WOODLANDS

1. Later Paleo-Indian: Lineal descendants of the Clovis and Folsom points include the Cumberland point, fluted, shorter than Clovis, with "ears" or a "fishtail"; and the extraordinary Dalton point, with its narrow triangular point sitting on a fluted "fishtail" base. (See Figure 35.)

2. Archaic: Early points stemmed and notched for use with the atlatl, such as Hardaway-Dalton, similar to Dalton but unfluted and having point much shorter and wider in proportion to base; Eva, of which there are two forms, stemmed and side-notched; and Palmer Corner-notched, a shorter triangular point with a flat base. The middle period was characterized by fine polished stone objects such as "banner stones," supposedly atlatl weights, and "bird stones," effigy stones pierced with lengthwise holes, possibly for the same purpose. Also adzes, gouges, and full-grooved axes. Projectile points are Neville and Stark from New England, the first flat-based and corner-notched, the second round-based with a shoulder. In the Great Lakes area, points may be made of copper, socketed and rattailed. Other copper articles appear in forms similar to their stone counterparts elsewhere. In other regions relatively large stemmed and notched points are found, an example of which is the Savannah River point, a hefty object with a stem and incurved base, found in the Southern Appalachian region. Some points are also made of ground slate. The late period introduced pottery (fiber-tempered), the ancestral style being called Vinette I and having a conical base. The ground stone ulu or curved-blade knife is also typical. Point types are Atlantic, medium-sized with a simple stem, and Susquehannah, small with a flared stem.

3. Woodlands: Pottery becomes generally more elaborate in decoration, sometimes with a flat rather than a conical base. Examples: Half Moon style from Pennsylvania

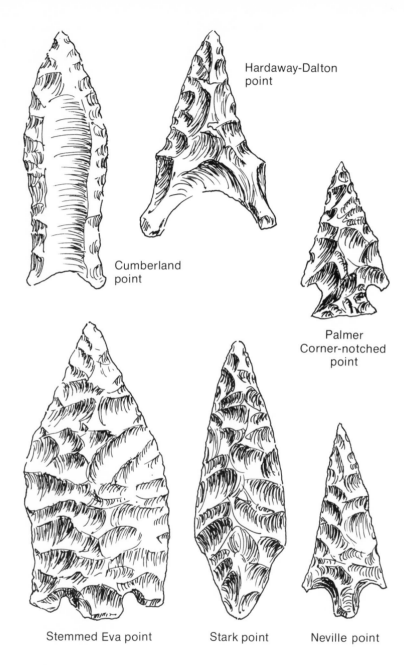

Hardaway-Dalton point

Cumberland point

Palmer Corner-notched point

Stemmed Eva point

Stark point

Neville point

FIGURE 36
Eastern Woodlands

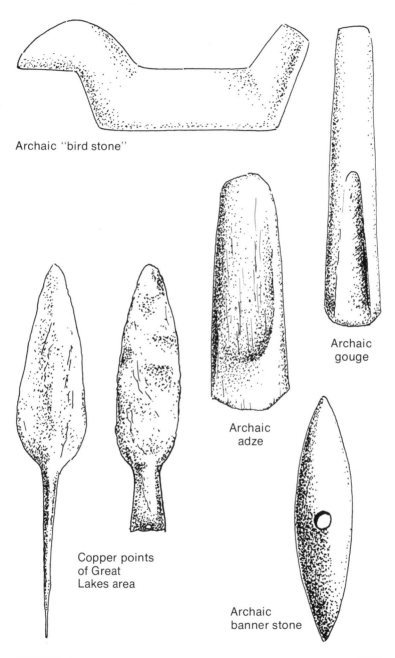

Archaic "bird stone"

Archaic
gouge

Archaic
adze

Copper points
of Great
Lakes area

Archaic
banner stone

FIGURE 37   277
Eastern Woodlands

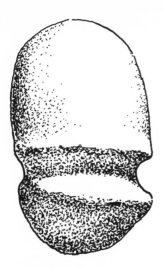

Archaic full-grooved axe

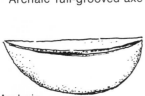

Archaic
ground stone ulu

Savannah River point

Archaic
ground
slate
point

Atlantic
point

Susquehanna
point

FIGURE 38
Eastern Woodlands

(flat-bottomed) and Forsyth style from Alabama (footed). Variations on these styles persist into historic times in outlying areas. Point types tend to be smaller, indicating use with the bow and arrow, and may have either side notches, corner notches, or contracting stems. Others are purely triangular.

a. Adena: Polished stone artifacts include reel-shaped (or, one might say, X-shaped) gorgets, the ungrooved axe or celt, stone tablets generally engraved with birdlike figures, and a particular style of flat-based grit-tempered pot called Montgomery Incised. Copper is generally in the form of jewelry.

b. Hopewell: Pottery is distinctive in shape and decoration, frequently having an expanded or flaring rim and with bases rounded, flattened, or footed. Designs are stamped or incised, with rather simple geometric motifs for everyday use, but with elaborate, swirling abstract or animal designs for funerary purposes. Exotic materials such as obsidian were apparently traded from distant points. Sheets of copper and mica were used to make cutout forms of geometric or animal shape and unknown purpose. So-called Monitor pipes for smoking are in the form of platforms with effigies carved on the top and are made of stone. They are peculiar in that the effigies face the user rather than the observer. Hopewellian points are large, broad-bladed, side-notched or corner-notched, and not vastly different from those familiar in the area from late Archaic through Woodlands deposits.

4. Mississippian: Pottery may be plain or painted with swirling or animal designs or in effigy forms not unlike the Hopewellian. New features are handles and unusual shapes such as the stirrup vessel, "Siamese twin" pot, and tripod bottle. Shell is used for temper. Polished stone axes are monolithic—made from a single stone, haft and all.

Southern Cult: Identified more by design motifs on exist-

 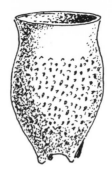 

Vinette I pot   Forsyth pot   Half Moon pot

Side-notched
Woodlands
point

Corner-notched
Woodlands
point

Contracting-
stemmed
Woodlands
point

Triangular Woodlands
point

FIGURE 39
Eastern Woodlands

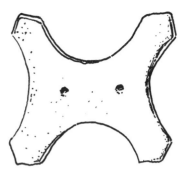

Adena polished stone gorget

Adena
celt

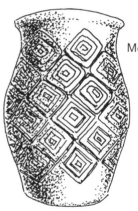

Montgomery
Incised
pot

Adena
engraved stone tablet

Hopewell
pottery

FIGURE 40
Eastern Woodlands

281

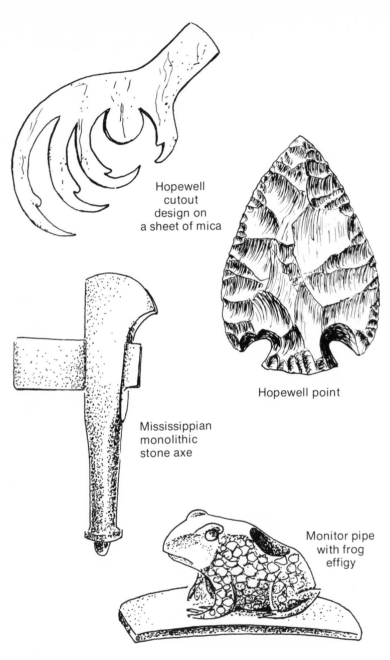

Hopewell cutout design on a sheet of mica

Hopewell point

Mississippian monolithic stone axe

Monitor pipe with frog effigy

FIGURE 41
Eastern Woodlands

Mississippian
effigy bowl

Mississippian
pot with handles

Mississippian
tripod
bottle

Mississippian
stirrup
vessel

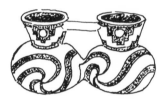

Mississippian
"Siamese twin"
pots

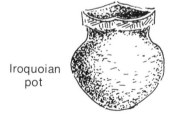

Iroquoian
pot

Arkansas
pot

Florida bowl

FIGURE 42
Eastern Woodlands

283

ing artifacts (see Figure 12, page 101) than by a change in form or function.

Outlying areas, later Woodlands Tradition: In western Florida, shallow, open-mouthed bowls. In the transitional area between the Plains and the Woodlands, roughly in northeastern Texas and southwestern Arkansas, is found engraved, polished black pottery. In the northeast, there is Iroquoian pottery with rounded bases and castellated rims.

Rock Art of the Eastern Woodlands

Rock art is comparatively sparse in the region except for a considerable concentration around the Ohio and Mississippi rivers and their tributaries. Most examples are pecked rather than painted. Even though sites tend to cluster around Adena, Hopewell, and Mississippian centers, the design elements are generally not closely related. They include thunderbirds, hands, footprints (human), bird and animal tracks, and meandering lines. In a few areas recognizable Southern Cult motifs may be seen. In the Southern Appalachian area is found a style much like the pit and groove designs of the Southwest and California, joined with concentric circles, animal tracks, and meanders. Some local authorities and even guidebooks attribute rock art of the east coast to anyone from Atlanteans to Norsemen, but there is no evidence at all that the carvings are anything but what they seem—the unaided work of various Native American peoples.

TYPICAL ARTIFACTS OF THE ARCTIC & SUBARCTIC

1. Eastern Subarctic: Virtually the same as those of the Eastern Woodlands, up through the Archaic Tradition.

2. Later Paleo-Indian (elsewhere): Points very like those called Agate Basin and Plainview, as already described (see

page 271). These may continue into the next tradition below.

3. Northwest Micro-blade: Small (generally less than 10 centimeters) blade tools, unretouched along the edges and with parallel sides, usually of very high quality obsidian. Various stemmed and notched points.

4. Arctic Small Tool: Similar in scale to those above, but much more finely flaked and of more familiar types.

5. Denetasiro: Polished stone tools suitable for woodcutting. Large quantities of bone and antler tools. Some copper.

6. Eskimo: Large quantities of carved walrus ivory. Early work is more abstract; later pieces are more realistic and generally plainer.

Rock Art of the Arctic and Subarctic

In the Eskimo area rock art has a curiously incidental quality, as if the various sites were only vaguely related to each other. Both petroglyphs and pictographs occur in isolated locations rather than in clusters. The latter are usually painted in red only. Designs are often those of masks or game animals. In some places there are human faces consisting of features only, without an outline. Some carvings appear to be little more than doodles containing parallel grooves, spirals, or dots. Certain Eskimo informants have stated that their representations of game animals were a part of the magic connected with the hunt.

In the Subarctic the emphasis is on naturalistic pecked and painted art showing large game animals, canoes, and some objects of historic date such as rifles. In the easternmost regions such as Nova Scotia there are some highly abstract petroglyphs attributed to the Micmac people.

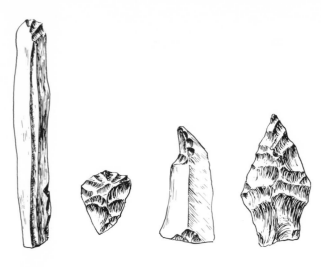

Northwest Micro-blades

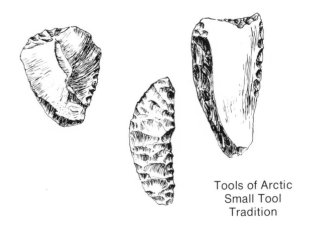

Tools of Arctic
Small Tool
Tradition

FIGURE 43
Arctic and Subarctic

Early Eskimo carved ivory polar bear

Late Eskimo carved bone snow goggles

Denetasiro bone tools

Early
Eskimo
carved
ivory
harpoon
point and
socket

FIGURE 44
Arctic and Subarctic

Appendix IV
Useful Addresses

PROFESSIONAL SOCIETIES

American Anthropological
Association (AAA)
1703 New Hampshire Avenue,
NW
Washington, D.C. 20009
Membership includes subscription to *The American Anthropologist*.

American Society for
Conservation Archaeology
(ASCA)
c/o Alexander J. Lindsay, Jr.
Treasurer, ASCA
Museum of Northern Arizona
Route 4, Box 720
Flagstaff, Arizona 86001
Membership includes subscription to ASCA newsletter. Individual membership: $10.00.

Archaeological Institute of
America
100 Washington Square East
New York, New York 10003

Association for Field Archaeology
(AFA)
c/o the Secretary, AFA
Department of Ancient Near
Eastern Antiquities
Metropolitan Museum of Art
Fifth Avenue at 82nd Street
New York, New York 10028

Society for American Archaeology
(SAA)
1703 New Hampshire Avenue,
NW
Washington, D.C. 20009
Membership includes subscription to *American Antiquity*. Individual membership: $15.00.

Society for Historical Archaeology
(SHA)
Michael J. Rodeffer, Secretary/
Treasurer

Ninety Six Historic Site
Box 418
Ninety Six, South Carolina 29666

Society for Industrial Archaeology
(SIA)
Treasurer, SIA
Room 5020, National Museum of
History and Technology
Washington, D.C. 20560
Individual membership: $15.00.

ARCHAEOLOGICAL OFFICERS AND AGENCIES

NOTE:
As of this writing the office of State
Archaeologist has not yet been
filled in all states.

U.S. State Archaeologists

Douglas Reger
State Archaeologist
Department of Natural Resources
323 East Fourth Avenue
Anchorage, Alaska 99501

Hester Davis
State Archaeologist
Arkansas Archaeological Survey
University of Arkansas
Fayetteville, Arkansas 72701

Francis Riddell
State Archaeologist
Department of Parks and
Recreation
Box 2390
Sacramento, California 95811

Bruce Rippeteau
State Archaeologist
Colorado State Museum
200 14th Avenue
Denver, Colorado 80203

Douglas F. Jordan
State Archaeologist
University of Connecticut
Storrs, Connecticut 06268

Ronald Thomas
State Archaeologist
Hall of Records
Dover, Delaware 19901

L. Rose Morrell
State Archaeologist
Florida Department of State
Tallahassee, Florida 32304

Lewis Larson
State Archaeologist
Office of Planning and Research
Department of Natural Resources
270 Washington Street, SW
Atlanta, Georgia 30334

Dr. James Kellar
State Archaeologist
Department of Anthropology
Indiana University
Bloomington, Indiana 47401

Duane C. Anderson
State Archaeologist
University of Iowa
Iowa City, Iowa 52242

Thomas A. Witty
State Archaeologist
Kansas Historical Society
Tenth and Jackson Streets
Topeka, Kansas 66612

Dr. R. Berle Clay
State Archaeologist
University of Kentucky
Lexington, Kentucky 40506

Dr. William G. Haag
State Archaeologist
Louisiana State University
Baton Rouge, Louisiana 70803

Tyler Bastian
State Archaeologist
Maryland Geological Survey
Latrobe Hall, Johns Hopkins
    University
Baltimore, Maryland 21218

Maurice Robbins
State Archaeologist
Bronson Museum
8 North Main Street
Attleboro, Massachusetts
    02703

John R. Halsey
State Archaeologist
Michigan History Division
208 North Capital Avenue
Lansing, Michigan 48918

Dr. Eldon Johnson
State Archaeologist
215 Ford Hall
University of Minnesota
Minneapolis, Minnesota 55455

Samuel McGahey
State Archaeologist
Department of Archives and
    History
Box 571
Jackson, Mississippi 39205

Stewart L. Peckham
State Archaeologist
Museum of New Mexico
Santa Fe, New Mexico 87501

Dr. Robert Funk
State Archaeologist
New York State Museum
Buffalo, New York 12222

Stephen J. Gluckman
State Archaeologist
Division of History and
    Archives
Archaeology Section
Raleigh, North Carolina 27611

Nick G. Franke
Research Archaeologist
State Historical Society
Bismarck, North Dakota
    58501

Martha Potter Otto
Curator of Archaeology
Ohio Historical Center
Columbus, Ohio 43211

Don Wychoff
State Archaeologist
University of Oklahoma
Norman, Oklahoma 73069

Berry Kent
State Archaeologist
William Penn Memorial Museum
Box 1026
Harrisburg, Pennsylvania 17608

Robert L. Stephenson
State Archaeologist
Institute of Archaeology and
   Anthropology
University of South Carolina
Columbia, South Carolina 29208

Robert Alex
State Archaeologist
Archaeological Research Center
Box 152
Fort Meade, South Dakota 57741

Joseph L. Benthall
State Archaeologist
Department of Conservation
5103 Edmonson Pike
Nashville, Tennessee 37211

Curtis Tunnell
State Archaeologist
Box 12276, Capital Station
Austin, Texas 78711

David B. Madsen
State Archaeologist
603 East South Temple
Salt Lake City, Utah 84102

Giovanna Neudorfer
State Archaeologist
Division for Historic Preservation
Pavilion Building
Montpelier, Vermont 05602

Joan E. Freeman
State Archaeologist
Wisconsin Historical Society
816 State Street
Madison, Wisconsin 53706

Daniel Fowler
Archaeological Administrator
Geological and Economic Survey
Box 879
Morgantown, West Virginia
   26505

George Frison
State Archaeologist
University of Wyoming
Laramie, Wyoming 82071

Additional Archaeological Contacts

W. Warren Floyd
Alabama Historical Commission
Montgomery, Alabama 36104

Charity Davidson
National Capital Planning
   Commission
1325 G Street, NW
Washington, D.C. 20576

Mario Delisio
Idaho State Historical
   Society
610 North Julin Davis Drive
Boise, Idaho 83706

Charles J. Bareis
Illinois Archaeological Survey
University of Illinois
Urbana, Illinois 61801

Randy L. Cottier and Susan B. Traub
Missouri State Park Board
State Historical Survey and Planning Board
909 University Avenue, Suite 215
Columbia Professional Building
Columbia, Missouri 65201

Dr. Dee C. Taylor
University of Montana
Department of Anthropology
Missoula, Montana 59801

Donald Tuohy
Nevada State Museum
Department of Anthropology
Carson City, Nevada 89701

Lorraine Williams
Archaeologist, Bureau of
  Archaeology, State Museum
185 West State Street
Trenton, New Jersey 08625

David L. Cole
Oregon Archaeological Survey
Museum of Natural History
University of Oregon
Eugene, Oregon 97403

John Senalis
Department of Anthropology and
  Sociology
University of Rhode Island
Kingston, Rhode Island 02881

Dr. William M. Kelso
Commonwealth of Virginia
Virginia Historic Landmarks
  Commission
221 Governor Street
Richmond, Virginia 23219

U.S. Forest Service Regional Offices

ALASKA REGION
Federal Office Building
Box 1628
Juneau, Alaska 99801

CALIFORNIA REGION
630 Sansome Street
San Francisco, California 94111

EASTERN REGION
633 West Wisconsin Avenue
Milwaukee, Wisconsin 53203

INTERMOUNTAIN REGION
324 25th Street
Ogden, Utah 84401

NORTHERN REGION
Federal Building
Missoula, Montana 59801

PACIFIC NORTHWEST REGION
319 SW Pine Street
Box 3623
Portland, Oregon 97208

ROCKY MOUNTAIN REGION
Federal Center
Building 85
Denver, Colorado 80225

SOUTHERN REGION
1720 Peachtree Road NW
Atlanta, Georgia 30309

SOUTHWESTERN REGION
517 Gold Avenue SW
Albuquerque, New Mexico 87101

And Finally

The Advisory Council on Historic
  Preservation
1522 K Street
Washington, D.C. 20005
  This is a sort of court of last resort in cases where you have ex-
  hausted all other avenues of
  preserving a threatened site.

CANADIAN ADDRESSES

Archaeological Survey of
  Canada
National Museum of Man
Ottawa, Ontario
K1A OM8

Heritage Canada
Box 1358
Station B
Ottawa, Ontario

Provincial Agencies

Director
Archaeological Survey of Alberta
10158 103rd Street
Edmonton, Alberta
T5J OX9

Provincial Archaeologist
Archaeological Sites Advisory
  Board
St. Ann's Academy
Parliament Buildings
Victoria, British Columbia

Staff Archaeologist
Historic Resources Branch
Department of Tourism,
  Recreation and Cultural
  Affairs
200 Vaughan Street
Winnipeg, Manitoba
R3C OP8

Provincial Archaeologist
Historic Resources Administration
Research and Development
  Branch
Box 6000
Fredericton, New Brunswick

Dr. James Tuck
Department of Anthropology
Memorial University
St. John's, Newfoundland
A1C 5S7

Coordinator of Historical
  Programs
Natural and Cultural Affairs
Government of the Northwest
  Territories
Yellowknife, Northwest Territories
X1A 2L9

Curator of History
Nova Scotia Museum
Halifax, Nova Scotia

Service d'Archéologie et
  d'Ethnologie
Ministère des Affaires Culturelles
6, rue de l'Université
Québec, Québec
G1R 4R7

Chief Archaeologist
Historic Planning and Research
  Branch
Ministry of Culture and
  Recreation
Whitney Block, Queen's Park
Toronto, Ontario
M7A 2R9

Supervisor of Historical
  Resources
Saskatchewan Museum of Natural
  History
Regina, Saskatchewan

Yukon Archaeologist
Archaeological Survey of Canada
National Museum of Man
Ottawa, Ontario
K1A OM8

Appendix V
Sources of Materials, Services, and Supplies

MAPS

U.S. Geological Survey quad maps and ortho-quads are available from:

Washington Distribution Section
U.S. Geological Survey
1200 South Eads Street
Arlington, Virginia 22202

Satellite photographs and other more sophisticated types of geological and geographic information may be had from:

Geographic Computer Search
EROS Data Center
Sioux Falls, South Dakota 57198

EROS's U.S. catalog and non-U.S. catalog are $1.25 each.

FIELD EQUIPMENT

Various useful items for field survey can be had from (among many others):

Eastern Mountain Sports, Inc.
1041 Commonwealth Avenue
Boston, Massachusetts 02215

EMS carries good inexpensive compasses and will send you a catalog for $1.00, which is refundable with your first order.

Recreational Equipment, Inc., is a user's cooperative with a $2.00 life-
time membership fee. The REI catalog is packed with useful items,
including compasses. Write to them at:

> 1525 11th Avenue
> Seattle, Washington 98122

Mail orders for members go to:

> P.O. Box 24827
> Seattle, Washington 98124

Their toll-free number for orders is 1–800–426–0351.

SCIENTIFIC GADGETS AND TESTING KITS

> The Edmund Scientific Company
> EDSCORP Building
> Barrington, New Jersey 08007

Edmund Scientific has things you never dreamed of, as well as soil test
kits and surveyors' equipment. Catalog 50¢.

OPERATORS OF ARCHAEOLOGICAL FIELD TRIPS ACCEPTING PAID PARTICIPANTS

> Earthwatch
> 10 Juniper Road
> Belmont, Massachusetts 02178

Free catalog.

> The Explorers' Club
> 46 East 70th Street
> New York, New York 10021

Free brochure.

ARCHAEOLOGICAL TESTING SERVICES

Geochron Laboratories
24 Blackstone Street
Cambridge, Massachusetts 02139

Teledyne Isotopes
50 Van Buren Avenue
Westwood, New Jersey 07675

Appendix VI
How to Determine
UTMG Coordinates

The letters UTMG stand for the Universal Transverse Mercator Grid system of coordinates. It is used on most U.S. Geological Survey topographical quadrangle maps (exceptions being the older editions), and is capable of pinpointing any location to within ten to a hundred meters.

A set of UTMG coordinates for North America takes the form of the letter E (for east) followed by a six-digit number, and the letter N (for north) followed by a seven-digit number. Numbers for the north coordinate increase as you read upward. Those for the east coordinate increase from left to right.

On U.S. Geological Survey maps the UTMG coordinates are marked along the map edges by blue ticks. (Do not be confused by black ticks, which apply to another system, or by latitude and longitude numbers in a form such as 37'30".) Each blue tick indicates another 1,000 meters (1 kilometer) east or north. A representative square might be the one 365000 meters east to 366000 meters east by 4721000 meters north to 4722000 meters north. However, the marks on the map edge will appear in the abbreviated form ^{3}65, ^{3}66, ^{47}21, ^{47}22. To locate your site on such a square, superimpose on it a real (transparent) or imaginary ten-by-ten grid like the one on the next page.

The small squares now represent areas 100 meters on a side. By counting squares left to right you can determine the next digit in the distance east. In the example it is 365700 meters east.

Similarly, by counting up, one finds the other coordinate to be 4721800 meters north. If even greater accuracy is desired, the 100-meter square may again be divided into 100 units 10 meters to a side in order to derive an additional digit. However, for many purposes an accuracy of 100 meters is enough.

The complete coordinates for this imaginary site may be written E 365700, N 4721800, and this information alone will serve to locate the site for any other researcher.

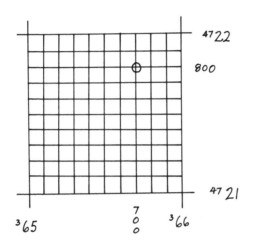

Appendix VII
Soil Identification

FIELD DETERMINATION OF SOILS

Sand: Loose and single-grained. The individual grains can readily be seen or felt. Squeezed in the hand when dry, it will fall apart when the pressure is released. Squeezed when moist, it will form a cast, but will crumble when touched.

Sandy loam: A soil containing much sand but which has enough silt and clay to make it somewhat coherent. The individual sand grains can readily be seen and felt. Squeezed when dry, it will form a cast which will readily fall apart, but if squeezed when moist a cast can be formed that will bear careful handling without breaking.

Loam: A soil having a relatively even mixture of different grades of sand and of silt and clay. It is mellow with a somewhat gritty feel yet fairly smooth and slightly plastic. Squeezed when dry, it will form a cast that will bear careful handling, while the cast formed by squeezing the moist soil can be handled quite freely without breaking.

Silt loam: A soil having a moderate amount of the fine grades of sand and only a small amount of clay, over half of the particles being of the size called "silt." When dry it may appear cloddy but the lumps can be readily broken, and when pulverized it feels soft and floury. When wet the soil readily runs together and puddles. Either dry or moist it will form casts that can be freely handled without breaking, but when moistened and squeezed between thumb and finger it will not "ribbon" but will give a broken appearance.

Clay loam: A fine-textured soil which usually breaks into clods or lumps that are hard when dry. When the moist soil is pinched between the thumb and finger it will form a thin "ribbon" which will break readily, barely sustaining its own weight. The moist soil is plastic and will form a cast that will bear much handling. When kneaded in the hand it does not crumble readily but tends to work into a heavy compact mass.

Clay: A fine-textured soil that usually forms very hard lumps or clods when dry and is quite plastic and usually sticky when wet. When the moist soil is pinched out between the thumb and fingers it will form a long, flexible "ribbon." Some fine clays very high in colloids are friable and lack plasticity in all conditions of moisture.

SOIL GLOSSARY

Aggregate soil: Many fine particles held in a single mass or cluster. Natural soil aggregates such as crumbs, blocks, or prisms are called peds. Clods are aggregates produced by tillage or other disturbances.

Alluvium: Soil material such as sand, silt, or clay that has been deposited on land by streams.

Bedrock: The solid rock underlying soils.

Consistence, soil: The feel of the soil and the ease with which a lump can be crushed by the fingers.

Common Terms:
    Loose: Noncoherent when dry or moist. Does not hold together in a mass.

Friable: When moist, crushes easily under gentle pressure between thumb and forefinger and can be pressed together into a lump.

Firm: When moist, crushes under moderate pressure between thumb and forefinger, but resistance is distinctly notable.

Plastic: When wet, readily deformed by moderate pressure but can be pressed into a lump. Will form a "wire" when rolled between thumb and forefinger.

Sticky: When wet, adheres to other materials and tends to stretch somewhat and roll apart rather than pull free from other material.

Hard: When dry, moderately resistant to pressure; can be broken with difficulty between thumb and forefinger.

Soft: When dry, breaks into powder or individual grains under very slight pressure.

Cemented: Hard and brittle; little affected by moistening.

Erosion: The wearing away of the land surface by wind (sandblast), running water, and other geological agents.

Hardpan: A hardened or cemented soil layer.

Glossary

Terms in SMALL CAPS indicate cross references.

adze   A tool of stone or, in historic times, metal, having a heavy, chisel-like end; used for dressing wood or timber.

artifact   In archaeology, any object made or created by human agency —including, according to some authorities, traces of human activity or occupation created accidentally or incidentally. Examples of the latter are POST MOLDS, CHIPPING WASTE, and MIDDENS.

atlatl   The so-called throwing stick, a device used in many preindustrial societies for launching a short spear or dart. (See drawing on page 38.) A typical atlatl consists of the launching shaft (with or without a handle) that is counterweighted on one end with a stone, the *atlatl weight.* The front of the launching shaft is notched or grooved in order to hold the spear or dart.

avocational archaeologist   Any person who devotes her or his time to archaeology as an avocation rather than as a full-time, paid profession. Often also called an *amateur archaeologist.* The term does *not* necessarily imply a contrast with the professional achaeologist in qualifications, training, or breadth of experience.

awl   In prehistoric archaeology, a pointed tool of stone or bone; used for piercing holes in leather or wood, and in the weaving of baskets.

barbed harpoon   See HARPOON.

bedrock mortar   A bowl- or U-shaped hollow ground into an outcrop of bedrock by certain early inhabitants of North America. In a bedrock mortar food materials were ground with a pestle.

biface (bifacial)   In archaeology, a stone tool that is worked (as by chipping) on both faces. Compare UNIFACE (UNIFACIAL).

buffalo jump   In the prehistoric and contact periods of North American archaeology, a cliff or bluff over which hunters drove herds of buffalo. Butchering sites appear at the foot of such drops.

burin   In prehistoric archaeology, a relatively small stone tool with a narrow, chisellike end; used in engraving bone, shell, wood.

chipping waste   The flakes of stone that fall from the main piece of stone as it is being worked. An important surface indication of archaeological sites.

conchoidal   Literally, shell-shaped. In archaeology, the term is used to describe the marks typical of a certain type of stone fracture that occurs when flakes are deliberately struck off in the process of toolmaking. Conchoidal marks resemble those on the back of a clamshell, being a series of more or less circular ridges radiating from a point on the edge of a round or oval scar.

conservation archaeology   Not a "school" or a technique, but rather a philosophical approach to archaeology. This approach views archaeological remains as a scarce and nonrenewable resource that must be conserved rather than squandered. Emphasis is therefore placed on site location and survey rather than on indiscriminate excavation and artifact collection.

context   In archaeology, the relation of artifacts and other cultural remains to the surrounding soil deposits. Like stratigraphy (see STRATIFICATION), context is vital for establishing relative dating and cultural associations.

core   In the manufacture of stone tools, a piece of stone from which blades are struck as a prelude to turning the blades into finished tools.

cultural diffusion   Any of several processes whereby a cultural trait, such as the use of pottery or a new technique for weaving, may spread from one area or people to another. Cultural diffusion may occur without the migration of peoples or the existence of formal trade routes, but merely as a result of a series of borrowings, one neighbor from another.

datum point   In archaeological survey, a geographical feature on or near a site, arbitrarily chosen as a reference point for other measurements made in maping the site. The datum point is located on the USGS survey map (see USGS) by means of QUADRANGULATION or TRIANGULATION. Distances and directions of other features of the site or of a test excavation may then be specified relative to the datum point.

dendrochronology The technique of dating wooden objects or remains by matching the growth rings displayed by the wood with a known series of such rings, which reflect climatic conditions. Not feasible with all species of trees, nor in places where reliable tree ring series have not been established. Also called *tree ring dating*.

diorama A scene, often in miniature, made by placing objects and figures in front of a painted or photographic backdrop or in a model landscape seen from above. A useful educational device for displaying reconstructions of historic or prehistoric scenes based on archaeological data.

effigy In North American archaeology, a representation in three dimensions of a human, animal, plant, or mythical figure; most typically found in pottery, stone carvings, and the shapes of earthen mounds, some of which are very large.

ethno-archaeology An approach to archaeology that gathers data on the lifeways of living preindustrial peoples in order to gain insight into the kinds of remains that might be left by certain activities. This is in contrast to the kind of reasoning that proceeds from known remains to a reconstruction of the activities that might have produced them.

ethnographic source An account of the lifeways of a people or group by an observer who is sometimes a member of another, possibly hostile or ill-informed culture. Invaluable to the archaeologist, but must be used with caution.

feature In archaeology, particularly excavation, an evidence of human activity that cannot be classified as an artifact in the usual sense. Examples are charcoal smears, indicating the presence of hearths, or POST MOLDS.

flint knapping The activity of chipping stone for the purpose of making tools or other artifacts. The term denotes stone tool working in general, whether the stone actually is flint (an Old World stone) or is chert, quartz, obsidian, or another stone type common in the New World.

gorget In North American prehistoric archaeology, a placque- or crescent-shaped ornament of stone, bone, shell, wood, or other material worn around the neck. Often carved, inlaid, engraved, or otherwise decorated. The term is probably often misapplied to objects whose actual functions are still unknown.

hafting The method by which a shaft or handle is fixed to a tool or weapon. In North American prehistoric archaeology, usually a binding or adhesive or combination of the two.

harpoon A weapon like a spear attached to a rope, used in the hunting of whales, seals, and other large sea creatures. In North American archaeology harpoons are of two basic types. The simpler *barbed harpoon* is held in the flesh by a series of barbs on the head and/or shaft. The more complex *toggle harpoon* incorporates a line fixed to the harpoon head by a swivellike device or *toggle;* once the prey is struck with this weapon the head turns at right angles to the line, thus making the harpoon even more difficult to dislodge than the barbed type.

historic archaeology The study of the material remains of any people or culture of which there are written records. In North America the historic period is generally considered to have begun with the arrival of European explorers in the late fifteenth and early sixteenth centuries.

house pit The pit dug when a house is constructed with its floor below ground level—a common practice in prehistoric North America; hence also the archaeological remains of such pits, often discernible by the disturbance and/or discoloration of soil within a roughly circular or rectangular area.

hydration A naturally occurring chemical process by which water molecules combine (often loosely) with the molecules of another substance. In archaeological dating of obsidian, the degree of hydration of the stone's surface provides an index of the date at which that surface was first exposed, as in the making of a tool.

industrial archaeology The study of the material remains of any people or culture in an industrial stage of development. The industrial period in North America is considered to have begun roughly in the middle of the nineteenth century with the building of mills or factories for the mass production of goods or processing of materials.

katchina (also *kachina*) Any of several ancestral spirits important in the religion of the Hopi Indians and represented in material culture by dancing masks, rock paintings of dancers, and painted figurines, the so-called (and miscalled) *katchina dolls.*

kiva A wholly or partly underground chamber constructed in Pueblo Indian villages for ceremonial, religious, and possibly other purposes; also the archaeological remains of such chambers.

leaching The percolation of water through soil or rock and the resultant dissolving of some of the minerals contained therein. In archaeology, leaching by ground water accounts for much of the disappearance of buried bone and shell, especially when soil conditions are acid.

lithics In archaeology, this term refers to stone artifacts and their study.

mano (and *millingstone* or *metate*) In North American prehistoric archaeology, a pair of utensils, usually of ground stone, used in the grinding of grain, seeds, or other foodstuffs. The mano is worked back and forth over the grinding surface of the stationary *millingstone* or *metate*.

maul In prehistoric archaeology, a heavy stone implement like a large pestle, possibly used for pounding, etc.

metate See MANO.

midden A refuse or trash heap. In North American prehistoric archaeology, a mound, sometimes very large, of discarded shells, bones, and other detritus; very useful to the archaeologist.

millingstone See MANO.

moraine In geology, a ridge or mound of boulders, gravel, sand, and clay created by the bulldozerlike action of advancing glaciers and left along the line of the ice front when the glaciers receded.

obsidian Naturally occurring volcanic glass, a highly prized material for the manufacture of stone tools.

olivella Genus name of several similar species of bivalves of the Pacific coast of North America and elsewhere. In North American prehistoric archaeology, olivella shells were used in the manufacture of disc beads.

paleopathology The study of the diseases of ancient peoples.

palynology In archaeology, the study of fossil pollen grains preserved in the soil of archaeological sites. Such a study is undertaken with a view to discovering the nature of prevailing flora at the time the site was made.

pebble tools Primitive stone tools made by chipping a rough edge on one end of a fist-sized stone. Such tools are known from the early (Paleolithic) sites of the Old World, but their occurrence in the New World (presumably at much later dates) is disputed.

percussion flaking Flaking of stone tools by means of sharp, hammerlike blows, leaving the characteristic marks of CONCHOIDAL fracture. Contrast with PRESSURE FLAKING, below.

petroglyph   See ROCK ART.

petrology   The study of rocks. In archaeology, the study of rock types in terms of their mechanical properties as they influence FLINT KNAPPING and of their chemical properties (especially unusual trace elements) as they may give clues to the geographical origin of artifacts from distant places.

pH   A chemical term referring to the concentration of hydrogen ions in a sample of material. In practical terms, pH measurements provide an index of acidity or alkalinity, low readings (on a scale of 1 to 10 where 7 is neutral) indicating acidity, high readings alkalinity. In archaeology, pH readings made on soil samples may sometimes assist in indicating the presence of prehistoric occupation sites.

pictograph   See ROCK ART.

pit house   A dwelling wholly or largely constructed underground, or the archaeological remains of the same.

plow zone   In North American archaeology, the disturbed layer of surface soil that has resulted from the widespread plowing of colonial and later times. Cultural material in plow zones can provide important information even though it has been disturbed.

post mold   An archaeological FEATURE that represents the remains of a post sunk in the ground for any of various purposes, most notably the supporting of a house roof.

pothunter   An irresponsible collector of archaeological artifacts who takes no thought for their CONTEXT, irreplaceability, and scientific value. A vandal, a boor, a lower form of life.

pre-Columbian   Describes the period of North (and South and Central) American culture before the arrival of Columbus—that is, the prehistoric period. See HISTORIC and PREHISTORIC ARCHAEOLOGY.

prehistoric archaeology   The study of the material remains of peoples and cultures of which there are no written records. Compare HISTORIC ARCHAEOLOGY.

pressure flaking   Flaking of stone tools by means of steady pressure. Fracture marks, though also CONCHOIDAL, are longer and thinner than in the case of PERCUSSION FLAKING.

projectile point   The more correct name for the stone weapon points often called arrowheads. The term includes arrowheads, harpoon points, spear points, lance points, and the points for atlatl darts.

quadrangulation   The use of four bearings in taking map sightings. See TRIANGULATION.

remanent artifacts Those artifacts that remain in an archaeological site, especially for a considerable period of time, well beyond the point by which organic materials have usually perished. Most common examples are stone, shell, bone, pottery, and, in historic contexts, glass.

replication In archaeology, the art and science of using authentic methods and materials to make artifacts of the type produced in historic or prehistoric societies. Replication is undertaken for the purpose of attaining a better understanding of the processes involved.

resist dyeing A dyeing technique whereby a pattern is made on the cloth with an impermeable substance before the dye is applied, so that the color appears on the background only.

ritual object An archaeological catch-all term, often applied to artifacts of unknown provenience and/or function. Properly, an object of no practical purpose that yet embodies a profound religious or mythological (symbolic) significance.

rock art A general term for figures, designs, or symbols on rock surfaces such as cliff faces, boulders, cave walls or ceilings, and so on. Includes both *petroglyphs,* which are pecked or incised, and *pictographs,* which are painted.

sherd (also shard) A fragment, especially of broken pottery or glass.

shovel test A small, informal test excavation for the purpose of assessing the nature of a known site or, where brush and undergrowth are heavy, of ascertaining the presence or absence of a suspected site. In conservation archaeology, shovel testing is rarely used in survey unless, as specified above, the ground is so overgrown as to make surface examination impossible. Occasionally, shovel testing may also be done in order to get more information about a site certain to be destroyed.

slag glass A fused and vitrified waste material left over from the process of glass manufacture, especially during the early industrial period; thus, in industrial archaeology, a useful indicator of the presence of an early glassmaking industry.

soil resistivity In lay terms, the soil's resistance to the flow of an electric current; the degree to which the soil is less than a perfect conductor. Variations in soil resistivity may be measured with a *resistivity meter* and may, under certain conditions, indicate the presence or absence of subsurface archaeological features.

steatite A soft, easily worked mineral, usually grayish or greenish in color, also called *soapstone.* Much used by prehistoric North American peoples for utensils and ornaments and by early historic inhabitants for hearths, washtubs, counter tops, and so on. Will not crack when placed in a fire.

sterile soil   In archaeology, soil that contains no traces or remains of human cultural activity.

stratification   In archaeology, the process of layer-by-layer cultural deposition, giving rise to the principle that "deepest is oldest." Though there are many exceptions to this rule, it is still the basis of most relative dating in archaeology, and *stratigraphy,* the formal study of stratification in rocks and soils, is an important archaeological tool.

tanged   In artifact description, a tool having a relatively slender, tonguelike projection at its base for use in HAFTING.

tempering   In pottery manufacture, the use of any of a number of materials such as grit or straw that, when mixed with the clay before firing, make it less likely to shatter when heated.

test pit   A more formal type of exploratory excavation than a SHOVEL TEST. Sparingly used in conservation archaeology.

thermoluminescence   In physical chemistry, the property possessed by certain materials of giving off light when heated. In archaeology, thermoluminescence of the constituent clay is the basis of a test for the age of pottery; this test, though still in the trial stages, may prove exceedingly useful.

tipi   The portable tent dwelling used by many groups of Indians of the Great Plains. The rings of stones used to weight down the lower edges of the tipi fabric are referred to as *tipi rings* and are an important indicator of the existence of archaeological sites in areas frequented by tipi dwellers. As tipis were sometimes pitched in a circle, the term "tipi ring" may also refer to a great ring made up of the lesser rings marking the locations of individual tipis.

toggle harpoon   See HARPOON.

trade beads   In the so-called contact period (the early years of encounters between Native Americans and European settlers), beads of European manufacture. An important item of trade, they were both more brightly colored and cheaper (in terms of labor) than the traditional shell, stone, and bone beads that had been used up to that time. Made most often of glass, sometimes of pottery or metal, trade beads are a useful type of REMANENT ARTIFACT for the archaeologist, as their origin can often be traced from their type and color.

transect   In archaeology, an arbitrary line cutting across a site or suspected site. In some cases, transects may be walked along in the course of a survey. If it is necessary to conduct a subsurface examination, test pits or shovel tests may be made along the transect. Thus the use of transects is one method of sampling.

tree ring dating   See DENDROCHRONOLOGY.

trepanning   A surgical operation in which a segment of the skull is removed. Skulls from prehistoric North America reveal that the procedure was surprisingly common in certain societies and periods, although the reason is not known.

triangulation   In mapping, the basic process used in the field to determine the exact position of an archaeological site, FEATURE, DATUM POINT, etc. In triangulation, compass bearings are taken on three landmarks that appear on the relevant survey map and lines are plotted on the map along the lines of the bearings; their point of intersection is then the location of the observer.

type collection   In biology, archaeology, and other fields, a collection of specimens made (usually by a museum or university department) for the purpose of compiling all the known types and variants of a given category of objects, such as Mississippian projectile points or Athapaskan pottery. Type collections are not made primarily for display, but for scientific study and for teaching purposes.

typical artifact   An artifact that, while not absolutely diagnostic of archaeological period or tradition, may still be considered an important clue to the dating or identification of the site or period from which it came.

ulu   A type of curved stone knife, often of ground slate.

uniface (unifacial)   In archaeology, a stone tool that is worked (as by chipping) on only one face. Compare BIFACE (BIFACIAL).

USGS   Abbreviation for the United States Geological Survey, whose 7.5-minute series quadrangle maps are the standard field reference in archaeological survey and site reporting.

utilized flake   A single flake struck from a piece of stone and used as a tool without retouching. Sometimes only microscopic examination can differentiate a utilized flake from a piece of CHIPPING WASTE.

Index

313

About the Authors

GEORGESS McHARGUE and MICHAEL ROBERTS write from an ideal combination of backgrounds and talents. Georgess McHargue is a professional writer with more than fifteen books to her credit, and has had a lifelong interest in archaeology. Michael Roberts has for years been a noted amateur archaeologist and has now gone professional with his new job as Administrative Director of the Institute for Conservation Archaeology of the Peabody Museum, Harvard University. He is a member of the Society of Professional Archaeologists. The authors, who are husband and wife, live in Groton, Massachusetts.

DR. THOMAS F. KING is Staff Archaeologist of the Interagency Archaeological Services Division, Office of Archaeology and Historic Preservation, National Park Service, Washington, D.C.